THE PYRENEAN HAUTE ROUTE

THE PYRENEAN HAUTE ROUTE

THE HRP HIGH-LEVEL TRAIL

by Tom Martens

CICERONE

JUNIPER HOUSE, MURLEY MOSS,
OXENHOLME ROAD, KENDAL, CUMBRIA LA9 7RL
www.cicerone.co.uk

Third edition 2019
ISBN: 978 1 85284 981 8
Reprinted 2022, 2024 (with updates)
Second edition 2009
First edition 2004

MIX
Paper | Supporting responsible forestry
FSC® C010256

Printed in China on responsibly sourced paper on behalf of Latitude Press Ltd.
A catalogue record for this book is available from the British Library.
All photographs are by the author unless otherwise stated.

Route mapping by Lovell Johns www.lovelljohns.com
Contains OpenStreetMap.org data © OpenStreetMap contributors, CC-BY-SA. NASA relief data courtesy of ESRI

Cicerone would like to thank dedicated HRP-lover Peter Forrest for his input and advice, and for keeping trekkers updated with the latest information on the trail. His website www.hrpguide.org is a useful resource for HRP trekkers. Thank you Peter.

Cicerone would also particularly like to thank Ton Joosten, author of earlier editions of this guidebook for his commitment to the trail over many years. Also thanks to all Cicerone users who have given us feedback over the years, it is very valuable. Thanks, and good trekking.

Front cover: Hikers between Col de l'Albe and the Juclar lakes (Day 34)

CONTENTS

Updates to this guide

While every effort is made by our authors to ensure the accuracy of guidebooks as they go to print, changes can occur during the lifetime of an edition. Any updates that we know of for this guide will be on the Cicerone website (www.cicerone.co.uk/981/updates), so please check before planning your trip. We also advise that you check information about such things as transport, accommodation and shops locally. Even rights of way can be altered over time.

The route maps in this guide are derived from publicly available data, databases and crowd-sourced data. As such they have not been through the detailed checking procedures that would generally be applied to a published map from an official mapping agency, although naturally we have reviewed them closely in the light of local knowledge as part of the preparation of this guide.

We are always grateful for information about any discrepancies between a guidebook and the facts on the ground, sent by email to updates@cicerone.co.uk or by post to Cicerone, Juniper House, Murley Moss, Oxenholme Road, Kendal, LA9 7RL.

Register your book: to sign up to receive free updates, special offers and GPX files where available, register your book at www.cicerone.co.uk.

The breathtaking view from the Vignemale peak (3298m) to Vallée de Gaube (Summit 2)

PREFACE

The Pyrenean Haute Route, originally an idea of Frenchman Georges Véron, takes adventurous hikers through regions where they will find themselves amid only mountains, lakes and wildlife. Véron undertook the first complete traverse of the Pyrenees by the central ridge in 1968; that it took so long before somebody attempted this adventure says something about the challenges involved. Ton Joosten and Peter Forrest further developed the route and made it accessible to a wider audience. This new edition builds on the superb work these hiker-writers have done, presenting the traverse of the Pyrenees in 44 stages. Some people will take more time, while others will do it faster. Every hiker can make their own traverse depending on their ambitions and capacities. For example, Georges Véron completed his original traverse in 41 days, together with two friends and aided by a car following with gear and supplies, while ultra-runner Mike Coppock recently ran the route in 12 days, self-supported. I personally believe that the route as it is suggested in this book is a good way to take in the ever-changing landscapes and hiking experiences. Doing it in 44 days, possibly spread over several years, will allow you to fully experience the Pyrenees, get to know some of the people who live there and see some of the abundant wildlife present in almost every corner.

Over the past 15 years I have spent a considerable amount of time in the Pyrenees, and I will definitely continue to explore this wonderful mountain chain. Some routes I have done so often that I feared I would grow tired of them, but on every outing I discover new aspects; corners I haven't noticed before, plants I haven't studied, animals whose behaviour I'm just starting to understand, caves I haven't explored yet… and there are people with whom I haven't shared a hiking experience yet. I conclude here by thanking everyone who has joined me so far on hikes on the French-Spanish border. I remember all of you, because Pyrenean adventures create intense memories. In particular I'd like to thank Brent D'Hooge, who introduced me to the Pyrenees, and Filip Bronchart and Jordi Catala, who joined me on some of the most extreme hikes.

Tom Martens

Mountain safety

Every mountain walk has its dangers, and those described in this guidebook are no exception. All who walk or climb in the mountains should recognise this and take responsibility for themselves and their companions along the way. The author and publisher have made every effort to ensure that the information contained in this guide was correct when it went to press, but, except for any liability that cannot be excluded by law, they cannot accept responsibility for any loss, injury or inconvenience sustained by any person using this book.

International distress signal *(emergency only)*
Six blasts on a whistle (and flashes with a torch after dark) spaced evenly for one minute, followed by a minute's pause. Repeat until an answer is received. The response is three signals per minute followed by a minute's pause.

Helicopter rescue
The following signals are used to communicate with a helicopter:

Help needed: raise both arms above head to form a 'Y'

Help not needed: raise one arm above head, extend other arm downward

Emergency telephone numbers
If telephoning from the UK the dialling codes are:
France: 0033; Spain: 0034; Andorra: 00376

France: PGHM (Peloton de Gendarmerie de Haute Montagne): tel 05 62 92 41 41
Emergency services: tel 112 (mobile phones)

Weather reports
www.meteo.fr or tel 3250
www.mountain-forecast.com
www.meteoblue.com
www.snow-forecast.com
www.meteoalarm.eu

Mountain rescue can be very expensive – be adequately insured.

The Cirque de Gavarnie is one of the best places to see how geological forces have shaped the Pyrenees (Day 16)

The colourful view from near Le Taillon (3144m, summit 3) over the Ordesa y Monte Perdido national park

ROUTE SUMMARY TABLES

Stage	Start	Distance (km)	Ascent (m)	Descent (m)	Time	Grade	Page
Section 1: Hendaye to Lescun							
1	Hendaye	24.5	1580	1350	8hr 15min	2	51
2	Col de Lizuniaga	25	1320	1270	7hr 15min	2	57
3	Arizkun	13	815	725	5hr	2	63
4	Aldudes	17	1095	535	5hr 45min	2	67
5	Roncesvalles	21.5	1080	1160	6hr 45min	2	73
6	Egurgui	15.5	1075	600	5hr 15min	2	79
7	Col Bagargui	18	1320	1335	7hr 15min	3	84
8	Cabane Ardané	22	1465	925	8hr 30min	2	89
9	Source de Marmitou	8.5	85	1035	3hr	1	95
Total (Section 1)		*165*	*9835*	*8935*	*9 days*		
Section 2: Lescun to Gavarnie							
10	Lescun	17.5	1565	480	6hr 45min	2	107
11	Refuge d'Arlet	18.5	995	1430	6hr 30min	2	111
12	Candanchu	14.5	1355	875	6hr 20min	2	115
13	Refuge de Pombie	15.5	1495	1450	8hr 10min	E	120
14	Refuge de Larribet	18	1300	1505	8hr 20min	3	126
15	Refuge Wallon	13.5	1510	720	7hr 20min	2	136

Stage	Start	Distance (km)	Ascent (m)	Descent (m)	Time	Grade	Page
16	Refuge de Bayssellance	17.5	510	1795	5hr 20min	2	145
Total (Section 2)		*115*	*8730*	*8255*	*7 days*		

Section 3: Gavarnie to Salardú

Stage	Start	Distance (km)	Ascent (m)	Descent (m)	Time	Grade	Page
17	Gavarnie	18	1285	1150	6hr 45min	2	160
18	Héas	27.5	1725	2125	10hr	3	165
19	Parzán	21	1675	1015	7hr 15min	2	172
20	Refugio de Viados	13	1055	1125	6hr 30min	3	176
21	Refuge de la Soula	11	1500	620	6hr 15min	E	181
22	Refuge du Portillon	16	1050	1480	7hr	E	184
23	Refugio de la Renclusa	15	1060	1575	7hr 45min	E	196
24	Hospital de Vielha	13.5	1125	740	7hr 15min	2	201
25	Refugi de la Restanca	20.5	795	1535	7hr 15min	2	205
Total (Section 3)		*155.5*	*11,270*	*11,365*	*9 days*		

Section 4: Salardú to l'Hospitalet-près-l'Andorre

Stage	Start	Distance (km)	Ascent (m)	Descent (m)	Time	Grade	Page
26	Salardú	17	1540	610	7hr 35min	3	230
27	Refugi Gràcia Airoto	8	260	1190	3hr 30min	2	235
28	Alós d'Isil	12	1535	515	7hr 25min	2	238
29	Refugi Enric Pujol	13.5	1045	1095	7hr 15min	2	245
30	Refugi de Certascan	12.5	1190	1060	5hr 10min	2	254
31	Refugi del Cinquantenari	10	820	970	5hr 20min	2	258

Stage	Start	Distance (km)	Ascent (m)	Descent (m)	Time	Grade	Page
32	Étang de Soucarrane	15.5	1090	1415	6hr 45min	2	261
33	Refugi de Sorteny	12.5	1385	1055	6hr 25min	2	265
34	Refugi de Cabana Sorda	17	920	1775	8hr 20min	2	269
Total (Section 4)		*118*	*9785*	*9685*	*9 days*		
Section 5: L'Hospitalet-près-l'Andorre to Banyuls-sur-Mer							
35	L'Hospitalet-près-l'Andorre	7.5	855	185	3hr	1	278
36	Refuge des Bésines	19	1280	1380	8hr 45min	3	281
37	Refuge des Bouillouses	17	370	815	4hr 45min	1	290
38	Eyne	20	1785	1125	8hr 15min	3	294
39	Refugi d'Ull de Ter	22	820	1330	7hr 15min	2	302
40	Refuge de Mariailles	27.5	2025	2235	9hr 50min	3	307
41	Mines de Batère	20	890	1695	7hr 20 min	2	316
42	Mas de la Fargassa	16	1255	1345	6hr 15min	2	320
43	Las Illas	23	1280	895	6hr 30min	2	325
44	Col de l'Ouillat	22.5	920	1855	8hr 25min	2	329
Total (Section 5)		*194.5*	*11,480*	*12,860*	*10 days*		
Total (Pyrenean Haute Route)		**748**	**51,100**	**51,100**	**44 days**		

	Summit	Altitude	Start	Distance (km)	Ascent (m)	Time (time to summit)	Grade	Page
Section 5: Classic summits								
1	Grande Fache	3005m	Refuge Wallon (Day 14/15)	11	1110	6hr 30min (3hr 30min)	F+	134
2	Vignemale	3298m	Refuge de Bayssellance (Day 15/16)	7	930	5hr 30min (3hr)	F+	141
3	Le Taillon	3144m	Campsite near Gavarnie (Day 16/17)	20	1950	10hr (5hr 55min)	F	149
4	Piméné	2801m	Refuge des Espuguettes (Day 17)	8.5	760	4hr 15min (2hr 15min)	F	163
5	Pic Perdiguère	3222m	Portal de Remune (Day 22)	4	460	2hr 45min (1hr 45min)	F+	191
6	Pico de Aneto	3404m	Refugio de la Renclusa (Day 22/23)	11	1255	7hr 30min (4hr)	F+	193
7	Montardo d'Aran	2826m	Coll de Crestada (Day 25)	2.5	280	2hr (1hr 10min)	F	210
8	Mont Roig	2868m	Refugi Enric Pujol (Day 28/29)	4	560	3hr 15min (1hr 45min)	F	243
9	Pic de Certascan	2853m	Coll de Certascan (Day 29)	2	235	1hr 10min (40min)	F	252
10	Pic des Bastiments	2881m	Pic de la Vaca (Day 38)	5	Ascent 345/ descent 605	2hr 55min (2hr 15min)	F	300

Hikers climbing through the Canigou cheminée *(Day 40)*

INTRODUCTION

Barrage d'Ossoue contains meltwater from the Vignemale (Day 16)

The Pyrenean Haute Route (PHR) is one of the greatest hiking challenges in Europe. It's a 750km thru hike that takes you from the Atlantic Ocean all the way to the Mediterranean Sea, following the high ridge of the Pyrenees as closely as possible. Those who hike it all the way, in a single expedition or in several hikes over a longer period of time, often describe it as the most varied and satisfying hike they've done.

The PHR (or HRP, for Haute Randonnée Pyrénéenne) does not have dedicated waymarking in the same way as the other trans-Pyrenean routes, the GR10 and GR11. These Grande Randonnée trails also cross the whole length of the Pyrenees but they offer hikers a distinctively waymarked route, whereas the PHR combines different routes with the aim of staying as high as possible on the way to the other side of the Pyrenees. It is therefore more demanding in terms of orientation and self-sufficiency. It also offers a chance to see parts of the Pyrenees where hardly anyone goes and where you can feel at one with the magnificent scenery.

The variation in landscapes is enormous: lush greenery in the Basque Country's hills, unearthly karst formations around Pic d'Anie, impressive high-mountain stretches in the Central Pyrenees, high snow-covered cols, half-frozen lakes, glaciers, emerald-green lakes, green pastoral areas, cork oak forests, dry Mediterranean vegetation and much more.

You will experience all of this – provided you're up for a serious challenge. It takes several weeks to cover the distance, the climate changes greatly as you progress, you will cover all sorts of terrain and you may encounter weather extremes of all kinds. There are many mountain huts to provide you with food and shelter, but you will also sometimes need to carry food for several days and find water on the trail.

The rewards, however, are numerous. You can take in the incredible scenery, sample local cheeses on the way, climb a peak to overlook the mountain chain, enjoy a night under the stars, share experiences with other hikers and go for the next challenge. The PHR isn't just a hike: it's a life-changing experience.

The Pyrenean Haute Route is effectively, in many places, a mountaineering route and should only be undertaken by experienced trekkers, even though throughout the traverse there are a number of alternative routes that avoid the most challenging obstacles. These can be taken in case of bad weather or other limiting circumstances. Likewise, there are several alternative routes that offer an even more exciting trail, in case you are in for a more serious challenge.

THE ROUTE

The first section of the Haute Route starts from the Atlantic Ocean in the

THREE WAYS TO TRAVERSE THE PYRENEES FROM COAST TO COAST

The GR10 and GR11 routes both traverse the whole length of the Pyrenees, respectively on the French and on the Spanish side. Being restricted to one country is one thing that sets them apart from the Haute Route, which doesn't hesitate to cross the border wherever there is a higher route on the other side. Another important difference is the waymarking: the GR routes are easy to follow thanks to their white-and-red markers which are found from coast to coast. The Haute Route on the other hand has no official status and you won't even see the French term 'Haute Route Pyrénéenne' or the Spanish equivalent 'Transpireneica Alta Ruta' on the way.

The Haute Route does, however, follow the GR routes regularly, at those places where they happen to take the highest tracks along the central ridge. At the Atlantic Ocean, GR10 and Haute Route hikers walk together for several hours. In the Central Pyrenees, the Haute Route is easy to follow as the GR10 and 11 routes also follow some of most challenging parts of the whole Pyrenean range. Many variants, which can be choosen if the weather is not in your favour, follow one of the GR routes, offering a low-level alternative that's easier to navigate. And during the final days of the Haute Route, you will mostly follow the GR10.

small town of Hendaye. After leaving the ocean behind, the route quickly heads into the green Basque hills. On Days 2 and 3 the trail passes a few typical Basque villages and Day 4 takes you above 1000m before heading down to the Col de Roncevaux – a place of great historic importance where the Haute Route joins the Camino de Santiago for a short while. On Days 5 and 6 the route goes higher into Basque country, and the crossing of Pic d'Orhy marks the first 2000m threshold. After this the route heads into what might be considered true mountain landscapes, and then on Day 9 there is a descent to the beautiful village of Lescun, sheltered by a cirque with several impressive peaks – it has lost nothing of its authenticity.

The second section is all about the transition to the High Pyrenees; on Days 10 and 11 the route follows relatively high paths, but it isn't until Day 13 that you encounter a mountain that makes a lasting impression, the memorably shaped Pic du Midi d'Ossau dominating the entire lanscape. Passes have been relatively easy so far, but this changes on Day 14 when you need to find and cross the Port du Lavedan – and the next day you are treated to an even higher climb to the Col de Cambales. It is now very clear that you have entered the Central Pyrenees; there are high mountains and beautiful lakes as far as the eye can see. You might be tempted to climb one or more of the classic summits before reaching Gavarnie, a small mountain village, on Day 16. Despite its isolation, the village is a very popular tourist destination and many hikers opt to take a break here to admire the unsurpassed views of the Cirque de Gavarnie with its Grande Cascade, one of Europe's highest waterfalls.

The third section is a rough hike through and over the Central Pyrenees. Day 17 is relatively easy, whereas the next day you are confronted with high passes and unforgiving terrain. The scenery is continuously impressive. Day 19 provides something of a break: an easy-to-follow route leads to a magnificent part of the Spanish Pyrenees, where you pass an ancient mountain community at Viados and walk next to the impressive slopes of the Posets mountain. The next day presents a high climb and a steep descent – a good warm-up for what is to come. Days 21 to 23 are a true confrontation with the most challenging landscapes of the Pyrenees: high, snow-covered mountain passes, long stretches over boulders with only cairns to guide you, and a couple of steep scrambles. Pico Aneto, the Pyrenees' highest mountain, is an optional climb along this route. The two final days of the third section take you through the beautiful Aigüestortes national park, with its sharp peaks and numerous lakes. After the previous days this might feel like a walk in the park!

In the fourth section there are far fewer extremes then in the previous one, but neither is it a hike to underestimate. The section starts with three days of exciting hiking in areas with little waymarking. There are again stretches with only cairns to follow and which include a few scrambles. The next three days you hike along long rivers and through large valleys in the Spanish Pyrenees, with a few small villages on the way. After a brief passage in France, the Haute Route goes into Andorra, where the magnificent Circ de Tristaina welcomes you. Flower-rich Andorra is crossed in two days and finally you descend back into France.

The final section of the Haute Route takes you over the impressive Pic Carlit, before descending to the Plateau de Cerdagne where you encounter authentic French villages. The high ridgewalk in Spain which then follows is an experience never to forget, with vast, colourful views. Another impressive mountain, Pic du Canigou, is then climbed. From its peak you can already spot the Mediterranean Sea. The temperature rises considerably as you hike down to the Tech river, but the route then takes you again into the mountains for two more days. On the last day, you are still above 1000m just a few hours before reaching the finish at the Mediterranean Sea.

TEN CLASSIC SUMMITS

Climbing to the Aneto peak (3404m)

If you've got time and energy, a worthwhile way of using them would be to climb one or several of the mountains that are close to the main route. Some of these have gained legendary status due to their height or history, while others may not be so famous but nevertheless offer magnificent views over the region. This guide describes the ascent of 10 classic Pyrenean summits.

None of these climbs are technically difficult: they are all either grade F or F+ (the two easiest levels of the alpine grades, these require no special training or experience). However, even in late summer an ice axe and crampons are required for the glaciers of the Vignemale and Pico de Aneto.

- Grande Fache (3005m, Day 14) provides a classic and easy ascent to a 3000m summit situated on the French-Spanish border that offers stunning views of the Balaitous massif.

- Vignemale (3298m, Day 15) is the highest mountain of the French Pyrenean summits and offers a magnificent glacier walk in Henry Russell's footsteps.
- Le Taillon (3144m, Day 16) is one of the many summits of the Cirque de Gavarnie. The walk, which contains the crossing of the famous Brèche de Roland, is a long, colourful excursion to a limestone wilderness.
- Piméné (2801m, Day 17) is a mountain of relatively modest height that has become famous because of the superb views of the Cirque de Gavarnie.
- Pic Perdiguère (3222m, Day 22) is the highest summit of the Cirque de Portillon, which contains about a dozen 3000m summits.
- Pico de Aneto (3404m, Day 22), the highest summit of the Pyrenees, offers a long hike over a glacier, an exciting scramble and amazing views.
- Montardo d'Aran (2826m, Day 25), just like the Piméné is not a high mountain but the summit offers excellent views over Val d'Aran and the Maladeta massif.
- Mont Roig (2868m, Day 28) is a frontier-summit that can be reached by a short, rough climb from Refugi Enric Pujol.
- Pic de Certascan (2853m, Day 29) is the highest summit of the vast region between the Mont Roig and the Pica d'Estats.
- Pic des Bastiments (2881m, Day 38) is a high peak at the easternmost side of the Pyrenees. It is reached after a long, beautiful walk on the frontier ridge.

GEOLOGY

There haven't always been mountains where the Pyrenees now stretch over 430km from the Atlantic Ocean to the Mediterranean Sea. The geological history of the area sheds a light on why we now find complex layers of mainly granite and limestone here. In the early Paleozoic era, 500 million year ago, there was an ocean in the place where we now find the mountain chain. About 400 million years ago, tectonic movement compressed the sedimentary rock that had formed on the ocean bed and began forming a gigantic structure: the Hercynian mountain chain. Eventually there grew a range with peaks as high as today's Himalaya. However, over millions of years the entire Hercynian mountains eroded away, leaving only the migmatite foot of the chain behind.

During much of the Mesozoic era, between 250 and 100 million years ago, the area was covered by a shallow sea, resulting in new layers of sedimentary rock. In the Cretaceous era, around 75 million year ago, a tectonic movement took place that shaped the early Pyrenees: the African plate pushed the Iberian crust (what is now Spain and Portugal) north, where it began crashing into the huge European crust. This process continued until well into the Cenozoic era, 20 million years ago, and formed the Pyrenean mountain chain.

Different forms of erosion have altered the Pyrenees into the shape we can now see. During long periods with a warm and humid climate, rainfall eroded the rock and transported billions of tons of debris down the rivers, forming valleys along the way. Some 200,000 years ago the temperatures fell drastically, and snow piled up extremely high in the valleys. The long glaciers that were thus created nibbled at the mountains and widened the valleys. Finally, from 5000 years ago, fluvial erosion started again, creating open, steep-sided valleys and gorges.

A few geological highlights along the Haute Route are mentioned in the route description. From west to east you can see Cretaceous flysch sedentary rock at Hendaye; karst limestone landscapes around Pic d'Anie; volcanic remains which now form Pic du Midi d'Ossau; the Ossoue glacier; the impressive cirques of Gavarnie, Estaubé and Barroude; the limestone mountains on the Spanish side of the Brèche de Roland; the dark granite mass of the Posets; the sinkhole of Aigualluts at the foot of the Aneto; glacial erosion at the Gallina lakes and much more.

PLANTS AND WILDLIFE

The Pyrenees are a wilderness with a large variety of landscapes and climate zones. With such variety also comes a wealth of plants and wildlife. The species mentioned below represent only a selection of those that might be seen in the region; further information can be found in guidebooks such as David Guixé & Toni Llobet's *Wildlife of the Pyrenees* (Gallocanta, 1st edition, 2016), and Christopher Grey-Wilson & Marjorie Blamey's *The Alpine Flowers of Britain and Europe* (Collins, 2nd edition, 2001), which contains a number of Pyrenean flowers.

Mammals

The Pyrenees are home to great number of mammals, some of which are endemic to the region. Hunting and diminishing natural habitats have at times led to the disappearance of a species, but in the last few decades great efforts have been made to protect and even reintroduce mammals in the area.

Two animals you will certainly spot are the isard and the marmot. The isard is a small, goatlike animal with vertical horns that usually lives in small herds. In the 20th century they were almost hunted to extinction, but nowadays there is a large, stable population.

An isard still in much of its winter fur at the end of June; a curious young marmot

When you hear the marmot's high-pitched alarm call, this usually means it has spotted you first. This small mammal, a member of the rodent family, died out in the Pyrenees as a result of the last ice age, but in 1948 marmots from the Alps were introduced and now there is a large population.

Another example of the reintroduction of a species is the Iberian ibex, also called the Iberian wild goat. The impressive males are much greater in size and have much longer horns than the females. The Pyrenean subspecies sadly died out in 2000, but since 2014 ibex from other regions have been released in France, resulting in the present population of around 120. The French are very fond of this animal, which they call the *bouquetin*.

The Pyrenean bear population has a broadly similar history. The original brown bear population died out in 2004, but genetically identical animals from Slovenia and Spain have been released since 1996. There is an ongoing debate between those for and against the presence of the bear in the Pyrenees, resulting in slow progress for the species. However, the population now seems viable at around 50. Only a few bears live in the western Pyrenees; the largest group lives in the central Pyrenees (between Parzán and Pic Carlit). The brown bear is largely a plant-eater, but it is also an opportunist, so occasionally it might attack another animal, for example a sheep. It's extremely unlikely that a hiker will encounter a bear. Bears associate the smell of humans with danger as a result of centuries of hunting practice; a bear will run to safety as soon as its excellent sense of smell detects any human presence.

The most curious mammal in the mountain chain is definitely the Pyrenean desman. The desman looks like a mole (and is about the same size), but has a tail like a rat's, webbed feet and a long snout which it uses as a snorkel. It lives in clean mountain streams, where it hunts for insects and sometimes small fish and frogs.

A relatively new mammal to the Pyrenees is the mouflon, a small number of which were introduced in the 20th century. A type of wild sheep, the male has impressive, curled horns. There is a chance of spotting mouflon on Days 37 and 39; it is found only in the eastern Pyrenees.

Other mammals in the Pyrenees include wolf, lynx, wildcat, common genet, deer, fox, squirrel, badger, wild boar, otter and stoat.

Reptiles and amphibians

The Pyrenean rock lizard can be seen sunbathing on warm days. This small reptile has a body of about 6cm long and its tail is slightly less than double that length. The species is endemic and occurs in a restricted area in the higher part of the central Pyrenees, between 1600 and 3000m. In the lower parts of the entire Pyrenean range, the common wall lizard is, as its name suggests, a regular sight. This lizard has a strongly marked grey back, whereas the Pyrenean rock lizard is a more uniform grey. A much larger lizard can be seen too: the western green lizard, which has a brilliant emerald-green body of up to 40cm long. Its preferred temperature is 32–33°C, so you are more likely to see it closer to the Mediterranean Sea.

Opposite: Heath fritillary on a Pyrenean thistle; common wall lizard; fire salamander; mountain Apollo; beautiful demoiselle; two-toothed goldenring

When it rains, most hikers think about finding shelter, but this is the fire salamander's favourite weather for an outing. Usually they are active only in the evening and the night, but on a rainy day you may well spot this black-and-yellow creature in a forest. They prefer deciduous forests where they like to hide in fallen leaves, when not hunting for spiders, slugs, newts and young frogs. The Pyrenean brook salamander is another endemic species in the Pyrenees; this largely aquatic variety grows to 16cm long and can be seen in slow-moving streams between 700 and 2500m.

The only venomous snake in the Pyrenees is the asp viper. This snake has a distinctive black zig-zag pattern on its back and is on average 60cm long. It likes warm areas that are exposed to the sun, with some plant cover. It occurs in the lower Pyrenees (below 2100m), notably in limestone mountains. In the unlikely event of a bite, medical care should always be sought immediately.

Butterflies, dragonflies and damselflies

The mountain Apollo is a typical Pyrenean butterfly. Given the

generally rough and barren terrain of the Haute Route, you will only see the following species occasionally – most likely on flowers or close to water: purple emperor, heath fritillary, silver-washed fritilary, Pyrenees brassy ringlet and Adonis blue.

The Aigüestortes national park with its many lakes is a great place for dragonflies and damselflies; there and in other places you may find the broad-bodied chaser, two-toothed goldenring (which lives primarily around mountain springs), western demoiselle, banded demoiselle, beautiful demoiselle, common blue damselfly and large red damselfly.

Birdlife

A full list of the birds that can be seen in the Pyrenees is beyond the scope of this guide; only a small selection is mentioned here.

The Pyrenean range boasts numerous birds of prey. You will easily spot vultures, kites and common kestrels.

Vultures are represented by the griffon vulture, the Egyptian vulture and the bearded vulture. Vultures are of great ecological value as scavengers and these three cooperate in cleaning up the carcasses of dead animals. The griffon vulture is a very large bird with a wingspan of up to 2.8m. It can often be seen soaring above open areas, looking for food. When a carcass has been found, large numbers of griffon vultures are likely to be seen descending to the location. While they eat most of the animal, Egyptian vultures can be seen waiting patiently for their turn. Whatever the griffon vultures leave is for them. When only bones are left, the beautifully coloured bearded vulture comes into action. This is the only animal that specialises in feeding on bones: it lives on a diet of 90% marrow. Its powerful digestive system dissolves even large bones, and those that are too large to swallow it picks up and drops onto rocks in order to break them into smaller pieces.

Kites have a wingspan of 150cm. Both the red and the slightly smaller black kites are easily recognisable by their distinctive forked tail. They are opportunistic hunters that feed on rodents, birds and small fish.

The common kestrel is a relatively small bird of prey that can often be seen hovering 10–20m above the ground, searching for prey. If a prey is detected, the bird makes a short, steep dive to the ground.

Among the many other birds in the Pyrenees are two species that live along mountain streams: the grey wagtail is a small, graceful, yellow-and-grey bird that feeds on insects; and the dipper is a small, stout, short-tailed brown-and-white bird that is exclusively seen on riverbanks and on stones in rivers. It is unique among small birds for its ability to dive and swim underwater. Their prey consists mainly of invertebrates and small fish.

Bird's-nest orchid; mountain houseleek, of the Sempervivum *('always alive') genus; Pyrenean columbine; southern marsh orchid*

Flowers

The Pyrenean flora is quite spectacular. There is an enormous variety of flowers and more than 160 of them are endemic – for example the Pyrenean saxifrage, a large pyramid saxifrage that decorates limestone boulders and rock faces; the Pyrenean Ramonde, a beautiful purple flower that belongs to a large tropical family and can be found only on shady limestone rocks in early summer; and the Pyrenean thistle, a pink thistle that survives in clusters at high altitudes on scree slopes.

Common flowers that decorate the lower slopes and pastures in spring and early summer are narcissi, asphodel and gentians. In summer, mountain slopes are often filled with great yellow gentian, rosebay willow-herb, alpenrose and Pyrenean iris.

A good number of species of orchids are quite easily found in the Pyrenees. The black vanilla orchid is a tiny red-and-black orchid commonly seen in the lower moutains. In a forest you may be lucky enough to see a bird's-nest orchid blooming and in meadows you can see fragrant orchid, burnt-tip orchid, pyramidal orchid and the beautiful lesser butterfly orchid with its white flowers.

Beside streams and in marshy areas there are globeflower, marsh marigold, common monkshood, marsh gelwort, white false helleborine and common butterwort. In forests and open spots on lower slopes there are martagon lily, Alpine sow-thistle, great masterwort or mountain sanicle, wood cranesbill, Pyrenean columbine, common columbine, Betony-leaved rampion, spiked rampion, fringed pink, St Bruno's lily and the beautiful Pyrenean lily.

In open fields at the sub-alpine level are Alpine aster, Pyrenean Eryngo, Merendera, trumpet gentian, Pyrenean gentian, sweet William and the endemic spotted gentian. Where snow has just melted in summer, Alpine snowbell and Pyrenean buttercup make their appearance.

Some flowers survive at high altitudes on rocks and scree: Alpine toadflax, purple saxifrage, mountain

Sunset from Pic Carlit (Day 36)

houseleek, Pyrenean thistle, Alpine hawksbeard and glacier wormwood.

MOUNTAIN WEATHER

Mountain ranges have a habit of creating their own climate. The weather you will experience depends a lot on the season and the hiking window you choose, but a few generalisations can be made.

First, July and August are the warmest months in the Pyrenees and below 2800m most snow will have melted by mid July. Secondly, in the western part of the Pyrenees rain and mist are much more likely than in the eastern part. And finally, the weather in Spain is often warmer, drier and sunnier than in France.

The Pyrenees' climate is to a great extent determined by the Atlantic Ocean. Clouds pushed in from the Atlantic start to rise against the western and northern slopes of the mountain chain, causing them to cool down and release their humidity as rain or snow. It's common to see clouds reaching up to a certain height on the northern side of the high ridge while in Spain there is blue sky. In the Basque country there isn't such a weather frontier, and as a result rain and mist can be persistent on both sides of the border.

There will often be nice, warm weather in the Pyrenees, but it's important to realise that a beautiful, warm day may evolve to a potentially violent thunderstorm in the afternoon. It's advisable to always make an early start, so you can cross high passes before this might occur. If you notice a thunderstorm approaching, try to find a safe shelter (but not a cave). Should you be high up, descend to a valley, even if that means turning back. If a thunderstorm suddenly begins and there is no safe shelter nearby, keep metal objects (such as hiking poles) at 30 metres or further away and make yourself as small as possible, while minimising contact with the ground. Crouch with your feet and knees together and cover your ears with your hands.

Even without thunderstorms, the heat can be extreme at times, especially on Spanish territory and close to the Mediterranean Sea. This may lead to problems like thirst, dehydration, sunburn and sunstroke. Make sure to take enough water and find shelter from the heat during the warmest part of the day.

Weather forecasts are available at every manned mountain hut and nowadays mobile phone reception is surprisingly good in many places, allowing you to check the latest forecast online. A general overview for the Pyrenean weather is posted daily (in the hiking season) on the Météo Pyrénées Facebook page. The www.yr.no website provides specific forecasts for most Pyrenean villages and some mountain peaks. Keep in mind that it is very complicated to predict the weather for a high mountain area, so depending on your exact location you might get worse or better conditions. Be ready for anything!

WHEN TO GO

In general, it's best not to start the traverse of the Pyrenees before the end of June. However, as many people spread the complete route over several years, you could easily hike certain sections in late springtime without the need to carry an ice axe and crampons.

June

This is a good month for hiking in the Basque territory and, from mid June onwards, the final section of the Haute Route. Pic Carlit might still be snow-covered, but the GR10 variant (Variant 6) provides a safe alternative for this route. June is a great month for enjoying the Pyrenees' fresh green springtime colours.

July and August

These months are the best time for a long hike in the Pyrenees. They are the driest and warmest of the year, but bear in mind that frost can still occur at night when bivouacking high in the mountains. The snow will have melted in most places, except around the highest passes. Areas with lingering snow will be few and most likely they won't be large, but it's essential to keep safe in those places. If you decide to take the routes that go over the high passes, it's essential to know how to use an ice axe and crampons. In popular areas, such as the Parc National des Pyrenees, you will meet a lot of fellow hikers, many of them day tourists. In a village like Gavarnie you might even feel uncomfortable when you find yourself in a crowd of people, but elsewhere it never gets too busy.

September

The days are already a lot shorter, and at some point the weather is going to get significantly colder. With winter on its way, significant frost at night is to be expected on a regular basis. In a tent, condensation may become an issue. However, during the day it can still be comfortably warm and sunny.

Barranc de Llavera (Day 29)

Snowfall is to be expected in the high mountains.

GETTING THERE

By rail

The easiest way to get to the start of the Haute Route is to take a TGV (high-speed) train (https://en.oui.sncf/en/TGV) from Paris to Hendaye. The journey takes less than 5hr and the train station is at walking distance from the Atlantic Ocean and the starting point of the Haute Route. The train leaves from Gare de Montparnasse in Paris, which can easily be reached from any other Paris train station or the Charles de Gaulle airport. The Eurostar from London, for example (www.eurostar.com/uk-en), arrives at Gare du Nord from where you can travel by metro to Gare de Montparnasse. At the end of the Haute Route, in Banyuls-sur-Mer, there is a train station from where you can travel back to Paris.

By air

The most straightforward option may be to fly to Paris (www.parisaeroport.fr/en) and take the train from there, or it may be possible to find a flight to one of the airports in or close to the Pyrenees. There are airports in Biarritz, San Sebastián, Pau, Tarbes, Toulouse, Carcassonne, Perpignan and Girona. From these airports you'll have to travel on by train or bus to start your hike.

Advice on how to get to the start of each section is provided in the section's introduction.

ACCOMMODATION AND SERVICES

At the end of each route description, contact details for the accommodation for that day are given. Information can also be obtained from www.gites-refuges.com and www.pyrenees-refuges.com, and in Appendix A. Only Days 5, 8 and 31 end in a place without accommodation, but suggestions for sleeping indoors are given at the start of the sections. Note, however, that several other stages end at a location where there is only unmanned accommodation so you will need to bring a sleeping bag and food.

Throughout the Haute Route you will find a range of services including mountain huts/refuges, *gîtes d'étape*, campsites, unmanned huts, hotels, pensiónes, *chambres d'hôtes*, cash dispensers, banks, post offices, shops, restaurants and bars. A comprehensive table in Appendix C shows the distribution of all facilities on route.

Mountain huts and *gîtes d'étape* offer indoor accomodation and meals. A *gîte d'étape* is a form of accomodation found in villages along long hiking routes. It typically has one or more dormitories, and bed linen is provided. Some have a separate kitchen where you can prepare your own meal.

Many manned mountain huts have an online reservation system,

The guardien *of the Portillon refuge gives advice to a hiker (Day 21)*

which sometimes also indicates the number of remaining places. Making reservations is strongly recommended, as walking from hut to hut has become very popular in the Pyrenees. Even if you're only having dinner it's best to make a reservation. Bed linen is not provided at huts but blankets and pillows are, so you only need a sleeping bag liner or a very light sleeping bag.

Hut prices are fairly similar throughout the region. You can expect to pay around €40–45 for half board, which includes €12–20 for a bed (often half that with a mountain club membership card – check if your national mountain club is party to the International Reciprocity Agreement on Mountain Huts), €18 for dinner and €8 for breakfast. Many huts offer a packed lunch for about €8 and they usually sell drinks and snacks too. It's possible to pay by card in some huts but not all, so make sure to take enough cash with you. The *gîtes d'étape* in villages have similar prices.

Other private lodgings such as *chambres d'hôtes*, pensións and hotels can be found in some places, but they are not mentioned in this book. A *chambre d'hôtes* is the French equivalent to a bed and breakfast and can be quite expensive. It is a room in a private house which is rented out to tourists. Breakfast and bed linen are always included. A *table d'hôtes* is similar, the only difference being that here the host also serves dinner.

Unmanned huts – variously called *cabane/cabana* and refuge/*refugio/refugi* – are free of charge and offer protection from the elements. They mostly have a table and benches and some even have beds, but there is never electricity. In the author's experience they do not get overcrowded, but on the weekends you can of course expect to see more people there.

Taking a tent allows greater freedom in where to sleep. In most cases it is possible to pitch a tent close to the manned mountain huts, in a designated area. Closer to civilisation there are dedicated campsites where you can also have a hot shower and wash your clothes. Finally, bivouacking (pitching a small tent for one night) is allowed in some circumstances. In France it is allowed at least an hour's walk from any surfaced road. Inside the borders of the Parc National des Pyrénées the same rule applies, but you are allowed to put up your tent only after 7pm and the following day you must take it down again before 9am. In Spain, strictly speaking any form of free camping is forbidden. This law is aimed at preventing people from setting up long-term camps. In practice however, bivouacking is tolerated in most places, but well away from roads and habitation and between 8pm until 8am only. In the Aigüestortes national park bivouacking is strictly forbidden.

FOOD, DRINK AND FUEL

If you don't mind paying for food that has been carried up to the mountain huts, it's possible to have almost every dinner and breakfast in a hut. However, many hikers will opt to carry cooking gear, fuel and food. About every third or fourth day it's possible to buy new supplies and fuel can be bought about every week. Many people use screw-on gas canisters (EN 417 standard); these can be bought in Hendaye, Lescun, Gavarnie, Benasque, Tavascan and Ax-les-Termes (near l'Hospitalet-près-l'Andorre). Sometimes it's necessary to go off-route to find supplies. Most shops have a wide choice of food, but there are also a few shops where you'll just have to buy what you can find. It's important to take into account that most French shops close for lunch, and most Spanish shops will respect the siesta from 2–4pm or even 5pm. Many hikers will sometimes cook and sometimes eat in huts. The food in the huts is generally good to excellent and in some local places the standard is so high that you'd be missing out on something great if you didn't eat there. Eating in a hut or gîte is also a great way to get in touch with other hikers or locals. More precise information is to be found in the facilities list (Appendix C).

Water is easy to find almost everywhere, although it's advised to treat water before drinking wherever it might have been contaminated by animals. Using a filter or purification tablets are good methods. If there are grazing animals upstream of your water source, then treatment is definitely required.

L'Hospitalet-près-l'Andorre offers welcome civilisation after the Andorran wilderness (Day 34)

If water is scarce on a certain route, this is clearly indicated in the route description. On those days you should take plenty of water from the last source on your way. A drinking supply of 2 litres should be sufficient.

WHAT TO TAKE

Your gear should be aimed at not getting cold or too warm, getting enough food and water, finding your way, keeping yourself safe on the track and having fun while hiking.

The choice for hiking gear is very personal. Lightweight gear is recommended but it is not unheard of for trekkers to cross the Pyrenees carrying a 20kg backpack. If you make your choices based on your experience, capacities and motivation, you should be fine. Nevertheless, keep in mind that with a light pack you're likely to have more fun.

Sending gear that you no longer need back home (ice axe, crampons and maps) is sensible – for example from the post office in Benasque or Vielha. Beyond Vielha there are no more snow-covered passes. Sending gear or supplies ahead to one of the post offices or campsites on the way is equally possible.

Essentials

- Good footwear – lightweight boots or trail-running shoes
- Sock combination – wool hiking socks offer the best breathability.

Use them with a liner sock to avoid blisters

- Backpack – a capacity of 45–60 litres if you're bivouacking and carrying your own food
- Clothing combination – a layering system gives you the greatest flexibility. Consider taking synthetic underwear, zip-off trousers, two or three short-sleeved t-shirts, a long-sleeved t-shirt in merino wool and a light insulated jacket (preferably with a hood). Carry a buff, gloves and a hat for the cold mornings and evenings
- Waterproofs – a light waterproof jacket is enough. Use a waterproof liner in your backpack to protect your gear from rain. (The popular backpack covers only work in light rain.) Ponchos have gone out of style but they're actually a great option for protecting both you and your gear from rain
- Sun protection – definitely take sunglasses and a sun hat, and those who burn easily should take sun sleeves
- Drinking system – this should have a capacity of a least 2 litres, preferably a bladder type with a hose. Don't forget a water purification system
- Wash kit – toothbrush, toothpaste, soap and lightweight towel
- Sleeping bag liner – for use in manned huts
- Sleeping bag – for use in unmanned huts
- First aid kit – a compact one for the usual cuts, sprains, blisters, stings, pains, etc. It should also include a survival blanket or bag

Evening light on the descent from Pic d'Orhy (Day 7)

- Torch – there are plenty of small, high-power torches to choose from
- Maps, waterproof map pouch and a quality compass
- Money and documents – cash, bank card, ID card, mountain club membership card
- Alpine gear – nowadays lightweight aluminium crampons and ice axes are available. These alternatives to true alpine equipment are very suitable for the circumstances encountered in the Pyrenees. (Note that ice axes have to be registered with EuroDespatch prior to travelling on Eurostar – see www.eurostar.com for details)

Non-essentials

- Hiking poles – the constant climbing and descending will be a lot easier on your knees with a pair of these. In steep and rocky places, they're also a great help for your balance
- Waterproof trousers – if you like to keep your legs dry
- Hiking watch with altimeter – knowing your altitude can be useful when navigation gets difficult
- Camera – for capturing your experience in images or videos
- Books – a notebook for your trip report, a field guide to the Pyrenean wildlife and flowers or a novel for the evenings
- Power bank or solar panel – gives you the freedom of charging your devices anywhere. Note that some mountain huts have limited electricity and may not allow charging; other huts usually ask a small sum for charging
- Binoculars or monocular – for spotting wildlife

Camping equipment

- Sleeping bag – should keep you comfortably warm, even in temperatures slightly below freezing point. A down sleeping bag is the best choice for the Pyrenees
- Tent – a lightweight one that is able to withstand high winds
- Sleeping mat – preferably a comfortable inflatable one. You will probably never need to pitch your tent in a place with stones, so the risk of punctures is low
- Stove, cooking pot, fuel and lighters – carry at least two lighters and store them in different places in your pack. Note that fuel and lighters are prohibited on aeroplanes and on Eurostar. Gas cartridges or other fuel can be bought at regular intervals, but careful planning is essential

MAPS

The Rando Editions maps are an excellent choice for hiking the Haute Route. This series of cross-border maps is the result of a collaboration between the French Institut Géographique National and the Spanish Institut Gartografic de Catalunya. Ten maps cover the complete route. The relevant map is always given at the beginning of each day's route description.

If you're hiking the whole route in one season you could send the maps you no longer need home, perhaps together with your ice axe and crampons once you're over the highest passes.

The maps required to complete the entire Pyrenean Haute Route are as follows:

- Rando Editions Carte de Randonnées, 1:50,000, no 1: Pays Basque Ouest
- Rando Editions Carte de Randonnées, 1:50,000, no 2: Pays Basque Est
- Rando Editions Carte de Randonnées, 1:50,000, no 3: Béarn
- Rando Editions Mapa Excursionista, 1:50,000, no 12: Gavarnie–Ordesa
- Rando Editions Mapa Excursionista 1:50,000, no 13: Aneto–Posets
- Rando Editions Mapa Excursionista 1:50,000, no 6: Couserans–Val d'Aran
- Rando Editions Mapa Excursionista 1:50,000, no 7: Haute-Ariège
- Rando Editions Carte de Randonnées, 1:50,000, no 8: Cerdagne–Capcir
- Rando Editions Carte de Randonnées, 1:50,000, no 10: Canigou
- Rando Editions Carte de Randonnées, 1:50,000, no 11: Rousillon

Route-finding is easy at the start (Day 1)

Path Conditions

There's a large variety in path conditions over the traverse: you will encounter grassy paths, scree slopes, boulder fields, rocky paths, forest tracks and much more. Depending on the year and the weather window you choose, the conditions can vary a little, but all paths are doable for experienced hikers. You will cross numerous streams of various widths. None of the crossings without a bridge pose real difficulties; only after prolonged rainfall will you risk getting your feet wet. Substantial snowfall in late springtime does occur, and in that case you will need an ice axe and crampons in the Central Pyrenees (between refuge d'Arrémoulit and Hospital de Vielha) until the second half of July. Always enquire at the refuges about the snow conditions on the high passes – the warden will usually be able to explain the precise situation. If you're hiking without ice axe and crampons early in the season, then opt for the alternative routes that avoid the high, snow-covered passes.

Insurance, Mountain Safety and Rescue

Before you set off to the Pyrenees, make sure that your travel insurance covers mountaineering activities. Most standard travel insurance policies don't cover these and a rescue service is extremely expensive. It's strongly advised to become a member of a mountaineering club that offers adequate insurance for mountain walkers. An additional benefit is that, as most of the mountaineering clubs enjoy reciprocal rights with other countries' clubs, members receive considerable discounts on overnight stays at mountain huts.

Accidents can occur, even when you take every possible measure to

Rules for Walkers in the Pyrenees

- Don't leave any rubbish in the mountains – carry it down
- Never light an open fire – it's strictly forbidden in the national parks and in the Spanish Pyrenees
- Walk on tracks as much as you can
- Don't pick any flowers or plants. Don't damage any trees or shrubs
- Close gates that are meant to keep cattle within a certain area
- Respect local habits and regulations
- Respect local properties, such as *cabanes*, as basic or simple as they may sometimes seem
- Don't make excessive noise
- Try not to disturb animals

A young shepherd at work in Val d'Arrious (Day 13)

prevent them. However, you can take various measures to reduce the risk.

Do not walk the Haute Route on your own. If you do start on your own, team up with other hikers. At the end of June and the beginning of July there will definitely be others embarking on the traverse. Give your family, relatives or a friend a detailed overview of your route and timing and keep them updated regularly while you are on the track.

Carry a survival blanket or bag to prevent yourself or someone else from becoming hypothermic (the most common emergency situation). Take shelter (but not in a cave) or move to a lower place if a thunderstorm is approaching. Keep in mind that the midday heat can be extreme at times, especially on the Spanish side. An early start will allow you to cover part of the route in the cooler morning temperatures. When it gets very hot, find shelter from the sun and take longer breaks. Make sure you're carrying sufficient water until the next point where you can refill.

When you see a shepherd dog with a herd of sheep, pass the herd at a safe distance.

Carry a first aid kit and a mobile phone. A personal locater beacon (a satellite tracker with which you can communicate your precise location – see for example www.findmespot.com) increases the possibility of being rescued in an emergency. There is mobile phone reception in some parts of the Pyrenees but there are also long stretches without. The European emergency phone number is 112, and other relevant emergency telephone numbers can be found on walking maps.

Take a whistle with you in order to give the emergency signal when necessary. Make the same signal (for example a blast on a whistle, a yell or flicker with a torch) six times in a minute at regular intervals. Then wait for a minute and repeat the signal until you receive an answer. The answer is three signals per minute, followed by a minutes' silence. There are still a few remote corners in the Pyrenees, visited by only very few hikers and help may take a long time to arrive.

Remember the international emergency signals for communicating with rescue helicopters: hold both arms above your head in a 'Y' shape if you need help (never wave with both hands at a rescue helicopter when you don't). A clear indication that you don't need help is to hold one arm up and the other down to form a straight line. Always carry a brightly coloured piece of clothing with you and wear it in case of an emergency. It will make it much easier for rescue workers to locate you.

USING THIS GUIDE

This book contains all the information needed to follow the Haute Route. The route is divided into 44 days and nearly every day ends at a place where it's possible to stay overnight inside. If you're carrying a tent you're more flexible to divide the hike according to your own tempo. Options for pitching the tent are mentioned in the route descriptions. Several variants are described, allowing you to choose a route free of high, snow-covered passes or a less demanding route in case the weather is not in your favour.

Practical information on the route is given at the start of the route description: the distance covered, total ascent and descent, grade of difficulty, duration, map or maps required, and the important passes on the route. Conditions underfoot are noted in the actual route descriptions.

Keep in mind that the times are walking times and take no account whatsoever of breaks for lunch, rests or taking pictures. Hikers who complete the route a little faster in the first couple of days are likely to be a little ahead most of the time. Walkers who are a long way behind the given times should work out by how much and apply that to their onward progress.

Maps and profiles in this book

The maps in this book are, of course, not meant to be used as walking maps, but are intended to help walkers find the Haute Route trail on the sheet maps. In the introduction to each section of the Haute Route the relevant maps are listed, and at the beginning of the route description for each of the 44 stages a note of the relevant map is given. Height profiles are found with each map in this guide, allowing you to see at a glance what you can expect from the walk.

Please note that spellings – and even the placenames themselves – may vary. The maps in this guide primarily use the French/Spanish names but sheet maps often give local forms, and on the most westerly section of the route, these are frequently in Basque.

Grading of the stages

A grade has been given to each of the 44 stages, to give an idea of what to expect.

- **1:** these routes are very short, easy walks on well-worn paths with waymarks. Walks in this category are suitable for anyone.
- **2:** the second category is for the classic PHR routes. These hikes involve a full day's walk with a fair amount of climbing and descending. Most of the time the route uses paths that are reasonably well waymarked and can be followed easily. There may be some rough sections that have to be negotiated. Under normal summer conditions these walks contain no serious obstacles. Most of the day sections of the route are graded 2.
- **3:** the walks that have been graded 3 are suitable only for experienced, well-trained mountaineers who are accustomed to very strenuous days. These walks are very long and/or demanding. There is a lot of rough terrain to be tackled. The days involve long climbs, long sections without a path or waymarks (orientation could become a serious problem in poor visibility), some exposed sections that require care and/or snowfields that have to be crossed.
- **E:** E stands for 'exceptional'. This category contains some very demanding and difficult walks with steep and potentially dangerous exposed sections that

require great care. Here and there some moderate scrambling is necessary, and steep snow slopes may have to be crossed. The E walks often enter remote areas where your navigation capabilities will be put to a serious test. There are four days graded E and for each of these routes there is a less demanding variant that can be chosen if the circumstances are not in your favour.

GPX tracks

GPX tracks for the routes in this guidebook are available to download free at www.cicerone.co.uk/981/GPX. If you have not bought the book through the Cicerone website, or have bought the book without opening an account, please register your purchase in your Cicerone library to access GPX and update information.

A GPS device is an excellent aid to navigation, but you should also carry a map and compass and know how to use them. GPX files are provided in good faith, but in view of the profusion of formats and devices, neither the author nor the publisher accepts responsibility for their use.

We provide files in a single standard GPX format that works on most devices and systems, but you may need to convert files to your preferred format using a GPX converter such as gpsvisualizer.com or one of the many other apps and online converters available.

SECTION 1: HENDAYE TO LESCUN

Looking back to La Rhune and the route to Lizuniaga (Day 2)

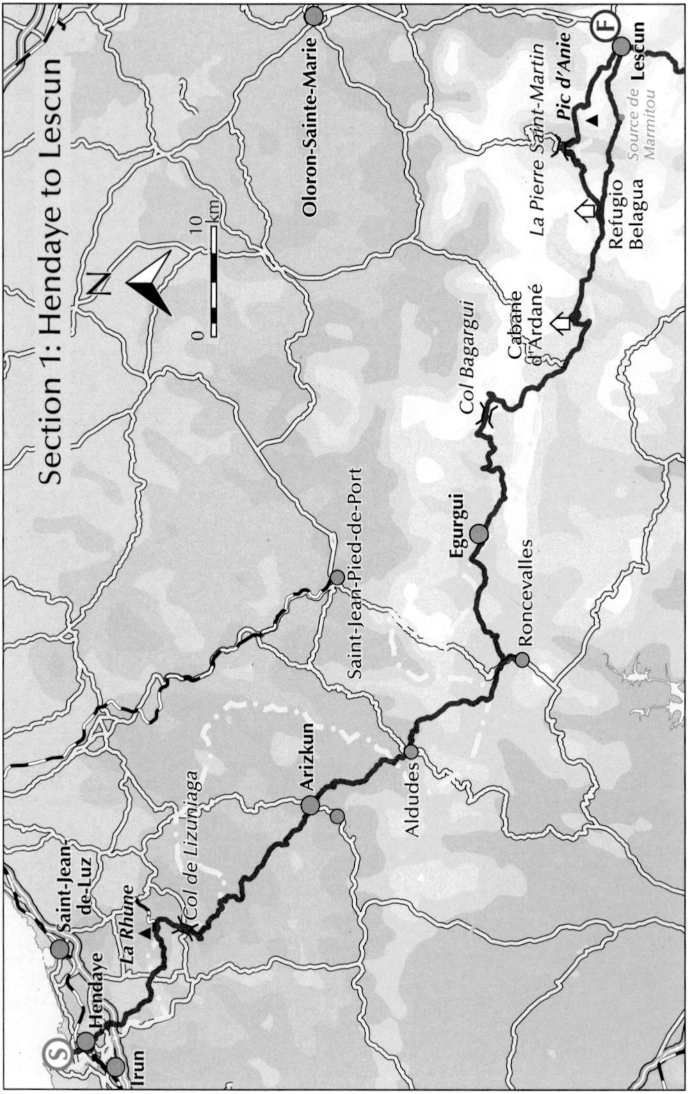
Section 1: Hendaye to Lescun
N
0
10
km
Oloron-Sainte-Marie
F
Lescun
Pic d'Anie
La Pierre Saint-Martin
Source de Marmitou
Refugio Belagua
Cabane d'Ardané
Col Bagargui
Egurgui
Roncevalles
Saint-Jean-Pied-de-Port
Arizkun
Aldudes
Col de Lizuniaga
Saint-Jean-de-Luz
La Rhune
Hendaye
S
Irun

The second day leads you higher into the Basque hills, from where you can still look back at the Atlantic Ocean

FROM SEA LEVEL TO THE FIRST MOUNTAINS

The route from the Atlantic Ocean to Lescun leads very gradually into the higher mountains of the Pyrenees. Initially crossing many beautifully green hills, it is some time before a 'real' mountain is encountered. The hike first goes over La Rhune (900m) and later passes modest mountains like Menditxipi (1376m) and Okabe (1466m) which are unlikely to leave a strong impression. The first real mountain is Pic d'Orhy (2017m), reached on Day 7. The Haute Route takes you over this summit by an exciting path that gives a taste of what the central Pyrenees have to offer. Finally, before descending to Lescun the trail passes through a high karst landscape with Pic d'Anie (2504m) being the highest point. The limestone plateau surrounding Pic d'Anie is a natural labyrinth of heavily eroded grey rocks and pine trees. It's an amazing and colourful adventure to hike across this bizarre plateau, where only few people venture. You are more likely to meet isards and marmots here.

The Basque Country (Euskal Herria in the Basque language, Pays Basque in French and Pais Vasco in Spanish) is truly beautiful with its small villages with traditional white-and-red stone houses, large forests and emerald-green grassy hills with herds of grazing sheep. It is an authentic region where you will probably meet more locals and herders than fellow hikers. The locals will happily tell you there's a good reason why their country is so lushly green: the influence of the Atlantic Ocean is particularly strong in this part of the Pyrenees, meaning an increased chance of rainfall.

At first, traversing the Basque country seems easy. There are no very high mountains or snowfields and just a few steep rocky slopes. Indeed, the author has hiked through the whole Basque Country under a blazing sun, enjoying every bit of the ever-changing views; while on other occasions there were times when mist and rain came in and stayed a whole day or longer, adding extra challenges to the hike. Visibility is often reduced to a couple of metres when mist comes down, and in such conditions your navigation skills will be put to the test.

HENDAYE

It's a tradition for hikers to have a swim in the Atlantic Ocean before embarking on the journey. Some hikers also put a little water from the ocean in a bottle which they carry all the way to mix with water from the Mediterranean Sea on the other side. Whatever you decide to do at the beginning of your adventure, Hendaye is a fine place to start. If you arrive there in the afternoon you might pitch your tent at the campsite and go for a walk along the 3km-long Hendaye beach. At the end of the beach you can admire flysch rock formations (beautiful sequences of sedimentary rock layers), and in the nearby Abbadia natural park you can see other fine examples of this geological phenomenon. The impressive Pointe Sainte-Anne is the northernmost point in this park; the cretaceous flysch rising up from the Atlantic Ocean make it a magnificent spot.

LESCUN

Lescun (900m) is a tiny village situated in a remote valley west of the Vallée d'Aspe. It is considered to be one of the most beautiful villages of the entire mountain range. The authentic, simple, grey stone-built houses are built on a steep grassy slope and overlook an enormous, lush green valley divided into small pastures. Isolated farmhouses, stone walls, small forests and hay barns punctuate this enchanting valley. But it is more than just a romantic valley: south of the village rise many sharp grey limestone peaks that together form a giant amphitheatre – the Cirque de Lescun. It's a remarkable contrast with the valley floor. Peaks like the Pic d'Anie (2504m), the Billare (2309m) and the Pic d'Ansabère (2377m) are not particularly high by Pyrenean standards, but due to the contrast with the valley they offer an impressive mountain landscape – one of the most admired in the Pyrenees. Lescun, with its authentic simplicity, fits perfectly within this landscape.

PRACTICAL INFORMATION

Public transport to Hendaye and the Haute Route

Hendaye is situated at the Atlantic Ocean, near the French-Spanish border. The village is accessible by train. From the Gare du Nord in Paris, take the subway to Montparnasse-Bienvenue and from there make your way to Gare Montparnasse (all together this transfer takes about an hour) where you can catch the TGV (high-speed train) to Hendaye.

The Haute Route itself begins near the Residence Croisière at the Hendaye beach. To get there from Hendaye's railway station, turn left after leaving the station and walk NE along the road that follows the railway. Turn left at the first junction, cross the railway by a bridge and walk N. Notice a small park on your left (with a pleasant view of Hendaye's port) and, a little further, a sports ground (also on your left). Leave the road that follows the coast and take the Boulevard du Maréchal Leclerc, which goes in a straight line to Residence Croisière. (Résidence Croisière is a large building with shops, bars and restaurants.) The Haute Route and GR10 begin here. The walk from Hendaye station to Résidence Croisière takes about half an hour.

Facilities in Hendaye

Hendaye has supermarkets, bakeries, bars, restaurants, cash dispensers and a post office. Camping is possible at Camping Alturan (tel 05 59 20 04 55) and Camping des 2 Jumeaux (tel 05 59 20 01 65); both are close to the beach. Camping gas can be obtained at the local Decathlon in the harbour. Hendaye has numerous, often quite expensive, hotels.

For information in English about Hendaye, see www.hendaye-tourisme.fr/en

Facilities in Lescun

Facilities in the village include a post office (no cash dispenser), chambres d'hôtes (Hébergement du Pic d'Anie), a gîte d'étape (Refuge du Pic d'Anie, tel 05 59 34 71 54), a refuge in the village (Maison de la Montagne, 23 places, tel 05 59 34 79 14) and a good food shop that also sells gas cartridges (carefully check the opening times as they vary from season to season). SE of the village along the GR10 trail is the campsite, Camping du Lauzart, with good sanitary facilities, free wi-fi and a tiny shop in summer. There's also a gîte on the campsite (tel 05 59 34 78 80).

Public transport from Lescun

There is no public transport that goes directly from Lescun. If you want to leave the Haute Route at this point you can walk or hitchhike out of Lescun on the D239, which starts at the church. Follow the D239 for 5km to Pont de Lescun, from where you can take a bus to Bedous or Oloron (see www.citrampyrenees.fr for the schedule). Both villages have a train station. Travel on to Pau, from where you can catch a high-speed train to Paris.

Variants

In case of poor visibility, Variant 1 offers a safer alternative route from Refugio de Belagua (Day 8) to Lescun (Day 9), following first a tarmac road to La Pierre Saint-Martin and from there the GR10. The GR10 route goes through a karst landscape that is just as beautiful and spectacular as that encountered on the main route.

Food

Food can be bought only in Arizkun (Day 2), Aldudes (Day 3) and on the Col Bagargui (Day 6). It's possible to have a meal at the Col d'Ibardin (Day 1), Col de Lizarrieta (day 2) Arizkun, Aldudes, Roncevalles, Chalet Pedro (Day 6), Iraty (day 6), Col Bagargui and Refugio de Belagua (day 8).

Maps

Rando Editions Carte de Randonnée, 1:50,000, no 1: Pays Basque Ouest; IGN Carte 1:25,000, 1346 OT: St Jean-Pied-de-Port; Rando Editions Carte de Randonnées, 1:50,000, no 2: Pays Basque Est; Rando Editions Carte de Randonnées, 1:50,000, no 3: Béarn.

Accomodation: contact details

All numbers and other information on accommodation along the Haute Route are also found in the route description.

- Hendaye: Camping Alturan – tel 05 59 20 04 55; Camping des 2 Jumeaux – tel 05 59 20 01 65
- Day 1: Hotel Lizuniaga – tel 948 631 031
- Day 2: Chambre d'hôtes Hordago – tel 07 86 79 41 14; Gontxea hostel – tel 948 453 433
- Day 3: Auberge Erreka Gorri – tel 05 59 83 83 04
- Day 4: La Posada – tel 948 790 322; Casa Sabina – tel 948 760 012
- Day 5: **no accommodation** – Refuge Aterbea on Day 6 is an option
- Day 6: Gîte Col Bagargui – tel 05 59 28 51 29
- Day 7: Cabane Ardané **(unmanned, no meals)**
- Day 8: Refugio de Belagua – tel 623 107 317 Variant: Refuge Jeandel – tel 05 59 66 14 46
- Variant: Refuge Jeandel – tel 05 59 66 14 46
- Lescun: Chambres d'hôtes and Gîte d'étape du Pic d'Anie – tel 05 59 34 71 54; Gîte La Maison de la Montagne – tel 05 59 34 79 14 or 06 75 48 43 95

DAY 1

Hendaye to Col de Lizuniaga

Start	Hendaye
Distance	24.5km
Total ascent	1580m
Total descent	1350m
Grade	2
Time	8hr 15min
Map	Rando Editions Carte de Randonnées, 1:50,000, no 1: Pays Basque Ouest
Route	Via the Col d'Ibardin (317m) and La Rhune (905m)

A long walk on footpaths, forest tracks and dirt roads. Navigation is easy under normal conditions. The Haute Route follows the GR10 from Hendaye as far as the slopes below Choldokogagna.

0.00 Residence Croisière (for the route here from Hendaye railway station see the introduction to this section, above). Opposite the Residence Croisière there is a roundabout and the first signpost for the GR10: turn your back on the Residence and the Atlantic and follow Boulevard du Général Leclerc to another roundabout.

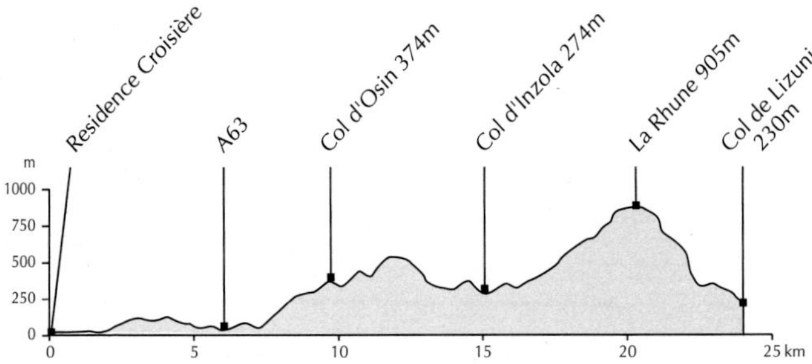

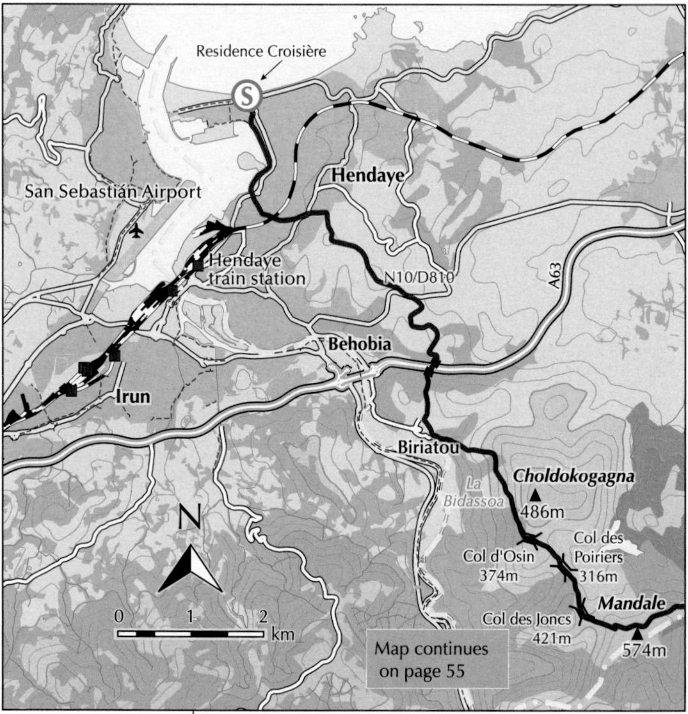

Turn right and take the third road, Rue des Citronniers. Follow the road to Boulevard de la Baie de Chingudy (a road by the water), turn left and walk along the water to the Jean Moulin roundabout, then continue along the water on a footpath, passing a sports ground, to reach a junction.

Turn left and go under a triple-arched bridge and follow Rue Pellot to another roundabout. Cross the roundabout and carefully follow the GR10 waymarks that lead you through a passage between a few buildings to find Rue Subernoa. Turn left and follow this small road until you reach a pedestrian tunnel under the railway; go through the tunnel and arrive at a roundabout then go

Hendaye, Baie du Chingoudy

straight ahead and climb E on Chemin de Biantenia until you reach the D358.

Turn left and after 150 metres, at a junction where the D358 turns left, climb further on Rue Errondenia. At a T-junction, where you meet Rue Pausoa, turn right and follow a track for 250 metres. Turn left at the highest point and follow a track that goes down slightly, then ignore a dirt road that branches off to the left and go up and down again. Pass a house (left of the track) and go down to the

1.20 N10/D810. Cross the road and turn left. Follow the road for 50 metres, then turn right and follow a track that goes down between trees. The path soon forks: turn right and follow a wider track that arrives near a few houses at a tarmac road. Go down this road to a junction and turn left (Route de Garlatz). Follow a small road, turn right on a minor pass and keep following the Route de Garlatz. Go straight on at an intersection and soon turn sharply left. Hike further down to the floor of the valley. Turn left again and follow the road for 100 metres, then turn right at a junction to climb S to a tunnel under the motorway (**A63**).

Looking back at Hendaye from Choldokogagna (486m)

Go through the tunnel and climb to a small road, then turn right at a junction and after a short, steep climb, turn left. Walk on a level road to a junction near a house (signpost), turn left and follow the road to another junction. Take the road on your right and follow this dirt road SE. Ignoring a path on your right, climb on a crest towards the **Choldokogagna** (486m) and arrive at a junction below a high-tension cable. Do not turn right; instead climb to an electricity pylon. After passing the pylon to the right, walk 250 metres E to reach another junction. Turn right and walk SE on the slopes of the Choldokogagna to arrive at the

3.15 Col d'Osin (374m), where the path from the Choldokogagna peak comes in from the left. Go SE down an obvious path to the **Col des Poiriers** (316m, signpost 'Pitara') and climb SSE towards the **Col des Joncs** (421m). Keeping the pass on your right-hand side, continue climbing, now E, and just before a small stream the path makes a sharp turn left. After a short climb N you reach a small plateau where the path turns to the right; pass the Mandale (574m), walking E on the northern slopes of the mountain. Beyond the Mandale, follow a forest track to the right of a pine forest, then go down to a tarmac road and descend steeply on this road, past numerous bars, restaurants and souvenir shops, to the

4.30 Col d'Ibardin (317m), at a T-junction on the French-Spanish border. This is where you leave the GR10, which turns left. For the PHR, turn right and go down into Spain for 50 metres, then turn left and follow a small tarmac road NE that climbs gently. After around 700 metres you'll notice a large restaurant (Restaurant Okalarre) on your right; leave the road, turn right and walk towards the building. Keeping the building on your right, you'll find a path. Follow this path, which soon bends to the right and arrives at a dirt road. Turn left and walk along a fenced picnic area (water available) to the

5.00 Col d'Inzola (274m), where a number of dirt roads meet and La Rhune (Larun) is signposted. Follow the track that climbs gently E and reach a dirt road that gives access to the summit of La Rhune. Climb this road, which passes **La Rhune** on its south side, pass below the

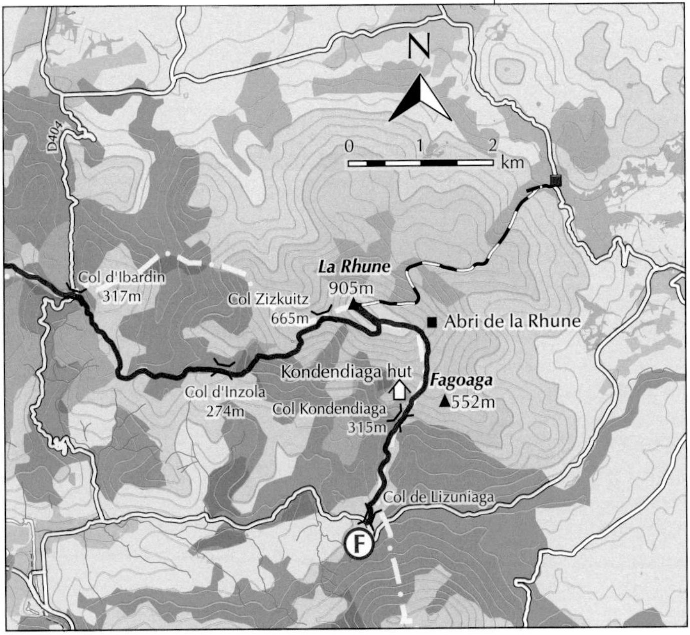

Col Zizkuitz (665m, border stone no 22), and at the end of the climb the road makes a turn to the left. (Walking all the way to the buildings on the top is optional; there are souvenir shops, a bar, restaurant, a *table d'orientation* and excellent views.) When you have the buildings in sight, past a small *cabane* (a shepherds' hut, closed) on the right, leave the road, turn right and find border stone no 25. Walk through the grass E towards border stone no 26; left of this stone the path goes down steeply to border stone no 27.

Continue descending SE on an obvious path until the path forks; take the right path and walk S to border stone no 29. The path bends a little to the left and arrives at a cairn where a steeper descent starts. Go down steeply SSW on the frontier ridge to reach the **Col Kondendiaga** (315m, border stone no 32 and an unmanned hut that sleeps 3–4), where several tracks meet. There are two parallel tracks that climb SSW: take the right track. Pass the point at which the tracks rejoin, take the right track at a junction and go down again. Turn left at the next junction and finally walk to

8.15 Col de Lizuniaga (230m, in Spain, close to the border). Hotel Lizuniaga, right at the col, also has a bar-restaurant and is open all year round, tel 948 631 031. Haute Route walkers are allowed to camp on the grass left of the path. There is a water point next to the road, a few metres west of the building.

DAY 2

Col de Lizuniaga to Arizkun

Start	Col de Lizuniaga
Distance	25km
Total ascent	1320m
Total descent	1270m
Grade	2
Time	7hr 15min
Map	Rando Editions Carte de Randonnées, 1:50,000, no 1: Pays Basque Ouest
Route	Via the Col de Lizarrieta (442m), Col d'Esquisaroi (515m) and the Col Bagacheta (793m)

An easy walk in normal conditions. The Haute Route partially follows the GR11. There is a lot of walking on dirt roads. Some improvisation is required on the descent to Arizkun.

0.00 Col de Lizuniaga. From the hotel, cross the road and follow a concrete road that soon turns into a dirt road. This climbs gently between pastures, and after 2km meets

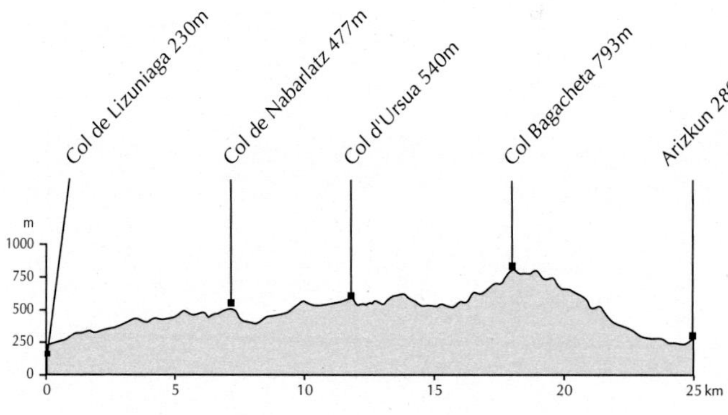

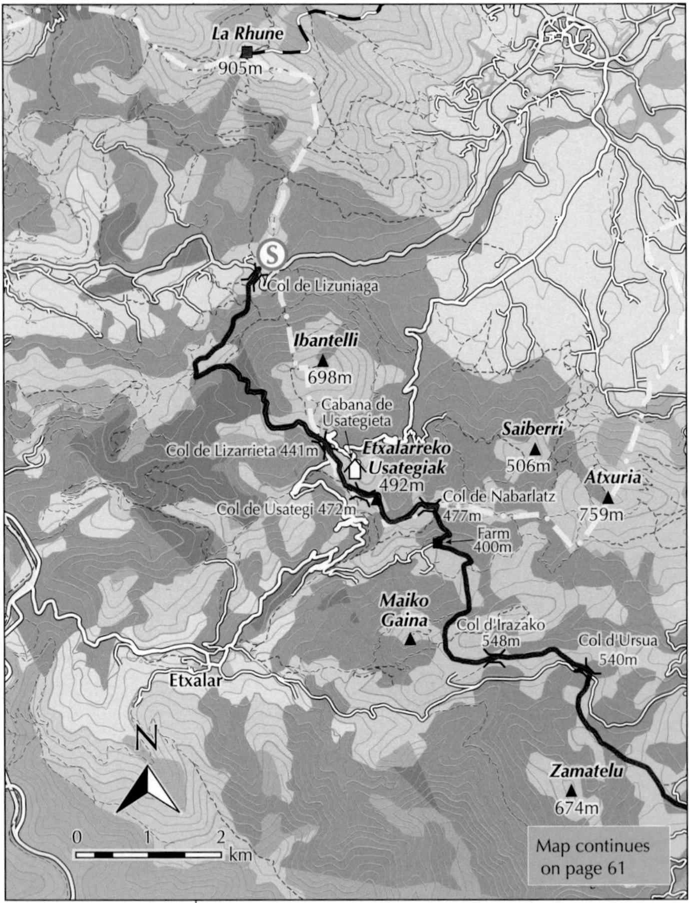

the GR11 coming in from the right. Don't turn right, but keep following the dirt road which bends to the left and climbs gently to the

1.25 Col de Lizarrieta (441m, border stone no 44). On the left there is chambre d'hôtes Hordago, where you can also eat lunch à la carte, tel 07 86 79 41 14, and on the right bar-restaurant Venta de Lizaieta (open 9–19h, closed on Mondays). Cross the tarmac road and climb SE on a dirt road. After 500m notice a path on your right, leading to small unmanned hut: Cabane d'Usategieta (basic, sleeps 2). If you don't need the hut, just continue on the dirt road and and pass **Col de Usategi** (472m, border stone no 46). Further on, notice a tall stone tower (a border fortification dating from the Peninsular war) on your left and keep following the road, on the French side of the border, as far as

2.00 Col de Nabarlatz (477m), at a junction. Turn right and after 100m reach a place where several paths meet near border stone no 50. Turn right, entering Spain, and go down S among bracken and turn left at a junction. Go down through forest to the Basate stream, cross the stream and climb W on a muddy track. Take the right branch where the path forks and walk to a farm; turn left and walk through the farm's courtyard, then follow the road to a junction. Turn right and arrive at another junction after 100 metres. Here turn left and climb SE on a dirt road through a small forest. Beyond the forest, pass

The Basque hills leading to Arizkun

the highest point (building on the left) and continue on a discrete path among bracken, which soon brings you to

3.20 Col de Irazako (548m, large trees), where a number of dirt roads meet. Climb the dirt road E, left of a fence. Notice a farm/barn on the right and walk underneath a high-tension cable, go down SE, cross a ridge and walk to the

3.40 Col d'Ursua (540m). Cross a small road and climb S on a dirt road, initially through forest, followed by meadows and hills covered with bracken. Climb gently to arrive at a minor pass, where the route forks: turn left and follow the road that descends to arrive at another pass with a junction, then turn right and go down the dirt road. Ignoring a dirt road on the right, continue to another pass (550m, old oak tree, several roads meet here), then turn left and descend SE. Notice a farmhouse at a distance on your left and follow the dirt road which bends to the right. After walking under a few beech trees, take a path on the right-hand side of the dirt road and walk on almost level terrain through bracken and a forest towards another dirt road. Turn left here and soon reach the

4.30 Col d'Esquisaroi (515m). Cross a small tarmac road and climb steeply SE between pastures on an eroded dirt road which becomes a regular path. Gradually the climb eases and you ascend gently for a while. In open surroundings the path forks; climb S to a dirt road, turn right and follow the almost level road to the

5.25 Col Bagacheta (793m, small iron cross).

In poor visibility it may be best to continue on the GR11 from Col Bagacheta and follow it for 7.5km to the village of Elizondo (shops, several hotels and restaurants). From there you can follow the N121B north for 5.5km to Arizkun and rejoin the Haute Route.

To continue on the Haute Route, leave the GR11, which goes S, and turn left to follow an unmarked trail NE. Initially almost level, the path goes down very

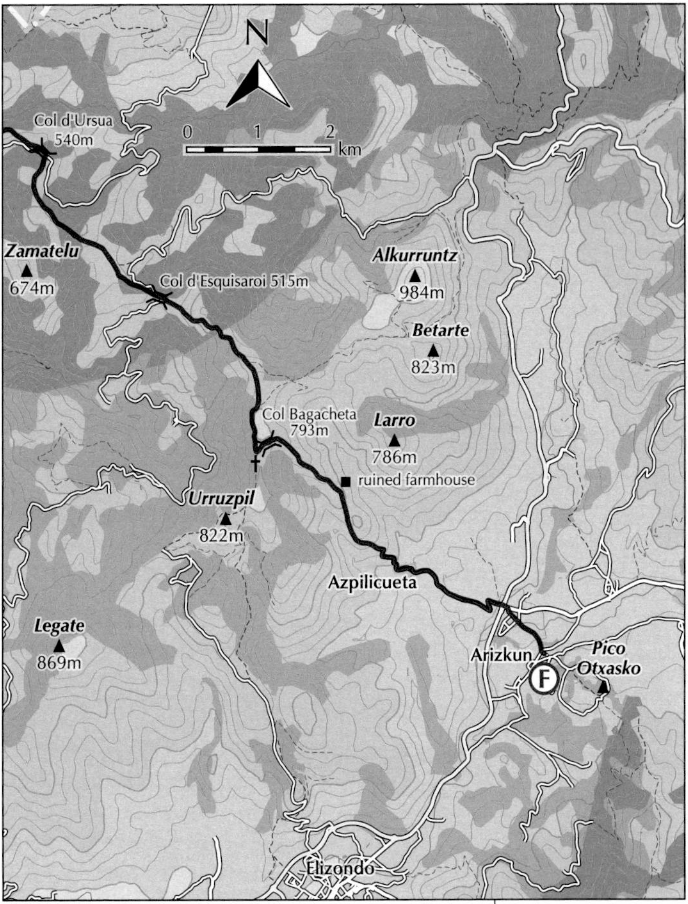

gently towards a ridge. Follow the ridge on the right side, rejoining it after a short descent, then keep the ridge for a short while on your left-hand side before rejoining it once more (670m). Cross the ridge and improvise a little as you descend E between trees to a **ruined farmhouse** which is surrounded by giant beech trees. Turn right and

Arizkun

follow the gently descending path, then cross the ridge (625m) once again and go down an eroded path. Turn right near a barn and follow a dirt road. After passing a cemetery, follow a small concrete road to the hamlet of **Azpilicueta** (370m, water point).

Turn left and walk on a road (NA-4457) to the N121B (250m, near the village of Arizkun), go straight ahead at the roundabout and turn right after about 50 metres. Follow the white-and-yellow marks which bring you to an old stone bridge (signpost for Arizkun), cross the bridge and climb finally to the centre of the village of

7.15 Arizkun (280m) – an attractive small Basque village.Turn right and follow the main road to the small village square where there is a bar. In the street to your left, near the church, is the Gontxea hostel, tel 948 453 433. There are no ideal places to pitch a tent near Arizkun.

DAY 3

Arizkun to Aldudes

Start	Arizkun
Distance	13km
Total ascent	815m
Total descent	725m
Grade	2
Time	5hr
Map	IGN Carte, 1:25,000, 1346 OT, St Jean-Pied-de-Port; and Rando Editions Carte de Randonnées, 1:50,000, no 2: Pays Basque Est
Route	Via Burga (872m) and the Col de Berdaritz (685m)
Note	It's essential to check availability at Auberge Erreka Gorri in advance as it is sometimes rented by large groups. Bookings should be made by email (alfarostatua@orange.fr) as there is no permanent staff.

An easy walk on paths and dirt roads. Navigation is straightforward in good weather.

0.00 Arizkun. Follow Calle Txuputo to the NE part of the village. Pass the church, turn right at a junction and

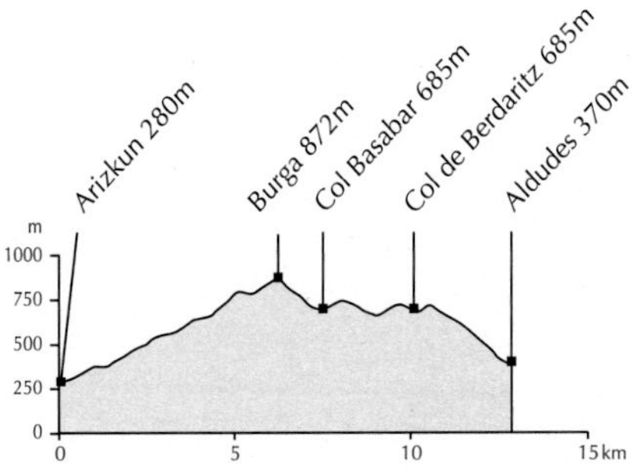

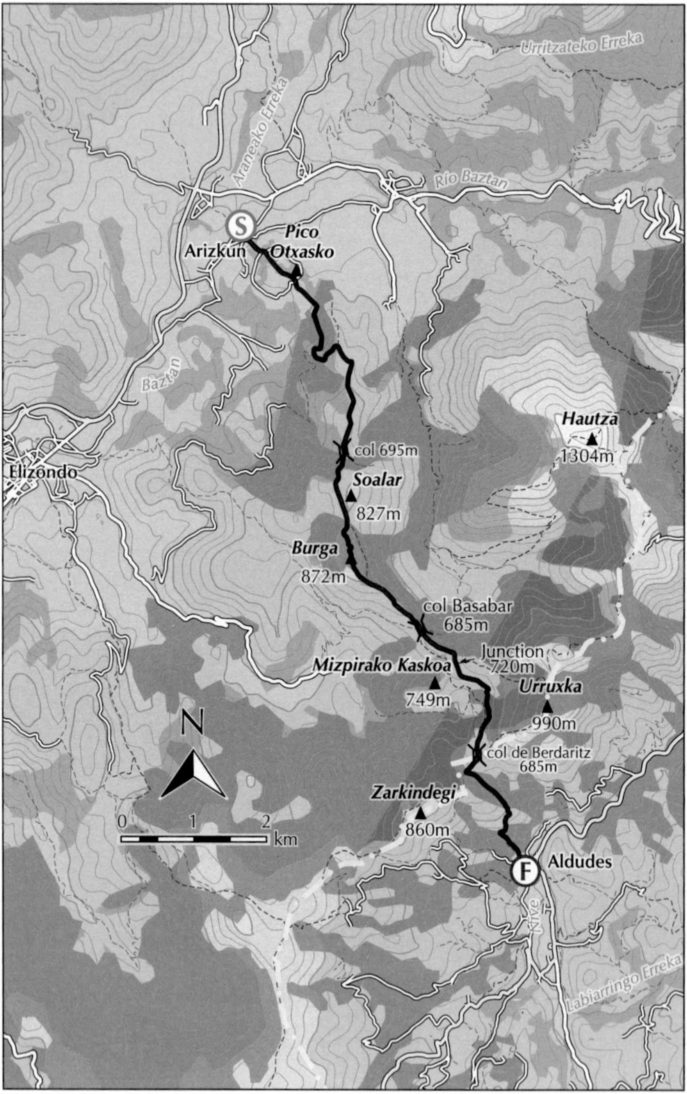
Urritzateko Erreka
Araneako Erreka
Río Baztan
Arizkun
Pico Otxasko
Baztan
Elizondo
col 695m
Soalar
827m
Burga
872m
Hautza
1304m
col Basabar
685m
Junction
720m
Mizpirako Kaskoa
749m
Urruxka
990m
col de Berdaritz
685m
Zarkindegi
860m
N
0
1
2
km
Aldudes
Nive
Labiarringo Erreka

follow a small road (San Kristobalgo Bidea) SE. After 200 metres, ignore a road coming from the right and turn right a few steps further on (when there is a house on your left-hand side). Climb on a path through a forest; this soon reaches its highest point and bends to the left.

The now level path arrives at a concrete road; turn right and follow this road which climbs gently and ends near a cattle grid. Ignore a dirt road to a farm on your right and instead follow the other dirt road. Then ignore a road that branches off to the left and keep climbing. Just a few metres past the highest point you will reach a junction; turn left and follow the road that goes around a barn and a pasture.

Ignore a road that comes in from the right and continue climbing. Notice a small white shed on your left, about 100 metres away. The dirt road now makes a sharp turn to the right. Ignore a small road that branches off to the left and keep climbing gently S on the dirt road until you arrive at a minor

1.50 col (695m) where there is a pasture with a barn on the right. Take the right-hand dirt road at a junction and climb further until the dirt road ends at a fence. On your left side there is a ladder going over a fence. Climb over the ladder and cross the field on the other side E, leading to an opening in the next fence. Follow a faint path SW and reach the Soalar peak (827m) after 200m. A few stones mark this broad peak. Follow a faint path S and soon cross a stile over a fence at the edge of a forest. Continue S on the other side of the fence, following a crest (no path, no marks) in a beech forest for 600m, leading to the summit of

2.50 Burga (872m), the highest point of the crest. The forest ends here and Burga offers fine views south. Turn left and descend on a path marked with some cairns alongside the forest, with a steep slope full of bracken on your right. Continue to a barn, walk between the barn and a stone wall, and then continue in the same direction, passing underneath a high-voltage cable and following a large track to the

Aldudes is situated in a valley along the river Nive

3.20 Col Basabar (685m, signpost). Cross a small road, ignore a dirt road on your left and the GRT5 path on your right, and climb straight ahead to enter a forest and arrive at a junction (720m). Turn right at this junction and, after the path makes a sharp bend to the left, walk SSE. The path now turns sharply right, passes the Urruskako farm/ guest house and continues to go down S to

4.10 Col de Berdaritz (685m, border stone no 117), where several dirt roads meet. Take the left of two tracks going SW and descend gently. After entering a forest, cross a stream and follow the path that bends to the left. On leaving the forest, you will see Aldudes down below in the Vallée des Aldudes. Turn left and descend SE on a dirt road which turns into a small tarmac road as you approach the village. Go all the way down, cross a stream, turn left and reach the centre of

5.00 Aldudes (370m), with the church on your left side. Cross the bridge and turn right to find the other facilities. Cross the bridge and turn right to find the other facilities. There's a good food store at the petrol station (ask here about pitching your tent) and a post office and a bar. Hikers without a tent can stay in Auberge Erreka Gorri (this hostel is sometimes fully booked by youth groups), tel 05 59 83 83 04.

DAY 4

Aldudes to Roncesvalles

Start	Aldudes
Distance	17km
Total ascent	1095m
Total descent	535m
Grade	2
Time	5hr 45min
Map	Rando Editions Carte de Randonnées, 1:50,000, no 2: Pays Basque Est
Route	Via the Redoute de Lindux (1220m) and the Col de Roncevaux (1057m)

Under normal conditions this is a pleasant walk on paths and dirt roads, through forest and pastureland. However, mist could make navigation very difficult, especially on the first part of the walk until Col de Méharroztéguy, as waymarks are not always present. You'll be walking above 1000m for the first time on this stage.

0.00 Aldudes. Walk from the village centre to the river Nive. Cross the bridge, turn right and walk S on the road towards the petrol station. Turn left just before the petrol station (Col Lepeder is indicated) and climb a staircase (yellow marks), then climb E on a well-worn path, first in zigzags and then in a straight line, to reach the **Col Lepeder** (495m, a few trees and cabins for hunters).

Beyond the col the path bends to the right; walk SE on the left side of the ridge on a slope covered with bracken. At a large track, turn left and follow the path, which arrives at a small concrete road. Turn right and climb a few metres to a small tarmac road (notice a barn and a fence for gathering sheep on your right), then turn left and walk on this more or less level road until you reach a junction. Here turn right and climb the road S to

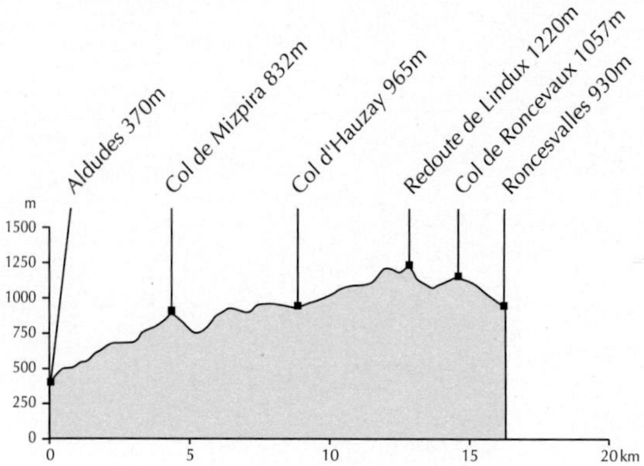

reach a minor pass (shepherds' hut on your right), then leave the road and climb straight ahead (E) on a large track. Where the track forks, take the left track and continue to climb E to a junction in a grassy area, where you turn right and leave the track that climbs steeply to Otsamunho.

Alternative route to the Col de Mizpira
In poor visibility it's easier to follow the route (yellow marks) to Otsamunho – a diversion that adds about 20min to the day's walk. From the junction on the grassy pass, follow a small but obvious track that climbs on slopes covered with bracken. Soon the path becomes more or less level and goes around the west slopes of Otsamunho. Arrive finally at a larger track, turn right and climb a few metres to a pass north of Otsamunho. Don't go down on the other side of the pass but follow a dirt road and walk S, keeping the bare summit of the mountain on your right. Descend to the **Col de Mizpira**.

For the main route, in good visibility, follow a large track that descends gently. Cross a small stream, climb a few metres alongside trees and walk to another minor pass,

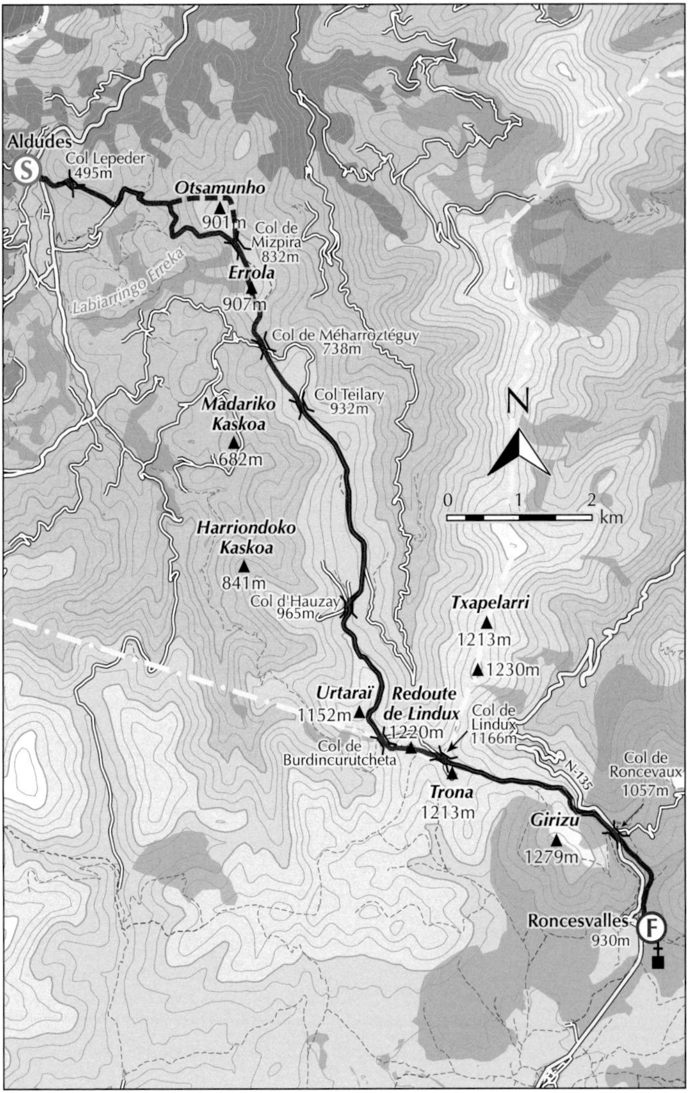
Aldudes
S
Col Lepeder
495m
Otsamunho
901m
Col de
Mizpira
832m
Errola
907m
Labiarringo Erreka
Col de Méharroztéguy
738m
Col Teilary
932m
Mâdariko
Kaskoa
682m
N
0
1
2
km
Harriondoko
Kaskoa
841m
Col d'Hauzay
965m
Txapelarri
1213m
1230m
Urtaraï
1152m
Redoute
de Lindux
1220m
Col de
Lindux
1166m
Col de
Burdincurutcheta
N-135
Col de
Roncevaux
1057m
Trona
1213m
Girizu
1279m
Roncesvalles
930m
F

View from Otsamunho (901m)

which offers fine views. The path now makes a sharp turn left and climbs E towards a few trees. Keep the trees on your left-hand side and make a right turn, then climb on an obvious path to a few rocks, where the path turns to the left and climbs gently to the large

1.40 Col de Mizpira (832m), near a drinking trough for cattle. Don't go down on the east side of the pass but follow a track SE that stays close to the ridge and soon arrives at a small pass. Continue climbing the crest SE on a vague dirt road to reach the **Errola** summit (907m), then descend steeply S on the ridge on an obvious track which turns into a dirt road. Notice a farm and a pasture on your left; turn right and arrive at the

2.15 Col de Méharroztéguy (738m), where on your left there is a construction used by farmers to gather and disinfect sheep. Cross a small road and climb on a broad track SE (there are numerous primitive constructions for hunters beside the track). In a forest the climb eases somewhat and you arrive at a ridge (900m); follow this ridge on the left, staying very close to it, and go down a little to arrive at a small road which you follow a short while to the **Col de Teilary** (932m, water point). Follow the same, almost level road SSE to the point where it forks, then turn right and climb gradually S on the road to the

3.30 Col d'Hauzay (965m, water available), where four small tarmac roads meet and Lindux is indicated. Turn left and climb gradually, mainly SE, on a road to arrive at the **Col de Burdincurutcheta** (1092m, border stone no 152); there is a shepherds' hut a few metres below the pass and it's sometimes possible to buy cheese here. Leave the road (in poor visibility it's better to follow the road all the way to Col de Roncevaux) and climb SSE on a grassy ridge that marks the border, staying to the right of a forest. The climb ends at the

4.30 Redoute de Lindux (1220m, border stone no 153), where there are excellent views of La Rhune and

Sunset at the Col de Burdincurutcheta

the Iparla ridge. There is a fence on the French-Spanish border: follow this, staying on the left of it, and go down to the **Col de Lindux** (1166m, border stone no 154). You'll arrive on the road you recently left; turn right, climb the road and cross a cattle grid near border stone no 155. Descend SSE on the road through a forest in Spanish territory to reach the

5.20 Col de Roncevaux (1057m, chapel and a monument to Roland), also called Puerto de Ibañeta.

THE LEGEND OF ROLAND

The medieval knight Roland was at the Roncevaux pass for entirely different reasons than the many pilgrims who later started crossing the Pyrenees here on the Camino de Santiago. In AD778 Roland was a Frankish military leader under Charlemagne. Charlemagne had personally led an army into battle with the Moors in Hispania and they were on the way back to Francia with a considerable amount of gold. During his time in the Iberian Peninsula, Charlemagne had enraged the Basques by destroying the city walls of their capital Pamplona. In retaliation, Basque forces attacked the rearguard of Charlemagne's army at a place where their knowledge of the mountainous terrain gave them an advantage: the Roncevaux pass at 1057m. Even though they were much less experienced warriors, the Basques slayed the whole Frankish rearguard, including Roland, in a surprise attack. The Basques, again thanks to their knowledge of the terrain, even managed to quickly disappear with the gold. It was Charlemagne's only military defeat.

Only much later, in the 11th century, was Roland's death elevated into legend with *The Song of Roland*. In this romanticised poem, Roland is cast as a role-model Christian knight who fights the Muslims until the end, after being betrayed by one of his own men. Due to the popularity of this poem, Roland's fame rose to such heights that several places were named after his feats. The Brèche de Roland near Gavarnie, for example, is the place where Roland supposedly tried to destroy his magical sword Durendal to prevent it from falling into the hands of his enemies. The sword, however, proved indestructible and created a giant opening in the Gavarnie cirque.

Perhaps only few pilgrims are aware of this history as they pass by the monument raised in honour of Roland on the pass. A metal sword used to be attached to the standing stone, but this memory of Roland has also disappeared. Most pilgrims are just relieved that they made it safely over the Pyrenees in their summer clothes and that they will soon be able to rest at the Roncesvalles monastery.

The pass is crossed by a road; cross the road, turn right and descend S on a track (white-and-red marks of the GR11; yellow marks of the GR65 to Santiago de Compostella) which soon enters a beech forest. Continue down until the forest ends and you arrive at a junction. Turn right here and walk on a broad track to the buildings of Roncesvalles, which you can see from afar.

5.45 Roncesvalles (930m) has bars, restaurants, two hotels, but no shops. ▶ The pilgrims' hostel only accepts pilgrims. Pitching the tent is possible an hour into tomorrow's route; make sure to take enough water.

Accommodation includes La Posada (tel 948 760 225) and Casa Sabina (tel 948 760 012).

DAY 5

Roncesvalles to Egurgui

Start	Roncesvalles
Distance	21.5km
Total ascent	1080m
Total descent	1160m
Grade	2
Time	6hr 45min
Map	Rando Editions Carte de Randonnées, 1:50,000, no 2: Pays Basque Est
Route	Via the Col d'Arnostéguy (1236m), the Col d'Orgambidé (988m) and the Col d'Errozaté (1076m)

A pleasant walk on roads, paths and dirt roads through forest and along grassy ridges that offer superb views. In good visibility there will be no difficulty in route-finding. The route is almost entirely along the GR11 for the first four hours. There is no accommodation at the stage end: unmanned huts on this stage and the next are an option if you are travelling without a tent.

0.00 Roncesvalles. Return to the Col de Roncevaux, turn right near the chapel and climb E on a small, winding road (it's possible to take shortcuts). After about 4km, arrive at a pass called **Port de Cize** (1430m, also called the Col Lepoeder; emergency telephone). Leave the road, turn left and follow a dirt road which descends gently to arrive, past the Menditxipi, at

1.30 Col d'Intzondorre (1375m), where several dirt roads meet and where you'll find a solid emergency shelter on your left. Keep walking NE on the dirt road which soon enters a forest. After about 2km you'll come out of the forest and find the inconspicuous **ruins of the cabanes de Bentarte** on your right. The dirt road makes a large curve to the left to go N to St Jean-Pied-de-Port (follow this road for 200 metres to find the Fontaine de Roland, where you can get water). Leave the dirt road a little beyond the ruins, turn right and follow the GR11 markers. Climb a few metres through the grass to a minor pass (1337m) and arrive at a fence that marks the French-Spanish border (there are three fences that come together here). Cross the fence and follow the border fence and border stones nos 200–204, staying on the French side of the border with the fence on your right. Continue along the border to the

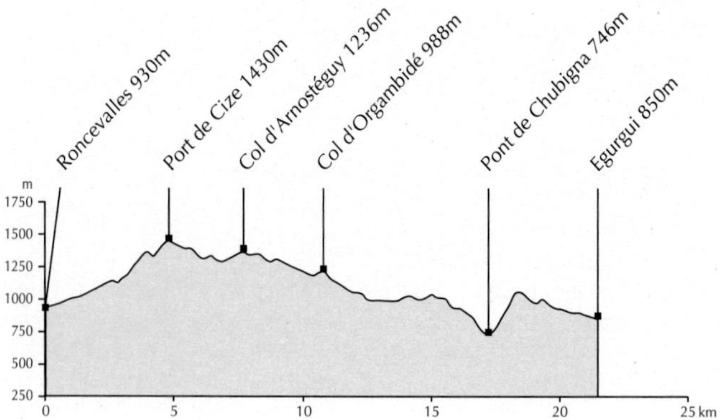

Battle of Roncevaux Pass monument, depicting the rearguard of Charlemagne's army being attacked by the Basques

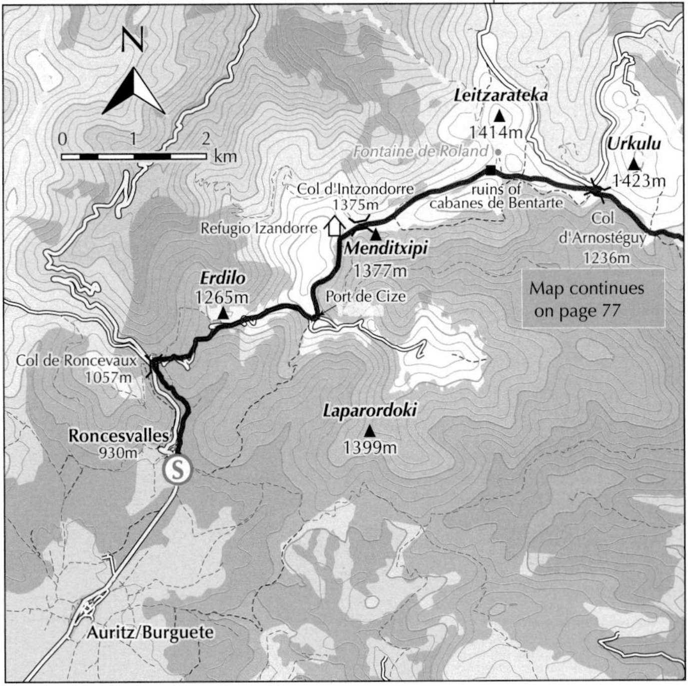

From the pass you can clearly see the Urkulu summit, with its remains of a tower.

2.45 Col d'Arnostéguy (1236m), near border stone no 205 and a small parking area beside the D428 – the road from St Jean-Pied-de-Port. ◂ Turn right, find a signpost and follow a broad, more or less level track SE. Ignore the path that climbs N to the Urkulu summit, and about 50 metres further on the path forks; leave the GR11 (which descends SE to Refuge d'Azpegi, an unmanned shelter with running water nearby) and go down E. Keeping all buildings and two small streams below on your right, walk to a concrete road (975m) where there is a large drinking trough for animals. Turn left and climb the road NE (after 200 metres you can cut across a field to avoid a very sharp hairpin bend) to reach the

4.00 Col d'Orgambidé (988m, border stone no 212). There is a green, unmanned emergency shelter a few metres below the col and a magnificent cromlech west of the pass.

The megalithic site at the Col d'Orgambidé holds more than meets the eye. The **cromlech** is easily found, but it is actually a very recent stone circle, which explains the contemporary artwork inscribed

The cromlech at Col d'Orgambidé

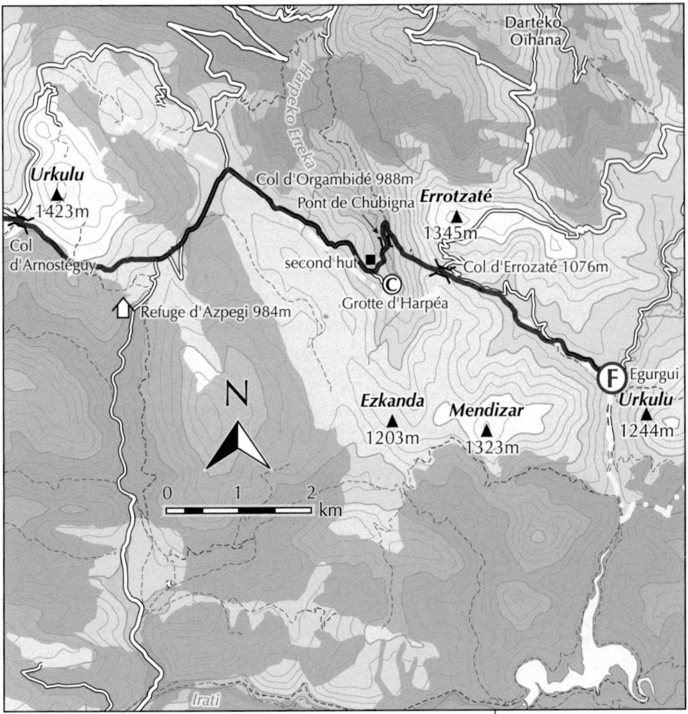

in some of the stones. The location was, however, not chosen arbitrarily: there is a megalithic dolmen just a short distance away, at border stone 212. This ancient burial site is, unlike many other dolmens, still underground and the border stone has been placed on top of the tumulus. The entrance to the burial place is clearly visible. Unfortunately, nothing is known about who the dolmen was made for.

Here you meet another road: turn right and walk SE, go past a first **shepherds' hut** and 300 metres further you'll notice a **second hut**. ▶ To continue, turn left, ignore the driveway to the second hut and walk towards

Here you can buy some of the best cheese in the whole Pyrenees and have a chat with the friendly cheesemaker.

a fence. Pass the fence on the right and go down steeply, following a faint path to reach the

4.55 Pont de Chubigna (746m; a great place to dip into the river). Cross the bridge, turn left and climb gently N above the stream. Very soon you'll pass a first gully; if you fancy a very steep climb, turn right here and ascend SE, keeping the gully on your right-hand side on your way to Col d'Errozaté. To follow the route shown on the map, continue N to reach a second gully. Turn right here and climb SE on a gentler path, then cross a fence close to the pass and walk to the

6.00 Col d'Errozaté (1076m). Don't go down the road below the pass but descend directly ESE on a vague path through a small valley in which there is no mountain stream in the highest section. Pass a *cabane* (closed) and a ruin and go down to the lower part of the valley. You'll find a small stream; follow this on its right side to the confluence of two streams and border stone no 223. Cross the stream and follow it (the best places for a bivouac today are to be found here) to the farmhouses of Uhartégain (915m). Go to the road and continue down to the bottom of a valley, where you'll find border stone no 224 at a confluence of two streams at

6.45 Egurgui (850m). Unfortunately, the unmanned Refuge d'Egurgui is no longer open. You'll find the building east of the stream; there are a few good places for a bivouac close to the refuge.

DAY 6

Egurgui to Col Bagargui

Start	Egurgui
Distance	15.5km
Total ascent	1075m
Total descent	600m
Grade	2
Time	5hr 15min
Map	Rando Editions Carte de Randonnées, 1:50,000, no 2: Pays Basque Est
Route	Via the Col Curutche (1285m), the Col d'Oraaté (1303m) and the plateau d'Okabe (1446m)

There are hardly any paths or waymarks in the first hour of the walk. Under normal conditions route-finding requires concentration; if there is thick mist it's better to wait until the visibility improves so you can see at least 50 metres ahead. From the plateau d'Occabé to Col Bagargui the route follows the GR10. Overall it is a pleasant route with attractive hills that offer both excellent views and dense forests.

0.00 Egurgui. From Refuge d'Egurgui, walk SW for 50 metres to a bridge. Cross the bridge, leave the road and

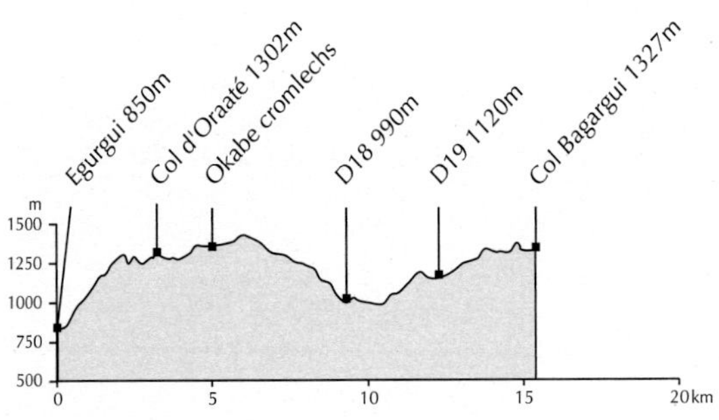

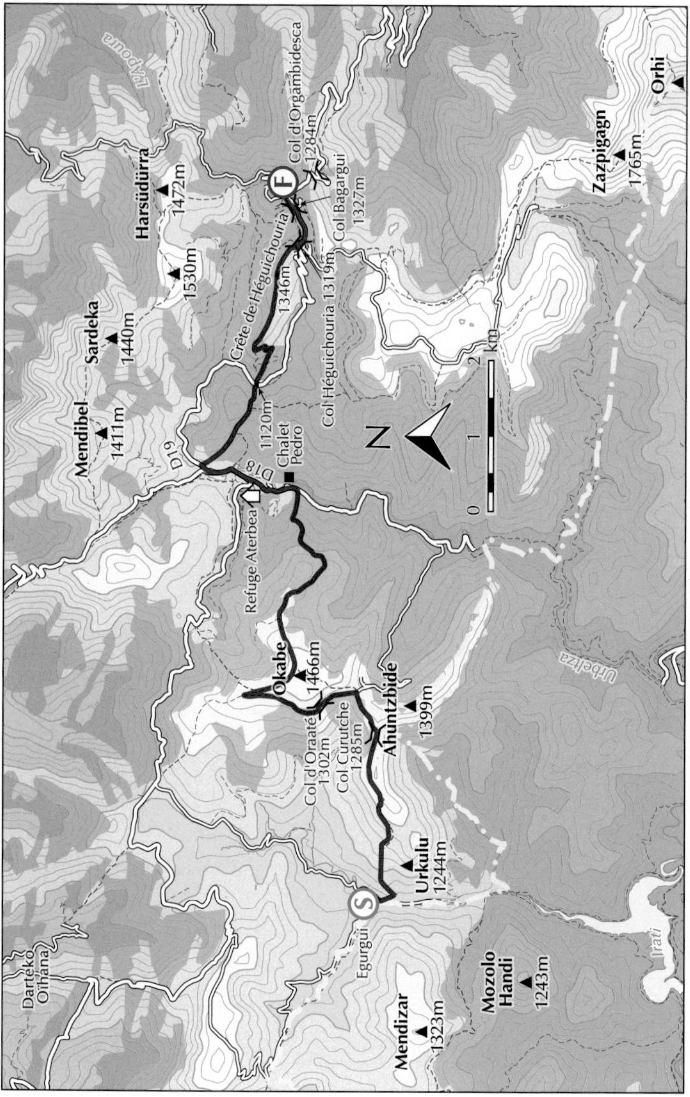
Darteko Oihana
Mendizar 1323m
Mozolo Handi 1243m
Egurgui
Irati
S
Urkulu 1244m
Ahuntzbide 1399m
Col Curutche 1285m
Col d'Oraaté 1302m
Okabe 1466m
Urbeltza
Refuge Aterbea
Chalet Pedro
D18
D19
1120m
N
0 1 2 km
Mendibel 1411m
Sardeka 1440m
1530m
Harsüdürra 1472m
Crête de Héguichouria 1346m
Col Héguichouria 1319m
Col Bagargui 1327m
F
Col d'Orgambidesca 1284m
Zazpigagn 1765m
Orhi

climb SE on a steep, grassy slope. As both path and marks are missing you'll have to find your own way. Keep a small valley below on your right and gain a large ridge. As you reach the highest point heading SE, you'll see another small valley in front of you. Turn left here and climb E towards a pass. Cross a false col at 1070m and walk towards the pass (1190m), situated between the southwest summit and the central summit of the Urkulu ridge. Turn left just before the pass, where you'll find white-and-red marks (wooden posts), and climb steeply through the grass to the ridge.

Pass the northeast summit (1333m) to the left and locate a faint track. Follow this more or less level path

Two-toothed goldenring dragonfly in the Iraty forest

which goes around a summit and approaches a minor pass. The path stays just below the pass and goes around another summit; keep following it to arrive at the large, grassy **Col Curutche** (1285m). Turn left here, follow the marks and walk NE in the upper section of a small forest (Bois de Néquécharre, water point), where you'll find a track. Follow the almost level track until, once out of the forest, you reach the

1.50 Col d'Oraaté (1302m), at the end of a small road. ◂ Ignore the road and follow a dirt road N, climbing very gradually and passing the **Okabe** (also called Occabé) summit on its west side. Past the Okabe you'll arrive at an extensive grassy plateau – the plateau d'Okabe. It's here that you'll meet the GR10, near the cromlechs of the Okabe; the Haute Route now follows the GR10 to Col Bagargui. Turn right and follow an obvious broad track that climbs S in the direction of the Okabe. Ignore a track on your left, and one that leads to the summit, and instead go E and then down NE to a plain covered with bracken, heath and bilberry. Don't turn left at a junction, but take the track that goes down into the Iraty forest as far as the bottom of the valley at the

Here you have fine views of tomorrow's obstacle: the Pic d'Orhy (2017m).

Two types of heather in the Iraty forest

3.15 D18 (990m, signpost). Turn left, noting **Chalet Pedro** on your right (reservation required for the restaurant, tel 05 59 28 55 98; the gîte is for longer stays only) and climb a little N on the road. Pass a large flat area on the banks of Rio Urbeltza (many tourists park their campervans here). On your left you'll find **Refuge Aterbea** – a non-guarded, comfortable shelter (10 places, toilets and showers). After a further 1.5km the road forks; turn right, taking the D19 that leads to Larrau, and turn right again after about 80 metres. Climb SE in a forest on a dirt road to reach a pass (1190m), and rather than turning right here, go down to the

4.15 D19 – the same road you just left. Cross the road, walk over the dam of an artificial lake (1120m), and the route bends to the right. Climb SE in long zigzags on a dirt road to the

5.05 Crête (ridge) de Héguichouria (1346m) with fine views of pic d'Orhy. Continue to climb along the ridge, passing two chalets, and go down to the **Col Héguichouria** (1319m) where you'll meet the D19 again. If staying at the gîte d'étape, check in here at the bureau d'accueil. In the same building there is a small shop that sells food and gas canisters (the gîte itself is located at Col Bagargui). Turn left and follow the almost level road E until you reach the

5.15 Col Bagargui (1327m, also called Col Bagargiak) in the Iraty tourist complex. It isn't the most attractive place to stay for the night, but there is a bar/restaurant and a gîte d'étape (15 places, tel 05 59 28 51 29).

COL D'ORGAMBIDESCA

If you continue on the D19 from Col Bagargui towards Larrau for about 500 metres you will arrive at the Col d'Orgambidesca (1284m), a grassy bluff next to the road. In autumn, ornithologists gather on this pass (where hunting is not allowed) to watch migratory birds crossing the Pyrenees. Bird lovers also come to the pass in summer, especially to watch vultures and birds of prey.

DAY 7

Col Bagargui to Cabane d'Ardané

Start	Col Bagargui
Distance	18km
Total ascent	1320m
Total descent	1335m
Grade	3
Time	7hr 15min
Map	Rando Editions Carte de Randonnées, 1:50,000, no 2: Pays Basque Est
Route	Via the Pic d'Orhy (2017m) and the Port de Larrau (1585m)

A demanding, tough walk. Even under normal conditions route finding can be challenging as there is often no path. In mist, navigation will be difficult. In strong winds, care is required on the Zazpigagn ridge. For the first time you'll be above 2000m. In good conditions this is a superb walk during which you stay very close to the frontier ridge. The stage ends at an unmanned hut so you will need to bring food.

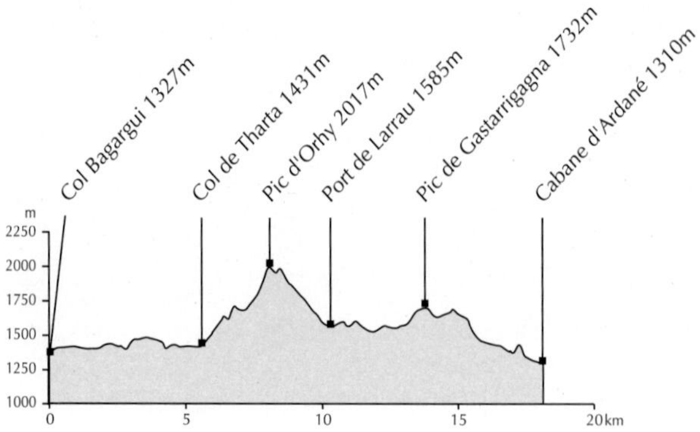

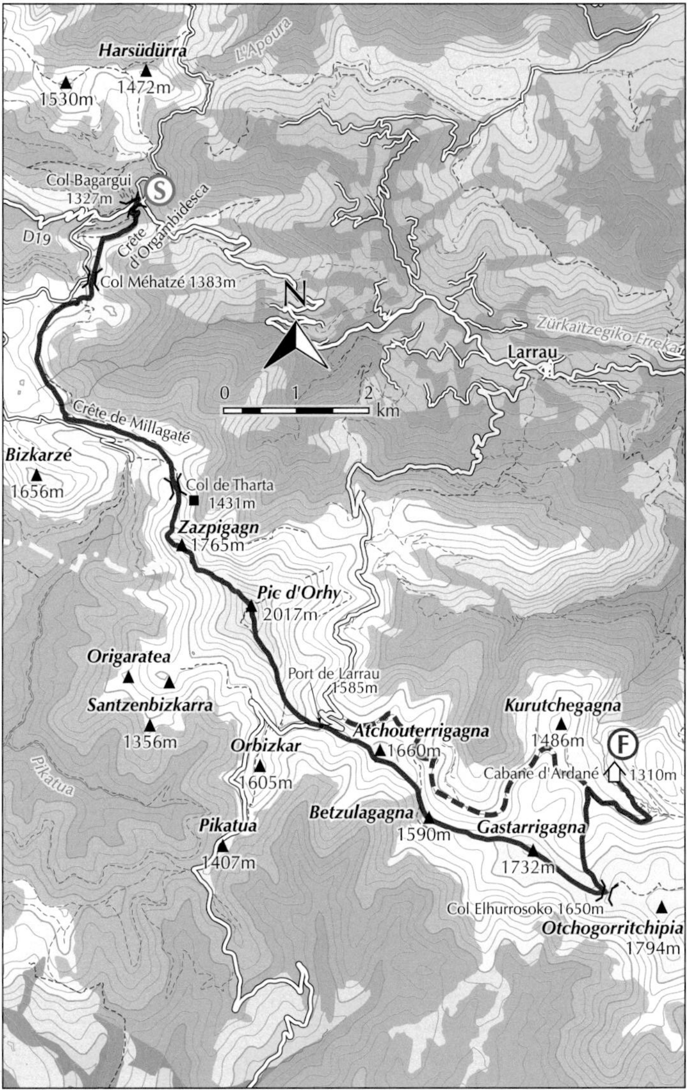
Harsüdürra
1472m
1530m
L'Apoura
Col Bagargui
1327m
S
D19
Crête d'Orgambidesca
Col Méhatzé 1383m
N
Zürkaïtzegiko Erreka
Larrau
0
1
2
km
Crête de Millagaté
Bizkarzé
1656m
Col de Tharta
1431m
Zazpigagn
1765m
Pic d'Orhy
2017m
Origaratea
Santzenbizkarra
1356m
Port de Larrau
1585m
Kurutchegagna
1486m
F
Atchouterrigagna
1660m
Orbizkar
1605m
Cabane d'Ardané
1310m
Pikatua
Betzulagagna
1590m
Gastarrigagna
Pikatua
1407m
1732m
Col Elhurrosoko 1650m
Otchogorritchipia
1794m

It's worth making a very early start to admire the sunrise at the Crête d'Orgambidesca.

0.00 Col Bagargui. ◂ Cross the D19 at the gîte d'étape and climb a small, winding tarmac road, passing several chalets. Near the highest chalet you'll notice a dirt road on your right; leave the road, ignore the dirt road and climb in a straight line on a very steep path S to the **Crête d'Orgambidesca** (1400m). Turn right, follow the ridge SW with the forest on your right-hand side, and walk towards a few antennas. Then turn left and descend S to the

0.30 Col Méhatzé (1383m), where there is a road on your right and a small hut below the road. Follow a track SSW to arrive at a drinking trough for cattle. Don't turn left but go past the trough and cross a small stream. After a short climb, arrive at a ridge with a dirt road, then turn right and follow the road which climbs a little to a junction.

Turn left, climb the road for a short while and then go down on the road towards a large hut for hunters. Turn right 50 metres before reaching the hut and continue S on an almost level path. There are several cattle tracks, making it difficult to stay on course: try to stay as level as possible. After crossing a few streams (possibly dry in summer) followed by a short ascent you'll reach the Millagaté ridge (1460m). Follow some ancient green marks and arrive at a hut (made of metal plates) beside a dirt road. Follow this dirt road SE, turn left at a junction and climb SE through grass to the

1.55 Col de Tharta (1431m), where the ascent of Pic d'Orhy really begins. Climb S on a grassy ridge, following a line of shelters for hunters (there is also a useful emergency shelter at the start), to reach the Crête de **Zazpigagn** (1765m). Follow a path that turns left and climbs SE on the limestone ridge, which becomes very narrow. Finally, descend steeply to reach a small gap. On your left there is a path that goes below the ridge (on the northeast side) for a while; leave the ridge temporarily, go down a few metres through loose scree and then climb steeply to reach the ridge again. Cross a fence via a triangular ladder and climb SE, staying close to the frontier ridge (ignore cattle tracks that will lead you away from the ridge), to reach the summit of:

Pic d'Orhy: the route's first peak over 2000m

3.55 Pic d'Orhy (2017m, concrete post) – the first 2000m summit of the route so far. Walk a few metres S on a level path, then descend SE on the right side of the ridge. Keeping close to the ridge, ignore a path that turns right towards a water reservoir and arrive at the

4.50 Port de Larrau (1585m, border stone no 237), with parking areas on both sides of the pass.

Bad weather route to Cabane d'Ardané

In bad weather it's advisable to leave the border ridge at the Port de Larrau. Descend N on the road for 1km to reach a junction, then turn right and follow a dirt road E for 6km to Cabane d'Ardané.

Cross the road, pass border stone no 237bis, and follow the frontier ridge SE (white-and-red markers). Pass a small summit to arrive at the **Pic de l'Achourterrigagna** (1660m, border stone no 238), then stay on the ridge and go down to the Port de Betzula (1540m, border stone no 239). Now ignore the markers and keep following the ridge as it climbs to the **Betzulagagna** (1590m), and then go down to the Col de Bildocharréko (1565m, border stone 240) before climbing (no path) E to the:

Cabane d'Ardané

6.10 Pic de Gastarrigagna (1732m, border stone no 241).

Pass the summit on its south side and descend SE on the ridge to the **Col Elhurrosoko** (1650m, border stone no 242), then turn left and descend N. There is no distinct path; just follow one of several cattle tracks on your way down to a dirt road on the French side of the border. Once there, turn right and follow the dirt road until you arrive at a junction. Turn left, pass a shepherds' hut (1330m) to the right and continue to the

7.15 Cabane d'Ardané (1310m, eight places, fireplace). There is a water source between the shepherds' hut and the cabane, next to the stream. Ask the shepherd if you can't find it.

DAY 8

Cabane d'Ardané to Source de Marmitou

Start	Cabane d'Ardané
Distance	22km
Total ascent	1465m
Total descent	925m
Grade	2
Time	8hr 30min
Map	Rando Editions Carte de Randonnées, 1:50,000, no 2: Pays Basque Est; and no 3: Béarn
Route	Via the Col Uthu (1664m), the Port de Belhay, Refugio de Belagua (1428m) and the Col d'Anaye (2086m)

The Haute Route stays very close to the frontier ridge for the first four hours of today's climb, then the second half is a beautiful climb through a fantastical limestone landscape, a natural labyrinth in which the waymarks have to be followed carefully to stay on course. The route between the Col Uthu and the Col d'Anaye is marked with white-and-red paintflashes. Today you'll enter the high mountains of the Pyrenees. The newly renovated Refugio de Belagua (around the midway point of this stage) offers a comfortable shelter and good food.

0.00 Cabane d'Ardané. Return to the shepherds' hut and to the junction of dirt roads. Turn left and follow the road that crosses the stream and makes a long zigzag. The road climbs on this zigzag and arrives at a minor pass, where it bends sharply to the left and starts to descend. Don't go left, but leave the road at this minor pass, following an obvious track ESE in the grass, and climb in a straight line to the

0.50 Col Uthu (1664m, fence, border stone no 247). ▸ Cross the fence and follow the track that bends towards the frontier ridge and skirts the southern slopes of the Chardékagagna (1893m). After reaching border stone

There are white-and-red markers from here until the Col d'Anaye.

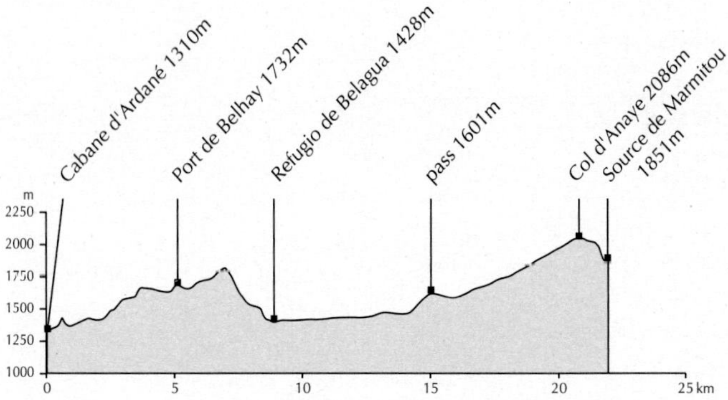

no 249, continue to walk along the south side of the ridge and arrive at the

1.55 Port de Belhay (1732m, border stone no 250). Go down on the French side to a fence, cross the fence, go down a few metres and turn right. Climb gradually E on a vague track through scree on the slope of the mountain to your right. Once past the mountain, walk through grass; the route (no path, only markers) climbs steeply SE in a straight line to a nameless pass (1810m) on the frontier ridge. ◄ From here, go down steeply on the Spanish side in a straight line and cross the **Port de Bimbalette** (1677m) on the south side of Pic de Bimbalette.

There are excellent views taking in the Pic d'Orhy, the Bisaurin (2668m) and the summits of the Lescun region.

The descent soon eases. Cross a stream and walk E along hills with a few pine trees. Cross several tiny streams (possibly dry in summer) and walk E on a more or less level path. A very large pass on the frontier (the **Port d'Ourdayté**, 1416m, border stone no 255) should be kept on your left-hand side; stay in Spain and walk ESE through grass.

After passing a drinking trough for cattle, notice a former customs house on the right, keep a farmhouse in the distance on your right and approach a road (which goes to the Col de la Pierre Saint-Martin). Keep the road

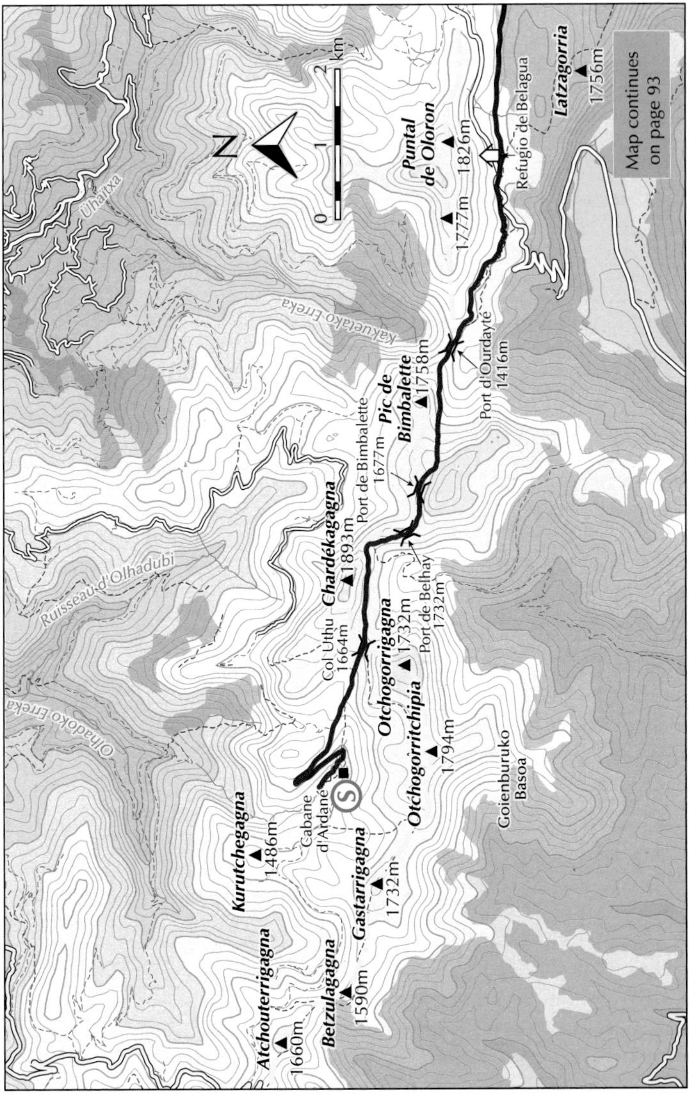
N
0
1
2 km
Uhaitxa
Kakuetako Erreka
Ruisseau d'Olhadubi
Olhadoko Erreka
Puntal de Oloron
1826m
1777m
Refugio de Belagua
Latzagorria
1756m
Map continues on page 93
Pic de Bimbalette
1758m
Port d'Ourdayté
1416m
Port de Bimbalette
1677m
Chardékagagna
1893m
Port de Belhay
1732m
Otchogorrigagna
1732m
Col Uthu
1664m
Otchogorritchipia
1794m
Goienburuko Basoa
Cabane d'Ardané
Kurutchegagna
1486m
Gastarrigagna
1732m
Atchouterrigagna
1660m
Betzulagagna
1590m

Karst landscape on the way to the Col d'Anaye

on your right-hand side for a few hundred metres, then cross the road, follow a path that climbs a little and reach

4.20 Refugio de Belagua (1428m), at the end of a large parking area. ◄ Open all year round, 56 places, tel 632 10 73 17.

Variant 1 leaves the main route here and offers a safer alternative in poor visibility. It takes you to Lescun (Day 9) via Refuge Jeandel and Refuge de Labérouat.

Pass the large hut and keep following the red-and-white markers, but make sure not to follow the GR track that goes down! Cross a stream and follow a cattle track NE on an almost level pasture towards a small rock face. Cross a tiny stream (possibly dry in summer) to reach the rock face and pass it to the right, then climb a few metres to a minor pass.

The route now enters a beech forest, in which you descend very gently E. At an open spot the route turns sharply to the right, then makes a curve to the left and climbs E through the dense forest. Here and there the route is blocked by fallen trees, but it is generally easy to follow. After a pass, a short descent and a short climb, you'll reach

5.50 a pass (1601m) offering a fine view over the Arres d'Anies, where only a few pine trees (and a few beeches initially) can survive. After a short descent

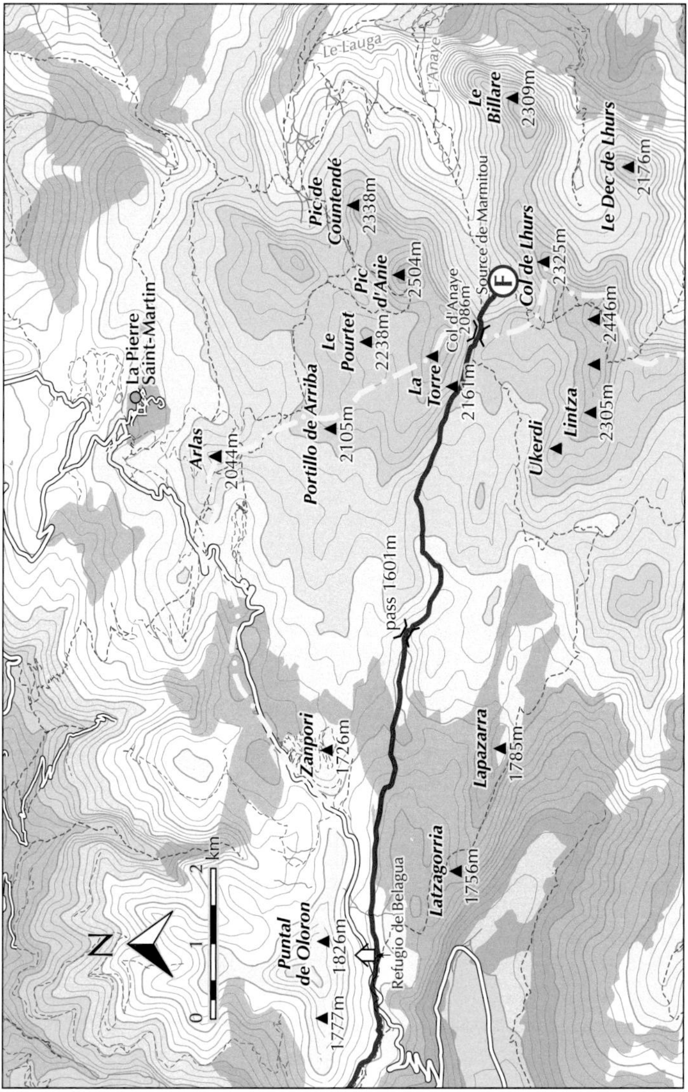

Le Lauga
L'Anaye
Le Billare
2309m
Le Dec de Lhurs
2176m
Pic de Countendé
2338m
Source de Marmitou
F
Col de Lhurs
2325m
Pic d'Anie
2504m
Col d'Anaye
2086m
Le Pourtet
2238m
2446m
La Torre
2161m
La Pierre Saint-Martin
Portillo de Arriba
2105m
Lintza
2305m
Ukerdi
Arlas
2044m
pass 1601m
Zanpori
1726m
Lapazarra
1785m
Latzagorria
1756m
Refugio de Belagua
Puntal de Oloron
1826m
1777m
N
0
1
2 km

Source de Marmitou at the bottom of a beautiful limestone wilderness

As you climb towards the Col d'Anaye the number of trees decreases dramatically and finally you find yourself walking in a completely bare karst landscape.

the path swings E between deeply carved limestone rocks. ◂ Close to the Col d'Anaye the path forks at a signpost where Lescun is indicated; leave the white-and-red markers and follow yellow stripes and dots. The route reaches a pass (2040m), descends a few metres, passes a pool (dry in summer) to the left and arrives at the

8.10 Col d'Anaye (2086m), a pass on the border that gives access to the Vallon d'Anaye in France. Descend E on a path to the floor of the Vallon d'Anaye, then pass some boulders and cross a clear stream that has its origin here and provides water of good quality. You are now at the

8.30 Source de Marmitou (1851m), a fine place to pitch a tent. At the very source of the stream you can find the remains of a *cabane*.

DAY 9

Source de Marmitou to Lescun

Start	Source de Marmitou
Distance	8.5km
Total ascent	85m
Total descent	1035m
Grade	1
Time	3hr
Map	Rando Editions Carte de Randonnées, 1:50,000, no 3: Béarn
Route	Via the Plateau de Sanchèse (1090m)

The first section of the Haute Route ends with a short, pleasant walk through a beautiful valley that is surrounded with bare limestone peaks. In Lescun you will have plenty of time to buy food, wash clothes and take a good rest before continuing on the long walk through the Parc National des Pyrénées.

0.00 Source de Marmitou. Follow a path east of the stream. Initially the path stays level and then it goes

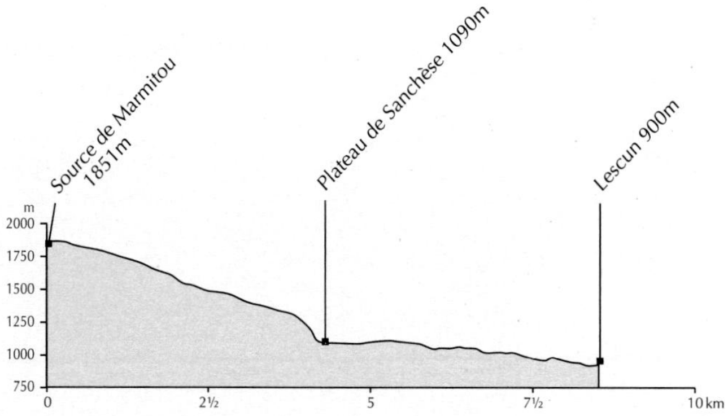

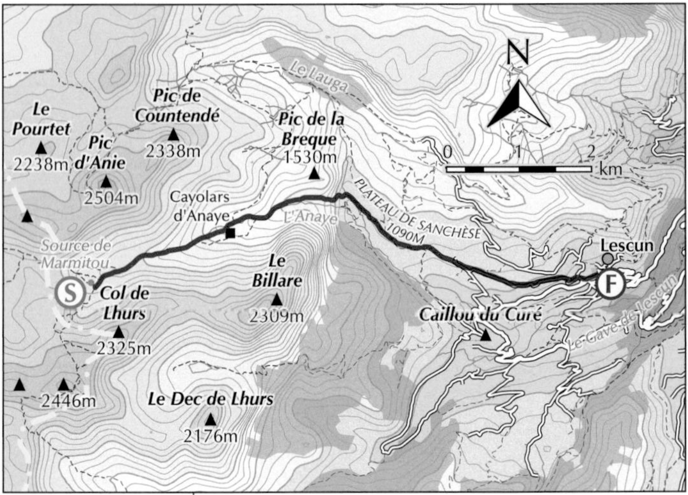

down gently into an open valley. The stream soon flows underground but reappears near the **Cayolars d'Anaye** (shepherds' huts), which will come into sight as you descend. Cross the stream, the Ruisseau d'Anaye, by a footbridge near the hut, then turn right and descend on a well-worn path (yellow marks) through forest and pasture on the left side of the stream, which could be dry

Lescun with its pastures and glacial cirque

in summer. Finally descend steeply in zigzags close to the impressive limestone walls of the Pic de la Brèque to reach the

2.00 Plateau de Sanchèse (1090m). Cross a stream immediately on a solid bridge, turn right and walk to a dirt road. Turn left onto this dirt road, which undulates for half an hour. At a minor pass, cross a cattle grid and from there follow a tarmac road that goes gently down to the village of

3.00 Lescun (900m). Near the village you'll reach the junction 'Sanchèse–Labérouat': turn right, ignore the road signed 'Anapia–Lac de Lhurs', then turn left and walk to the centre of Lescun. For practical information about Lescun see the introduction to this section.

VARIANT 1

From Refugi de Belagua to Lescun via La Pierre Saint-Martin

Start	Refugio de Belagua (Day 8)
Finish	Lescun (Day 9/10)
Distance	27km
Total ascent	1060m
Total descent	1585m
Grade	2
Time	8hr 10min
Map	Rando Editions Carte de Randonnées, 1:50,000, no 3: Béarn
Route	Via La Pierre Saint-Martin, Pas de l'Osque (1922m) and Refuge de l'Abérouat

This route provides a safer alternative, in case of poor visibility, following the tarmac road from Belagua to La Pierre Saint-Martin and from there the GR10 to Lescun. The GR10 route takes you through an equally beautiful and spectacular karst landscape as the normal route would have.

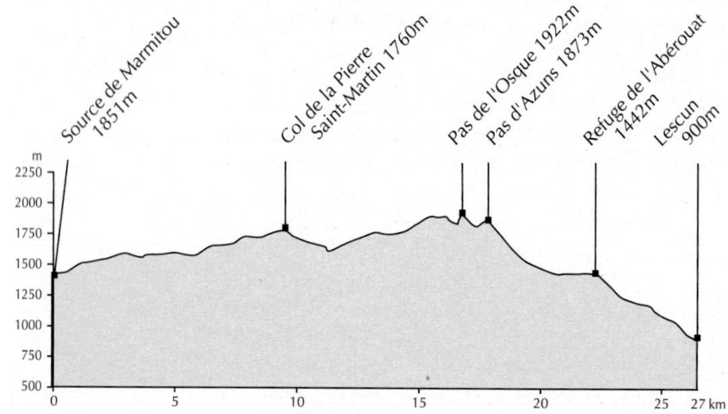
Source de Marmitou
1851m
Col de la Pierre
Saint-Martin 1760m
Pas de l'Osque 1922m
Pas d'Azuns 1873m
Refuge de l'Abérouat
1442m
Lescun
900m
m
2250
2000
1750
1500
1250
1000
750
500
0
5
10
15
20
25
27 km

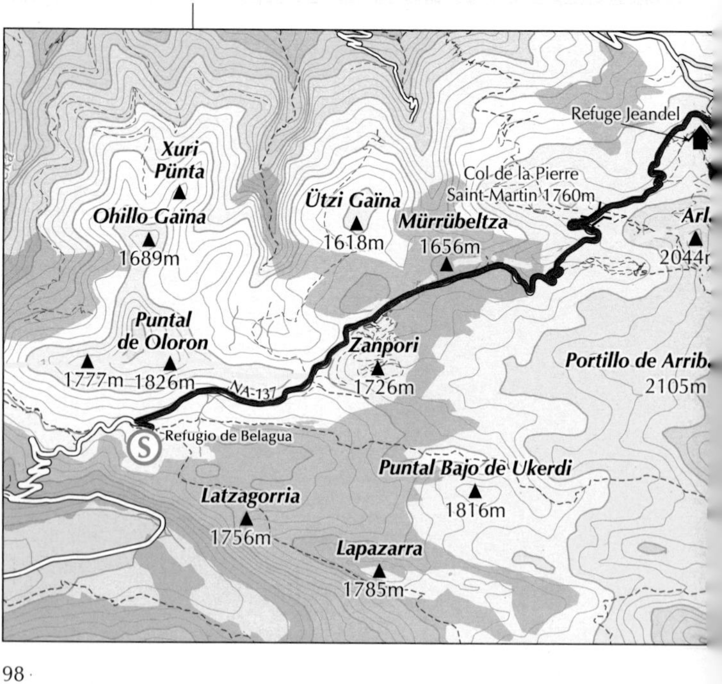
Refuge Jeandel
Xuri
Pünta
Ohillo Gaïna
1689m
Ützi Gaïna
1618m
Col de la Pierre
Saint-Martin 1760m
Mürrübeltza
1656m
2044m
Puntal
de Oloron
1777m
1826m
NA-137
Zanpori
1726m
Portillo de Arrib
2105m
S
Refugio de Belagua
Puntal Bajo de Ukerdi
1816m
Latzagorria
1756m
Lapazarra
1785m

0.00 Refugio de Belagua. From the refugio, go back to the tarmac road (NA-137) and follow it NE for 9km, and shortly after walking into France you reach the

2.30 Col de la Pierre Saint-Martin (1760m) Continue on the same road (now D132) for another few kilometres until you reach the village of **La Pierre Saint-Martin**. Turn right at the first large building and walk 250 metres on the D332, then turn right, following the sign to

3.15 Refuge Jeandel, a hut with 19 places, meals available, snacks for sale, tel 05 59 66 14 46. To join the GR10 path, go down from the refuge and turn right to go under a ski lift. You are now on the GR10. Follow the white-and-red markers on a dirt road until you reach the **Plateau de Pescamou** (1744m), a small green plain.

Turn left and leave the dirt road, and continue on a small path through an exceptionally beautiful landscape of limestone and pine trees. The path joins a wider track,

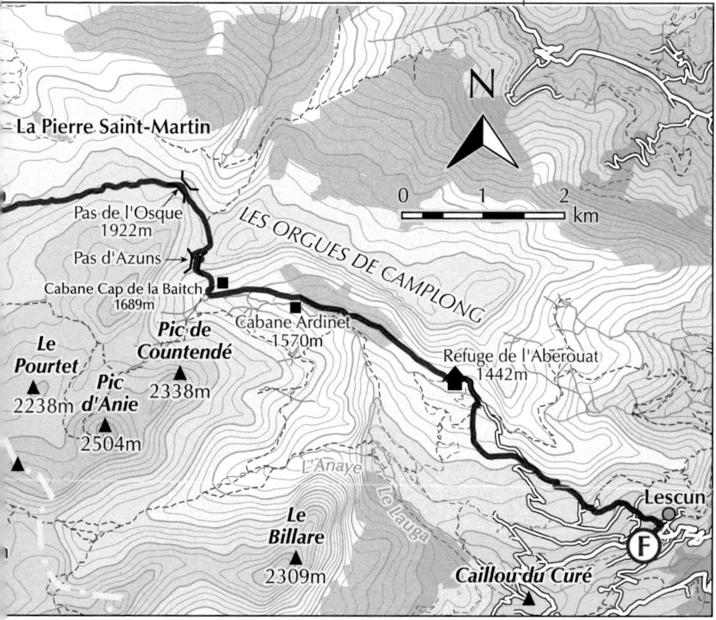

The path leading up to Pas de l'Osque

which leads under a ski lift. Keep a little to the left and go under another ski lift before again joining a small path. Climb, with a short scramble at the end, to

5.00 Pas de l'Osque (1922m), a fairytale passage in-between two peaks. Go down on the path and then go up again to the **Pas d'Azuns** (1873m), and then descend to **Cabane de Cap de la Baitch** (1689m, shepherds' hut, cheese for sale). From here continue E, noting another *cabane* (**Cabane Ardinet**) above the path, and enter a forest. Soon after emerging from the forest you arrive at the

6.45 Refuge de l'Abérouat (1442m, tel 05 59 34 71 67). ◂ Walk SE along the road for 200 metres and then follow the GR10 that branches off to the right. Descend on a wide track and finally cross a stream, then walk S through a muddy area and take the left branch where the path forks.

In bad weather you could opt to walk all the way to Lescun along the tarmac road that starts at the refuge.

The path climbs a little and arrives at the road again. Turn right, follow the road for just a few metres, and then leave the road by turning left onto a dirt road. Walk along this dirt road and turn left at a junction, then make a sharp turn to the right and go down in zigzags on a small path to reach a road. Turn left and follow the road for a short while, then turn right and descend on a small path between meadows. After crossing a meadow you'll arrive once more at the road; turn left and follow the road for a short while before turning left again. Follow a dirt road to the centre of

8.10 Lescun (900m). For practical information about Lescun see the introduction to this section.

SECTION 2: LESCUN TO GAVARNIE

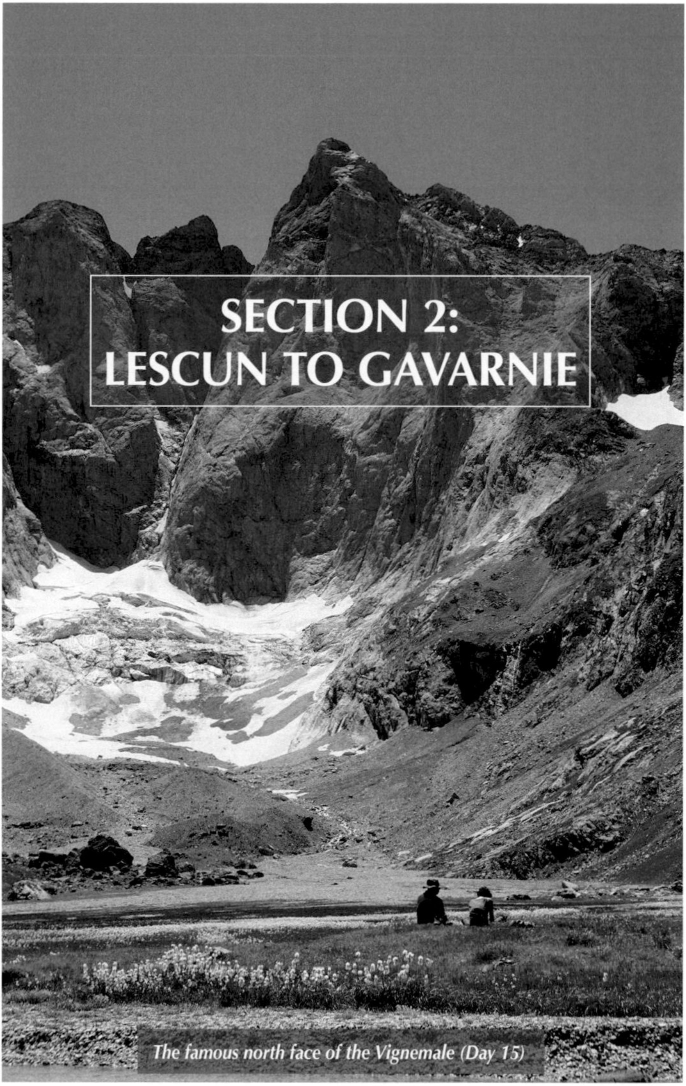

The famous north face of the Vignemale (Day 15)

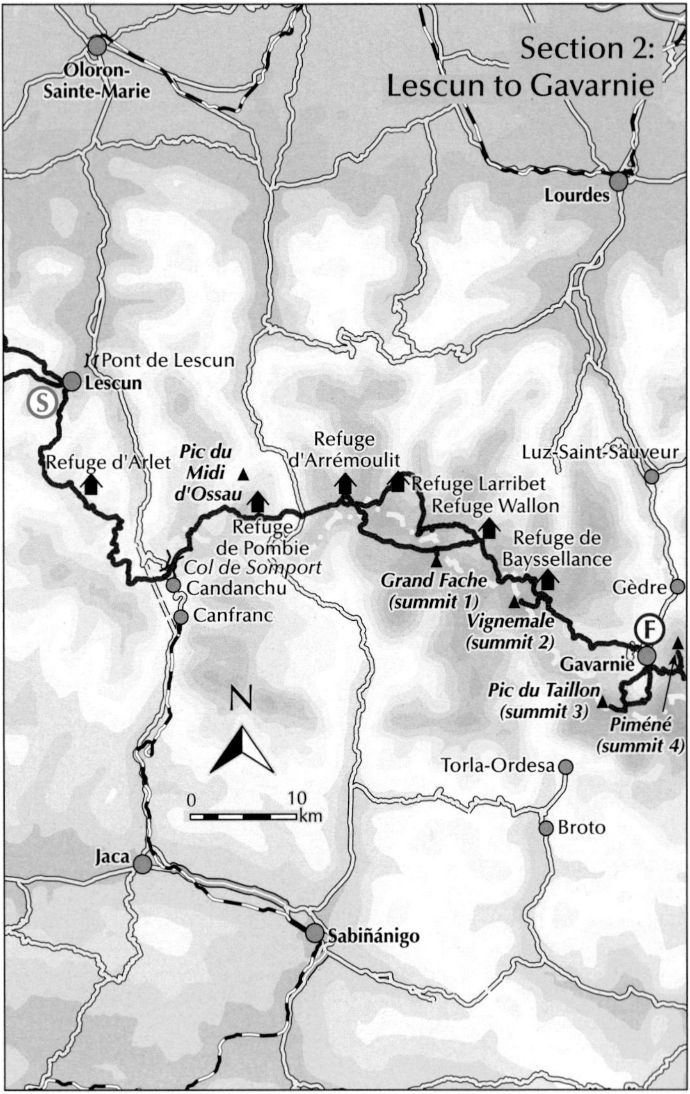
Section 2:
Lescun to Gavarnie
Oloron-
Sainte-Marie
Lourdes
Pont de Lescun
Lescun
S
Refuge d'Arlet
Pic du
Midi
d'Ossau
Refuge
d'Arrémoulit
Refuge Larribet
Refuge Wallon
Refuge de
Bayssellance
Luz-Saint-Sauveur
Refuge
de Pombie
Col de Somport
Candanchu
Canfranc
Grand Fache
(summit 1)
Vignemale
(summit 2)
Gèdre
F
Gavarnie
Pic du Taillon
(summit 3)
Piméné
(summit 4)
N
Torla-Ordesa
0
10
km
Broto
Jaca
Sabiñánigo

HIGHLIGHTS OF THE PARC NATIONAL DES PYRÉNÉES

This second section of the PHR takes you into the high Pyrenees. The moment you cross the Col des Moines on Day 12, you enter a new world: the beautifully shaped Pic du Midi d'Ossau (2884m) immediately catches your attention and leaves no doubt as to the nature of the route ahead. The trail passes right next to this extinct volcano and leads to some serious obstacles including the Passage d'Orteig, the Port du Lavedan and the Col de Cambales. Exposed ridges, steep sections, rough terrain and snowfields add extra excitement to the hiking. In early summer you'll need crampons and an ice axe on some of these crossings. Always check at the refuges about the conditions ahead and carefully consider the possibility of opting for one of the alternative routes that avoid these potentially dangerous passages. These routes provide a safe option where crampons and ice axe aren't needed. But whatever route you take, it will be a tough hike to Gavarnie.

Soon after leaving Lescun you enter the Parc National des Pyrénées. This protected area was created over 50 years ago and is the only national park in the French Pyrenees. The central zone of the park is a thin ribbon that stretches from the Vallée d'Aspe in the west to the Vallée d'Aure in the east. The national park is approximately 100km long and covers an area of 45,707 hectares. For obvious reasons, it's a popular hiking area.

The route from Lescun to Gavarnie reveals many of the highlights of the Parc National des Pyrenées: the green Vallée d'Aspe with its herds of sheep and small *cabanes*; the granite wilderness of the Balaitous massif which hosts numerous lakes and pools; the enchanting Vallée du Marcadau with its bubbling streams and old pine trees; the impressive north face of the Vignemale (3298m); the glacier d'Ossoue; and, of course, the monumental Cirque de Gavarnie. Every day is full of surprises, each pass marking the threshold of another landscape. The walk from Lescun to Gavarnie is not only a walk from hut to hut, but also a walk from one highlight to another.

You may wish to climb one or more of the classic summits described in this section: Grande Fache (Day 14), the Vignemale (Day 15) and Le Taillon (Day 16). Without exception, these are beautiful climbs that offer magnificent views.

GAVARNIE AND THE CIRQUE DE GAVARNIE

In recent times the village of Gavarnie has come to attract enormous numbers of tourists, both day-hikers and trekkers. It's certainly not the village itself that makes Gavarnie so popular, as it is not much more than a long street surrounded by bars, restaurants and souvenir shops. What attracts tourists is the gigantic natural amphitheatre that lies a few kilometres south

After crossing Col des Moines the route enters a world of high mountains (Day 12)

of the village – the famous Cirque de Gavarnie. The vertical walls are up to 1500m high from the valley floor to the top; all the summits of the cirque exceed 3000m in altitude; and there are dozens of waterfalls, all relatively small except one – the Grande Cascade (422m), one of Europe's highest.

The main attraction for tourists in Gavarnie is a visit to the cirque, sometimes on the back of a horse or mule. The simple walk takes about an hour. As for trekkers, Gavarnie is an ideal base for a backpacking expedition. Options include a walk to the Refuge des Sarradets to cross the French-Spanish border by the famous gap in the Cirque de Gavarnie, the Brèche de Roland (2807m); an exploration of the Ordesa National Park; or the start of the third section of the Haute Route!

PRACTICAL INFORMATION

Public transport to Lescun

It's possible to get close to Lescun by public transport, but unfortunately there are no buses that go all the way to the village. Take a train to Paris Gare du Nord, take the subway to Montparnasse-Bienvenue and from there take the TGV to Pau. There is a train service from Pau to Oloron-Sainte-Marie; in Oloron take the bus to Pont de Lescun (for the schedule see www.citrampyrenees.fr). From there it is a 5km walk along the road to Lescun.

Facilities in Lescun

Facilities in the village include a post office (no cash dispenser), chambres d'hôtes, a gîte d'étape, a refuge and a good food shop that also sells gas cartridges. SE of the village along the GR10 trail you'll find a campsite and gîte.

Facilities in Gavarnie

Facilities in the village include the Office du Tourisme, the Maison du Parc National, a small but decent supermarket, a basic campsite south of the village (in the direction of the Cirque de Gavarnie), a picnic spot (next to the church), a cash dispenser, hotels, restaurants, bars and souvenir shops.

There is a fine place for walkers to spend the night in the north section of the village: Gîte d'étape Le Gypaète, 45 places, tel 05 62 92 40 61. The campsite is called Camping La Bergerie, tel 05 62 92 48 4, open from early June to late September. It's highly recommended to make a reservation, as this is a very popular campsite.

Public transport from Gavarnie

There is a bus stop in front of the tourist office from which you can catch a bus to Lourdes (see http://summer.gavarnie.com for the schedule). From there you can travel on by train to Paris.

Variants

Variant 2 offers an alternative route from Refuge d'Arrémoulit (Day 13) to Refuge Wallon (Day 14) avoiding Col de Cambalés. It does, however, include Col de la Fache, which itself should not to be underestimated. From the Col de la Fache it's possible to climb the Grande Fache (3005m) en route.

Classic summits

Grande Fache (3005m) can be climbed from Col de la Fache, which is passed on Variant 2 (route description is provided from Refuge Wallon on the main route). Vignemale (3298m) can be climbed from Refuge de Bayssellance (reached at the end of Day 15). Le Taillon (3144m) can be climbed from Gavarnie.

Food

Food supplies for several days have to be carried, as food can only be bought in a small shop in the village of Candanchu (Day 11). If you need a supermarket, then go to Canfranc-Estacion, 4km south of Candanchu. It's easy to catch a ride in this area and there is also a bus service to Canfranc.

If you decide to have dinner in the refuges, remember to ask the guardian in advance whether you can join the table.

Maps

Rando Editions Carte de Randonnées, 1:50,000, no 3: Béarn; and Rando Editions Mapa Excursionista, 1:50,000, no 12: Gavarnie–Ordesa.

Pitching a tent in the Parc National

Bivouacking (meaning in the Parc National pitching a small tent for one night, between 7pm and 9am) is allowed to a certain extent within the borders of the national park: the location must be at least an hour's walk from any paved road. A bivouac near all the refuges in this section (except the Spanish hut Refugio de Respomuso, Variant 2) is allowed. There's often a designated area near the hut where walkers can pitch a tent.

Mountain huts

This second section provides information for spending each night in a refuge. Note, however, that walking from one hut to another is becoming increasingly popular, and as a consequence you will have to make a reservation at each hut in order to ensure a place.

Accomodation: contact details

All numbers and other information about accommodation along the Haute Route is also found in the route description.

- Lescun: Chambres d'Hôtes and Gîte d'étape du Pic d'Anie – tel 05 59 34 71 54; Gîte La Maison de la Montagne – tel 05 59 34 79 14 or 06 75 48 43 95
- Day 10: Refuge d'Arlet – tel 05 59 36 00 99
- Day 11: Hostel Valle del Aragon – tel 974 373 222; Refugio El Aguila – tel 974 373 291
- Day 12: Refuge de Pombie – tel 09 88 77 39 44
- Day 13: Refuge d'Arremoulit – tel 09 88 77 32 85 or 05 59 05 31 79; Refuge de Larribet – tel 09 88 66 61 22

Lescun is a great place to have a rest after crossing the Basque Country

- Day 14: Refuge Wallon – tel 09 88 77 37 90; Variant: Refugio de Respomuso – tel 974 337 556
- Day 15: Refuge des Oulettes de Gaube – tel 09 88 18 41 46; Refuge de Bayssellance – tel 09 74 77 66 52
- Day 16: Refuge des Granges de Holle – tel 05 62 92 48 77
- Gavarnie: Gîte Le Gypaète, tel 05 62 92 40 61; Camping La Bergerie – tel 05 62 92 48 41

DAY 10

Lescun to Refuge d'Arlet

Start	Lescun
Distance	17.5km
Total ascent	1565m
Total descent	480m
Grade	2
Time	6hr 45min
Map	Rando Editions Carte de Randonnées, 1:50,000, no 3: Béarn
Route	Via the Col de Pau (1942m) and the Col de Saoubathou (1949m)
Note	In summer it can be hard to find water between Cabane de Bonaris and Refuge d'Arlet.

A very pleasant walk that will cause no problems on a clear day. There are top-class views over the Aspe region during this long walk close to the French-Spanish border. Today you'll encounter a Pyrenean lake for the first time.

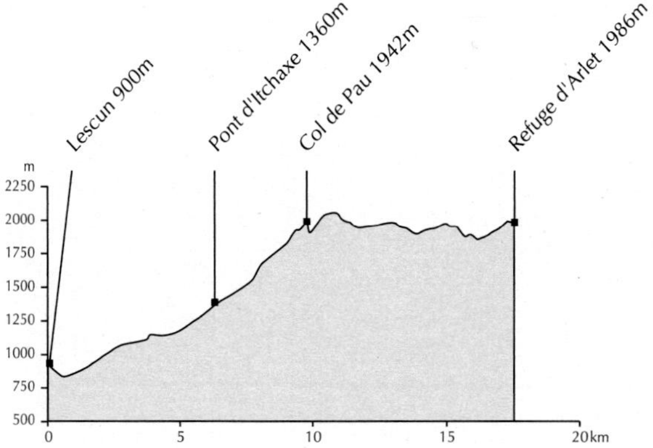

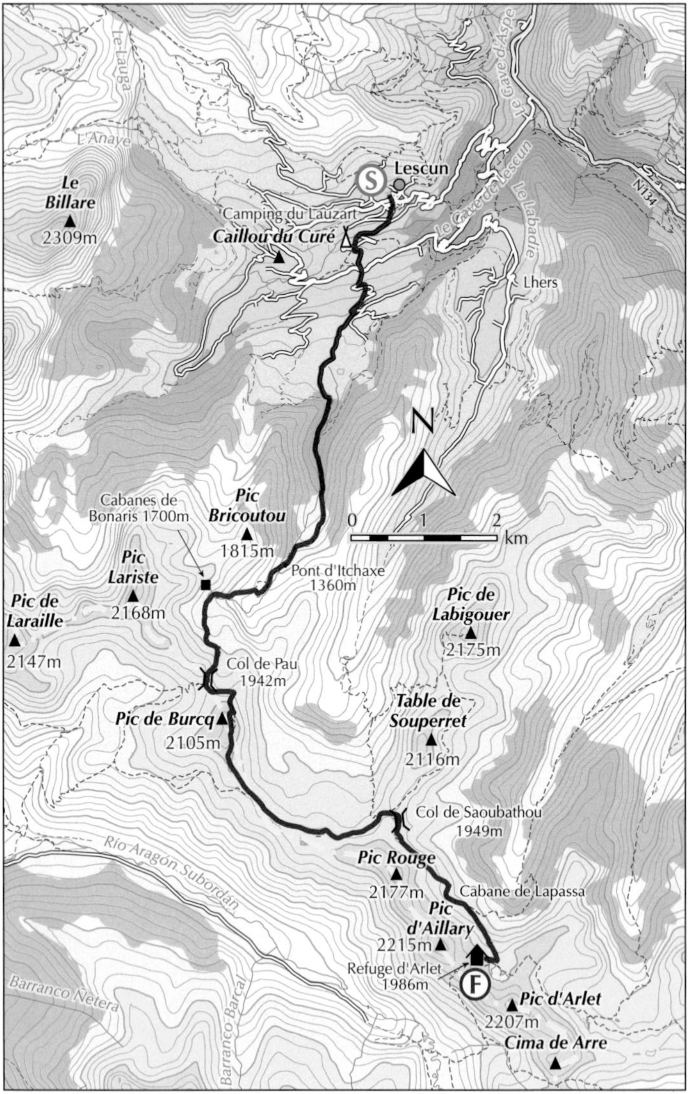
Le Lauga
L'Anaye
Le Billare
2309m
Lescun
Camping du Lauzart
Caillou du Curé
Le Gave d'Aspe
Le Gave de Lescun
Le Labadie
N134
Lhers
N
0
1
2
km
Pic Bricoutou
1815m
Cabanes de Bonaris 1700m
Pont d'Itchaxe 1360m
Pic Lariste
2168m
Pic de Laraille
2147m
Pic de Labigouer
2175m
Col de Pau 1942m
Pic de Burcq
2105m
Table de Souperret
2116m
Col de Saoubathou 1949m
Río Aragón Subordán
Pic Rouge
2177m
Cabane de Lapassa
Pic d'Aillary
2215m
Refuge d'Arlet 1986m
Pic d'Arlet
2207m
Cima de Arre
Barranco Ñetera
Barranco Barcal

0.00 Lescun. From the *épicerie* (grocery shop) in the centre of the village, GR marks lead you from the south side of Lescun down to the Pont du Moulin. Cross the bridge, leave the road and follow the path that climbs steeply to **Camping du Lauzart** (there's also a gîte here), where you'll meet the road again.

Follow the road S to a junction and continue S on the road that leads to La Brénère (indicated at the junction), climbing initially with the GR10. Take a shortcut left of the road and reach the road again near a house, then take another, longer shortcut and return once again to the road. Turn right, leave the GR10 and walk to a junction.

Turn left and climb in zigzags, following the sign to Col de Pau, and then continue S, always on the road. Pass several farms and barns, and a few metres past a barn on your left the road makes a very sharp curve to the right (1090m). Leave the road, turn left and walk on a level dirt road that soon enters a valley through which the Labrénère stream flows. Walk S with the stream on your left-hand side, and continue to follow the dirt road S after it has crossed the stream. Pass a water point and climb to the

1.45 Pont d'Itchaxe (1360m), a small bridge on the Labrénère stream. Cross the bridge, enter the Parc National and climb SW, initially through a forest and later through open fields. Notice a few old *cabanes* on your right and climb in zigzags to the **Cabane de Bonaris** (1700m), a hut that is always occupied by shepherds in summer. The *cabane* is situated beside a small plateau and there is a water point. Cross the plateau (no path here) and climb S along rocky slopes on an obvious path to the

3.45 Col de Pau (1942m), situated on the French-Spanish border and offering fine views over extensive Spanish sierras. ▶ Don't cross the pass, but stay in France, turn left and follow a well-worn path E to another pass. Climb a little on the northern slopes of the **Pic de Burcq** (2105m), go down a few metres and follow a more or less level path that stays very close to the border ridge.

Around Col de Pau you are on the 'Freedom Trail' where guides (*passeurs*) helped WWII refugees (*évadées*) escape from France to Spain.

Semi-wild horses on the ridge walk between Col de Pau and Refuge d'Arlet

The path then bends a little away from the border and climbs a little E. Ignore a path that descends and climb a few metres to the **Col de Saoubathou** (1949m).

On the east side of the pass, follow the undulating path SE. Make a short descent, a short climb north of the Pic Rouge (which is indeed purplish-red) and then a descent to the grassy Lapassa plateau. Notice **Cabane de Lapassa** on your left, ignore the path that descends NE towards the hamlet of Borce, and finally climb in a number of short zigzags to

6.45 Refuge d'Arlet (1986m), overlooking the Lac d'Arlet. This manned mountain hut is owned by the Parc National des Pyrénées. Open from June to September, it offers accommodation for 45 people and a meals service, tel 05 59 36 00 99. Bivouac is possible near the lake.

DAY 11

Refuge d'Arlet to Candanchu

Start	Refuge d'Arlet
Distance	18.5km
Total ascent	995m
Total descent	1430m
Grade	2
Time	6hr 30min
Map	Rando Editions Carte de Randonnées, 1:50,000, no 3: Béarn
Route	Via the Col de Lapachouaou (1891m), the Pla d'Espélunguère (1400m) and the Pas de l'Échelle (1775m)

A pleasant walk mainly through pastureland and sometimes forest. The route follows the GR11 from Ibón de Astanés. There will be no route-finding problems under normal conditions.

0.00 Refuge d'Arlet. Cross a small dam close to the refuge and follow a path SE. After the lake the path makes

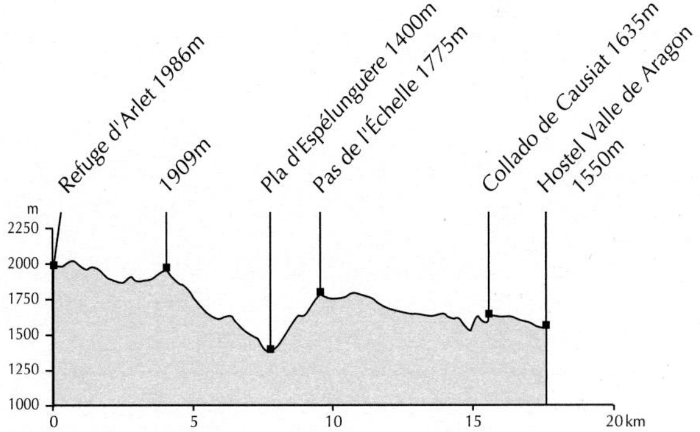

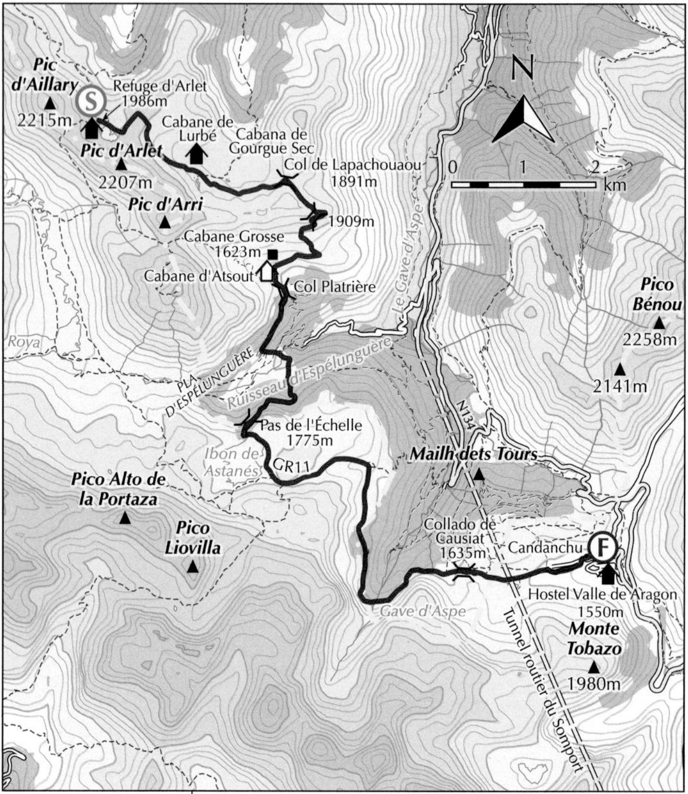

From the pass there are very fine views over summits like the Pic d'Anie, the Peña Colorada, the Pic d'Anayet and the Pic du Midi d'Ossau.

a sharp turn to the left and climbs gently to a minor pass NE of Pic d'Arlet. ◂ Turn right at an obvious junction and descend SE into the Montagne de Barnasse. Pass **Cabane de Lurbé** (1845m, closed) and reach another junction; ignore the path that goes down towards Cabane de Gourgue Sec (a shepherds' hut (closed) on the left, below, near a tiny lake) and go straight on to the

1.00 Col de Lapachouaou (1891m). Follow the path as it bends to the right and leads SE to the next **col** (1909m). Start the descent to the Pla d'Espélunguère

Herders milking sheep near Cabane Grosse

here, heading S in zigzags. Pass **Cabane Grosse** (a shepherds' hut, 1623m) and continue on a dirt road. A little further on, notice **Cabane d'Atsout** (a good emergency shelter), then continue NE, cross two tiny streams and climb a few metres to the **Col Platrière** (not identified on the 1:50,000 map).

Turn right, leave the dirt road and go down on a path through the Espélunguère forest. In this forest you'll find a dirt road; follow this until you come out of the forest. Immediately upon leaving the forest, turn left and descend E on a path along the edge of the forest until you reach the dirt road again on the

2.45 Pla d'Espélunguère (1400m), a small plateau with a *cabane* on its NW side where a herder sells cheese. Cross the dirt road, follow a small path NE down to the **Ruisseau d'Espélunguère** and cross the river by a metal footbridge, then climb a few metres through grass to the junction 'Sansanet–Estaëns' (indicated with a signpost). Turn right here and take the path that goes generally S towards the Ibón d'Astanés.

Climb steeply on a track marked with cairns, cross a small stream and enter a beech forest. Cross the stream

Bivouac near Pla d'Espélunguère

once more and keep climbing steeply on a path that eventually goes up in zigzags. Cross the stream for a third time and pass a *cabane* (closed) in an open, flat spot. Near the end of the climb, out of the forest, the path bends to the right, makes a few zigzags and leads over a metal ladder before reaching the

4.00 Pas de l'Échelle (1775m), on the border. Pass **Ibón de Astanés** (1754m) along its eastern shore and find, SE of the lake, an obvious path going E. You are now on the **GR11** for a short while. Climb a little way and then descend for a bit longer after a grassy pass. At a large pass (1704m), with Val d'Aspe down in front of you, leave the GR11, turn right to walk S through grass and leave Spain for a while near border stone no 293 (30 metres left of the path). After a short descent, cross a stream and enter a forest.

The undulating path is rather faint in places. Once out of the forest, cross a stream (gully) and a dry stream. Enter another forest, and when you come out of it, reach the **Gave d'Aspe**. Cross the stream carefully and take great care on the other side of it, where a steep eroded scree slope has to be crossed. Follow the path NE, and after a short section among bracken the route bends towards the east. Enter a forest and climb steeply. Once out of the forest, cross a few streams and climb to the

6.00 Collado de Causiat (1635m, signpost), on the border. Cross the border and walk E through the ski area of Candanchu to reach a road, then follow this to the Candanchu ski resort. Notice a military school on your left, Refugio Santa Christina on your right, and enter the village where the main road makes a hairpin bend. Turn right and walk along the *galleria commercial* (cafés, shops, some closed in summer). Go down the road to a junction, turn right and walk a few metres to

6.30 Hostel Valle de Aragon (1550m), on the left side of the road, 98 places, tel 974 373 222. A charming hostel, where meals are provided. Another possibility is Refugio El Aguila, the neighbouring building, tel 974 373 291.

DAY 12

Candanchu to Refuge de Pombie

Start	Candanchu
Distance	14.5km
Total ascent	1355m
Total descent	875m
Grade	2
Time	6hr 20min
Map	Rando Editions Carte de Randonnées, 1:50,000, no 3: Béarn
Route	Via the Col des Moines (2168m) and the Col de Peyreget (2310m)

A tough but pleasant hike on well-worn paths. This route takes you past the symbol of the Pyrenees: the Pic du Midi d'Ossau (2884m). There are some boulders to negotiate near the Col de Peyreget.

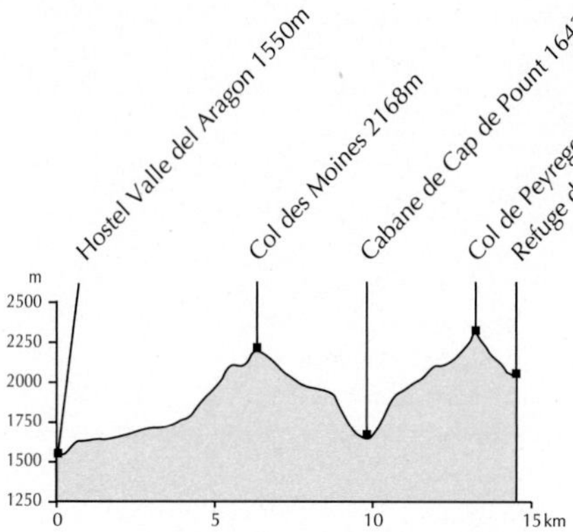

Almost everything is closed here in summer but the last restaurant is open every day in July and August.

0.00 Candanchu. Return to the main road and climb NE until you arrive at the **Col du Somport** (1632m), then stay in Spain and walk ENE on a road towards the ski resort of

1.00 Astun (1710m). ◀ Climb N past the last buildings on a small path which comes back to the small road that also starts at Astun. Follow the road, cross a minor stream three times and approach the Barranco del Escalar. The road turns into a path which you continue following on the east side of the stream until you reach **Ibon de Escalar** (2078m), a lovely spot situated in a grassy bowl and an excellent place for a bivouac. Pass the lake to the right (water source) and climb, first N and then E, to the

2.15 Col des Moines (2168m, border stone 309) on the French-Spanish border, offering excellent views of the Pic du Midi d'Ossau. Descend gently NE; the path eventually becomes steeper, bends a little N, crosses a few minor streams and reaches a junction (1995m) west of Lac Castérau.

Turn right, go down to **Lac Castérau** (great places for a bivouac) and pass it on its southern side. Then climb a few metres and descend NE on an eroded path to the floor of a valley, where you will reach a concrete road. Turn left here, and after a few metres (signpost) turn right

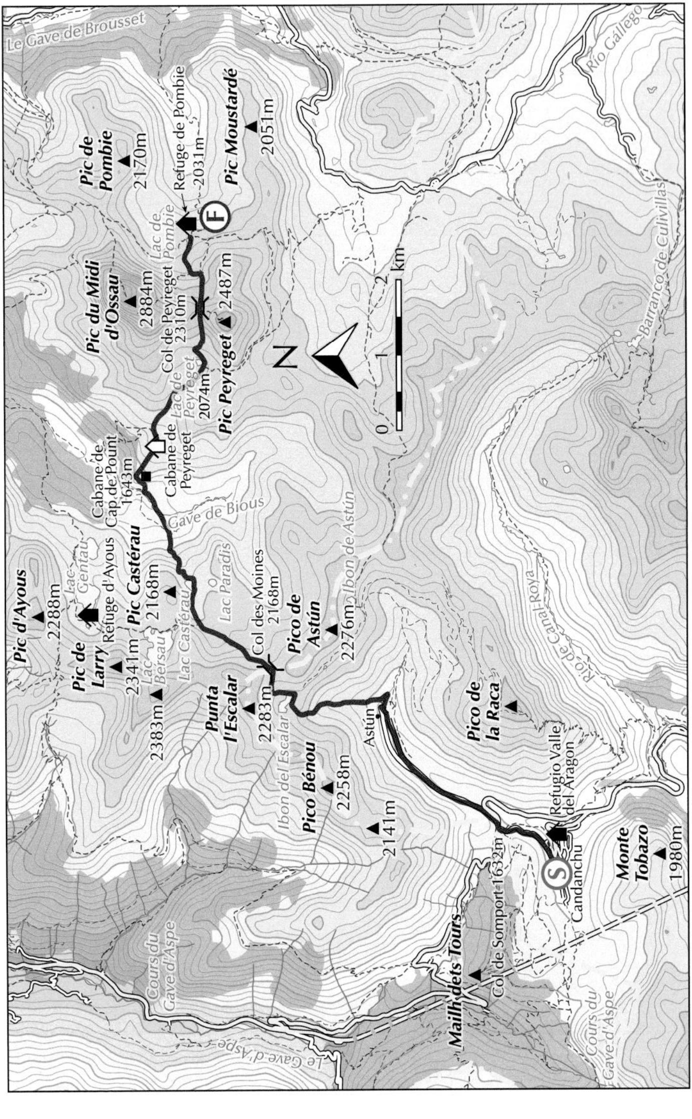

Le Gave de Brousset
Pic de Pombie
2170m
Refuge de Pombie
2031m
Pic Moustardé
2051m
Rio Cállego
Lac de Pombie
Pic du Midi d'Ossau
2884m
Col de Peyreget
2310m
2487m
Pic Peyreget
Lac de Peyreget
2074m
N
0
1
2
km
Cabane de Cap de Pount
1643m
Cabane de Peyreget
Gave de Bious
Barranco de Culivillas
Pic d'Ayous
2288m
Lac Gentau
Refuge d'Ayous
Pic Castérau
2168m
Lac Paradis
Ibon de Astún
Col des Moines
2168m
Pic de Larry
2341m
Lac Bersau
Lac Castérau
Pico de Astún
2276m
2383m
Punta l'Escalar
2283m
Ibon del Escalar
Astún
Pico de la Raca
Rio de Canal Roya
Pico Bénou
2258m
2141m
Refugio Valle del Aragon
Col de Somport 1632m
Candanchu
Monte Tobazo
1980m
Cours du Gave d'Aspe
Mailh dets Tours
Le Gave d'Aspe

and go down to the **Gave de Bious**. Cross the stream by a footbridge (1644m) and walk ENE on more or less level terrain to

3.45 Cabane de Cap de Pount (1643m, always occupied by shepherds). Turn left just in front of the *cabane* and find a small path that climbs NE in the direction of two rock faces. The path is marked with cairns. Climb steeply E in short zigzags and continue to climb until you reach a plateau where the **Cabane de Peyreget** (1920m, a tiny part is open for hikers and makes a good emergency shelter) is situated. Reach a well-worn path a few metres further NE, turn right and climb this obvious path SE to the

5.00 Lac de Peyreget (2074m). The path forks at the south side of this tiny lake; turn left and climb E on a path marked with cairns close to the impressive Pic du Midi d'Ossau. After passing a tiny pool, cross a section of boulders and climb on a steep slope to the

5.45 Col de Peyreget (2310m), from where there are excellent views. Descend E on rough terrain to the small Lacs du Col de Peyreget, and beyond the lakes follow the path as it turns to the left and takes you down to

Hikers near the Col de Peyreget

6.20 Refuge de Pombie (2031m), situated east of the charming Lac de Pombie. The hut is manned from June to mid October and belongs to the FFCAM (Fédération Française des Clubs Alpins et de Montagne). It has 45 places, tel 05 59 05 31 78. Bivouac is allowed on designated terrain nearby. The hut offers extensive views to the east, with high summits including the Balaïtous (3144m), the first 3000m summit you'll encounter. ▶

Refuge de Pombie (2031m)

A large part of tomorrow's walk can be seen from here.

DAY 13

Refuge de Pombie to Refuge de Larribet

Start	Refuge de Pombie
Distance	15.5km
Total ascent	1495m
Total descent	1450m
Grade	E
Time	8hr 10min
Map	Rando Editions Carte de Randonnées, 1:50,000, no 3: Béarn
Route	Via the Col d'Arrious (2259m), the Col du Palas (2517m) and the Port du Lavédan (2615m)
Note	Snow may be encountered on the route even in early summer; ice axe and crampons recommended

This stage of the Haute Route offers more serious challenges. The area around the two high passes that have to be crossed at the end of the day could be covered with snow even in the second half of July. Ice axe and crampons may be necessary. In poor visibility the best thing to do is to stay in Refuge d'Arrémoulit. Good visibility is vital for the final section between Arrémoulit and Larribet. Check at Refuge d'Arrémoulit about the snow conditions on this section and, if advised, take Variant 2 instead.

0.00 Refuge de Pombie. Find a signpost next to the refuge that indicates 'Caillou de Soques', follow this and go down, crossing a small stream. The route now bends to the east and makes a few long zigzags. Follow a stream on your way down to **Cabane de Pucheaux**. The *cabane* (1720m, shepherds' hut) remains at a small distance on your left-hand side; as soon as it is passed, the route turns left.

Cross the Gave de Pombie (two footbridges, the first crosses a dry stream), turn right and follow the stream on a little way. Cross the stream again by a footbridge (1625m) just before you enter a forest and descend E

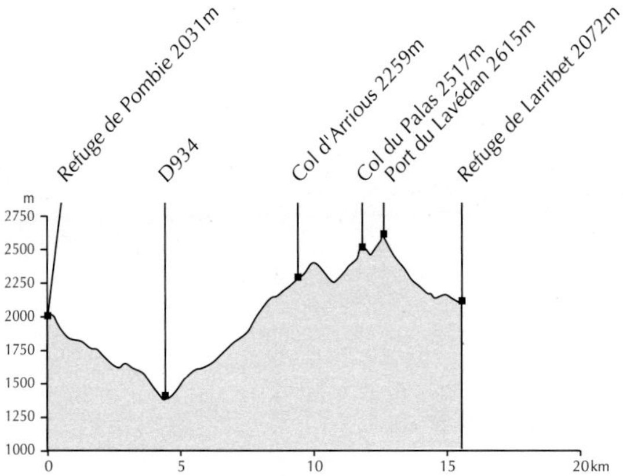

until you reach an open valley. Go down to the **Gave de Brousset** (1350m), cross the stream and after a short climb SE you'll meet the

1.35 D934, the road that links the Vallée d'Ossau with the Valle de Teña in Spain by the Col du Pourtalet. Cross the road at a small hut (cheese for sale) and you'll see the **Cabane de Caillou de Soques** (a very basic shelter built onto a rock) a few metres higher up. Turn left and walk to a signpost (on the other side of the stream) that indicates the climb to the Col d'Arrious and Refuge d'Arrémoulit, then follow a path that climbs in zigzags NE through a forest until you reach a bridge (1560m) on the Ruisseau d'Arrious at the edge of the forest.

Cross the bridge and climb E in an open valley, staying left at a little distance from the Arrious stream. Arrive at a *cabane* that has been built against a giant rock (1883m), then keep climbing on a path that bends away from and then arrives again at the stream. Follow the stream for a short while and cross it again on a minor plateau before reaching a false col (appears to be a pass, but the climb continues), then go across another small plateau, cross the stream once more and make the final climb to

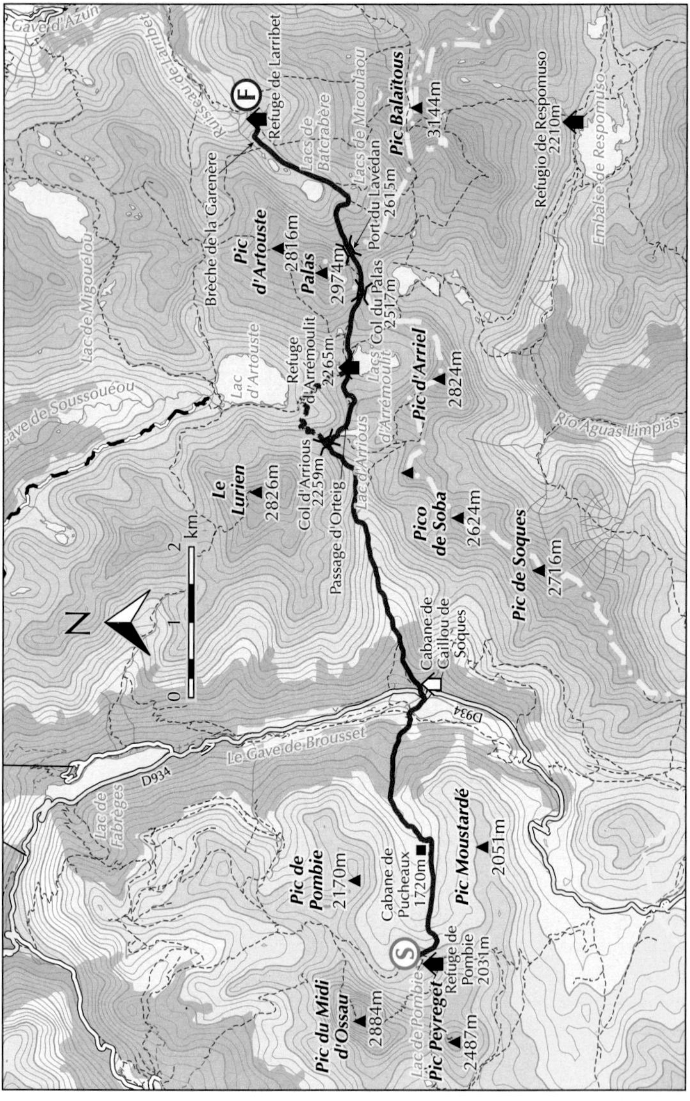
Gave d'Azun
Ruisseau de Larribet
F
Refuge de Larribet
Lacs de Batcrabère
Lacs de Micoulaou
Pic Balaïtous
3144m
Refugio de Respomuso
2210m
Embalse de Respomuso
Brèche de la Garenère
Pic d'Artouste
2816m
Palas
2974m
Port du Lavédan
2615m
Col du Palas
2517m
Lac de Migouélou
Lac d'Artouste
Refuge d'Arrémoulit
2265m
Lacs d'Arrémoulit
Pic d'Arriel
2824m
Gave de Soussouéou
Col d'Arrious
2259m
Lac d'Arrious
Passage d'Orteig
Río Aguas Limpias
Le Lurien
2826m
Pico de Soba
2624m
Pic de Soques
2716m
N
0
1
2 km
Cabane de Caillou de Soques
D934
Le Gave de Brousset
Lac de Fabrèges
D934
Pic de Pombie
2170m
Cabane de Pucheaux
1720m
Pic Moustardé
2051m
S
Refuge de Pombie
2031m
Lac de Pombie
Pic du Midi d'Ossau
2884m
Pic Peyreget
2487m

Crossing the Passage d'Orteig

4.05 Col d'Arrious (2259m). The path forks here, and you need to decide at this point whether you want to undertake the Passage d'Orteig. The Passage d'Orteig is not technical, but it is impressive; it can be awkward for those who sometimes suffer from vertigo and is best avoided in bad weather.

To avoid the Passage d'Orteig

Descend NE in zigzags from the Col d'Arrious towards the Lac d'Artouste. Cross a tiny stream on a small plateau and go down until the path forks at about 2090m, still well above the Lac d'Artouste. Turn right and follow a path that climbs in numerous zigzags to the **Refuge d'Arrémoulit** (2265m). This variant adds 30min to the day's hike.

To continue via the Passage d'Orteig, turn right and walk SE to the nearby **Lac d'Arrious** (2285m). The path immediately turns away from the lake, to the left, crosses a minor pass, turns right and approaches a rock face that has been secured with steel cables. Climb steeply above a deep abyss and finally, past the Passage d'Orteig, walk E through a wild rocky landscape and go down to

5.05 Refuge d'Arrémoulit (2265m; bivouac possible near the hut), with a fine view onto the largest Arrémoulit lake, which is dominated by the pyramid summit of Pic d'Arriel (2824m). The FFCAM owns the hut; there are guardians from the end of May until early October, and meals are available. There are 24 places in the hut and 16 camping, tel 05 59 05 31 79.

Walkers who decide to spend the night in or near Refuge d'Arrémoulit and don't want to lose a day can take the alternative route (Variant 2) described at the end of Day 14. This option avoids the challenging terrain of the Col de Cambalés.

Turn left after leaving the hut and climb NE on boulders and rocks through a narrow valley to find a small lake (Lac du Palas). From the lake, climb steeply E through rocks and scree (probably over snow in early summer) to the

6.10 Col du Palas (2517m) on the French-Spanish border. Go down a short way on the east side of the pass

The challenging terrain around the Port du Lavédan

and make a traverse of roughly 500 metres NE on rocks towards the Port du Lavédan. About halfway, go over a small ridge on a rock face, or alternatively go down to a grassy area beneath the rock face. Whatever option you take, climb NE once you get past the rock face, aiming for a narrow opening in the frontier ridge ahead of you. At the narrow opening you will find white-red-white markers on the rocks; this is the

6.55 Port du Lavédan (2615m). ▸ Carefully follow the Parc National markers (white-red-white) on the other side of the pass. Don't be tempted to descend steeply NE to the Lacs de Batcrabère, which you can already see; instead, go down a little NE and then move E on rocks and scree or (in early summer) snowfields. If there is snow on the S side of the Port du Lavédan, crampons and ice axe should be used.

In some years the route can be covered with snow even until the end of July. If this is the case, don't cross here without crampons.

At 2450m the path turns SE for a short while, before descending more steeply NE to the small **Lacs de Micoulaou** (2325m). ▸ Go N down to the two **Lacs de Batcrabère** (the largest lake lies at 2180m) and pass the lakes, keeping them at a little distance on your left-hand side. Beyond the lakes you'll reach the **Brèche de**

The challenging part is over when you reach these lakes.

Refuge de Larribet

la Garenère, a small gap between rocks. Cross the gap, or follow the easier path that goes left around it, and go down to the

8.10 Refuge de Larribet (2072m), a FFCAM-owned hut manned from early May until the end of September, 60 places, tel 09 88 66 61 22. Meals available. There's a nice atmosphere in the hut, and a bivouac is possible on a beautiful plateau.

DAY 14

Refuge de Larribet to Refuge Wallon

Start	Refuge de Larribet
Distance	18km
Total ascent	1300m
Total descent	1505m
Grade	3
Time	8hr 20min
Map	Rando Editions Carte de Randonnées, 1:50,000, no 3: Béarn
Route	Via the Col de Cambalès (2706m)
Note	Snow may be encountered on the route even in early summer; ice axe and crampons are advised

A tough walk with the Col de Cambalès as a serious obstacle. There is rough terrain and possibly snowfields on both sides of the pass. It's also a delightful walk, with the romantic Vallon de Larribet, the Cambalès lakes and the arrival at the large Pla de la Gole with its old pine trees as highlights. A variant route from the Refuge d'Arrémoulit (Day 13), avoiding the difficult sections of this route, is described in Variant 2.

0.00 Refuge de Larribet. From the hut, descend NE in zigzags on a well-worn path to a plateau where you have the water rushing down from the Lacs de Batcrabère next to you. Cross the stream and a few others (you

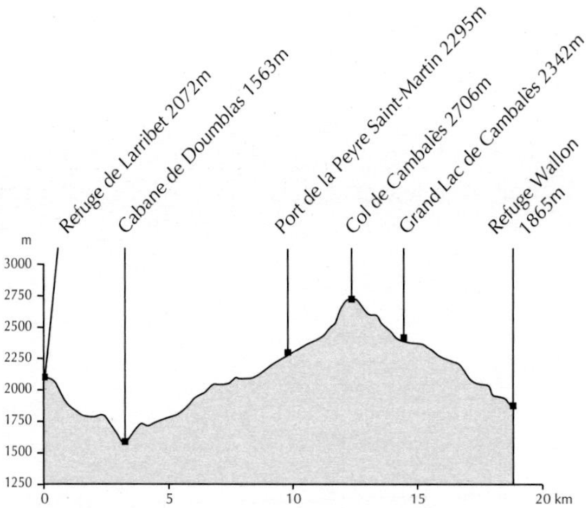

might get your feet wet after heavy rain, but these crossings are not difficult) and continue to descend, eventually reaching the **Claou de Larribet** (1740m, signpost) – a beautiful natural garden where the water rests a little before plunging down in waterfalls. Go down E between pine trees towards the Vallée d'Arrens, and on down to where the path forks (signpost), well above

1.15 Cabane de Doumblas (1563m, hut with four places, basic but useful; sometimes in use by a shepherd), situated on the other side of the Gave d'Arrens. It's not necessary to descend to the bridge and the *cabane*; instead take the path that climbs SE to the main path in the valley. ▶ Once you reach this path at 1700m, continue S towards the Port de la Peyre-Saint-Martin and soon reach **Le Labassa**, a small plateau in which the Gave d'Arrens meanders.

There may be plenty of delicious billberries here in July.

Cross a footbridge, follow a faint path across the plateau, ignore the path that climbs to the unmanned Refuge Ledormeur (signpost) and cross another footbridge. Climb a number of zigzags, after which the path goes straight ahead S. Notice the beautiful **Lacs de Remoulis** below on

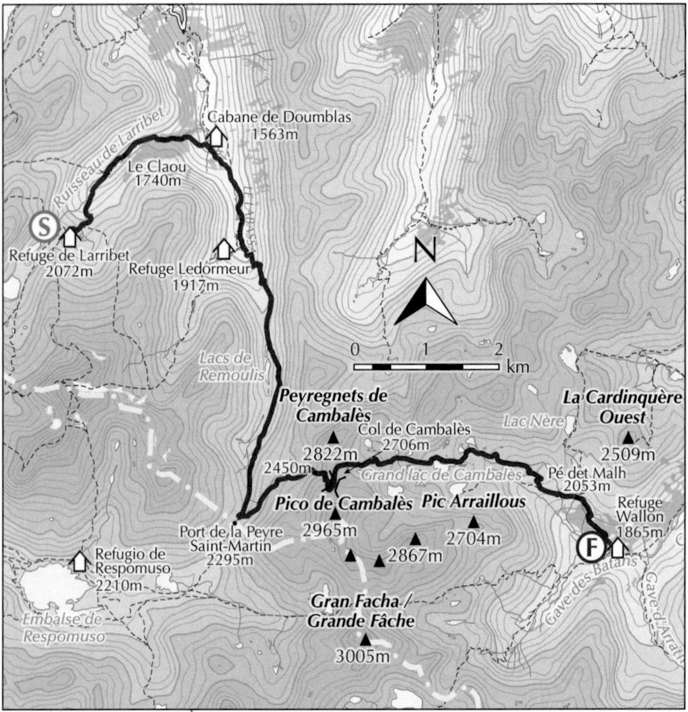

your right and keep climbing. After a few short zigzags the path again goes straight ahead and almost reaches the

4.00 Port de la Peyre Saint-Martin (2295m), a large pass on the French-Spanish border with beautiful bivouac places on the Spanish side. A few metres north of the port, Col de Cambalès is indicated (signpost). Follow this path NE, cross a stream (2372m, possibly dry in summer) and climb a few zigzags. At **2450m** the path forks; ignore the cairns that climb S and instead cross a small valley, following cairns E. At 2500m the final climb to the col begins. Climb steeply at first in zigzags, then more gently E for a short while, and finally climb again in zigzags to the

The Lacs de Cambalès in late June, with Pic de Cambalès and Col de Cambalès (far right) in the background

5.15 Col de Cambalès (2706m, signpost) with fine views to the east side of the Balaïtous and the Glacier de las Néous. On the east side of the pass, descend very steeply S for a few metres and then turn left to descend NE on rocks and (probably) snowfields. The route then bends to the right to an elevated part in the valley and descends E towards the Lacs de Cambalès.

Pass the **Grand Lac de Cambalès** (2342m) to the left, notice two smaller lakes on your left and go down ESE, crossings several streams to arrive at a small plateau called **Pé det Malh** (2053m). Cross another stream and turn right, ignoring the path that goes N to Lac Nère (signpost). Cross another stream and descend SE between pine trees to the large Pla de la Gole, where you will find a chapel and

8.20 Refuge Wallon (1865m), on the banks of the Gave des Batans. ▶ Owned by the FFCAM, the hut is being renovated and enlarged at the time of writing. Reopening is planned for the 2022 season, check www.refuge-marcadau.csvss.fr/en/the-refuge for the latest updates and reservations. Bivouac is allowed on a designated area on the plateau. This is a beautiful place to stay for the night, but you won't be alone!

The ascent of Grande Fache starts from the refuge and takes 6hr 30min (return) – see 'Summit 1', below.

VARIANT 2

Refuge d'Arrémoulit to Refuge Wallon

Start	Refuge d'Arrémoulit (Day 13)
Finish	Refuge Wallon (Day 14/15)
Distance	16.5km
Total ascent	1060m
Total descent	1465m
Grade	2
Time	7hr 45min
Map	Rando Editions Carte de Randonnées, 1:50,000, no 3: Béarn
Route	Via the Col d'Arrémoulit (2448m) and the Col de la Fache (2664m)
Note	Snow may be encountered near the Col de la Fache even in early summer

A long hike that avoids having to cross the Port du Lavedan and the Col de Cambalés. It does, however, involve a crossing of the Col de la Fache, which itself is not to be underestimated. From the Col de la Fache, it's possible to climb the Grande Fache (3005m) en route (see Summit 1).

0.00 Refuge d'Arrémoulit. Walk from the hut to the northeast side of the lake and climb SE through a chaos of rocks (there are some cairns to guide you) to the

0.30 Col d'Arrémoulit (2448m), a large frontier pass that can be seen from the refuge. Go down steeply on the east side of the pass towards the two northern lakes of the **Ibones del Arriel** and follow the cairns until you are between the two lakes. Turn right and walk S along the western shore of the second lake; turn left as soon as you are past this lake and meet a path southeast of the lakes. Turn right and follow this path.

Keep a small lake on your left-hand side, cross a small stream and go down along the next lake to a small plateau. Cross the stream once more, just before a tiny

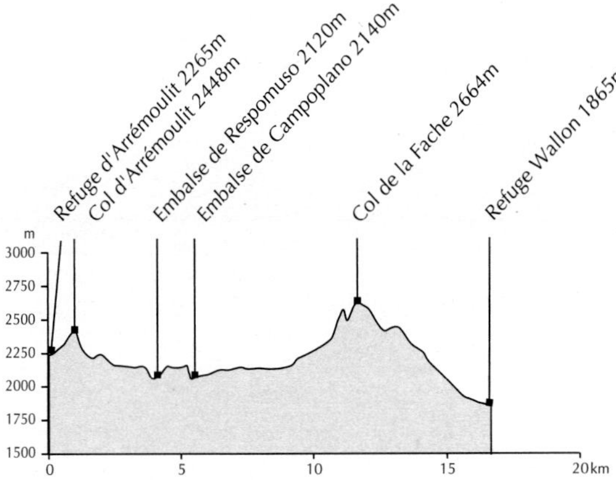

lake with a dam, climb for a short while and go down to the remains of a few buildings (notice another lake on your left below). Turn left here and walk SE for about 1hr on a well-worn path that undulates high above the valley of the Rio Aguas Limpias to the large dam of the

3.10 Embalse de Respomuso (2120m), where you'll meet the white-and-red marks of the GR11. Turn left, climb a little and walk above the northern shore of the lake. Go left at a junction and cross the Barranco Respomuso, keeping **Refugio de Respomuso** (2200m, open all year, 105 places, meals available, bivouac not allowed, reservation obligatory, tel 974 337 556) below on your right. Leave the GR11 and continue E as soon as you are east of the lake, pass a few tiny lakes (excellent places for a bivouac) and arrive at the

3.50 Embalse de Campoplano (2140m, signpost). Stay left of the unfinished dam as you walk along the southern shore of the lake. (There are fine places for a bivouac on the east side of the lake.) Cross the stream flowing from the lake, and then the stream coming from the Lacs de la Fache, and climb E on a path marked with cairns, keeping the stream coming from the Lacs de la

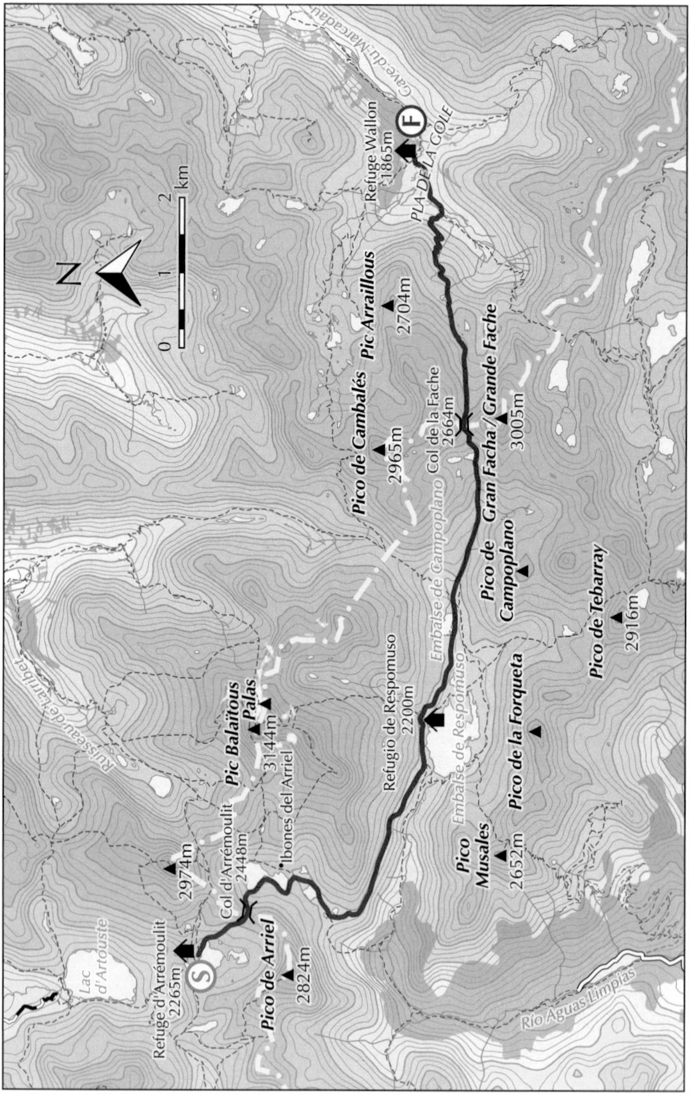
N
0
1
2 km
Refuge d'Arrémoulit
2265m
Lac d'Artouste
2974m
Col d'Arrémoulit
2448m
Pico de Arriel
2824m
Ibones del Arriel
Pic Balaïtous
3144m
Palas
Ruisseau-de-Larribet
Refugio de Respomuso
2200m
Embalse de Respomuso
Embalse de Campoplano
Pico Musales
2652m
Pico de la Forqueta
Pico de Tebarray
2916m
Pico de Campoplano
Pico de Cambalés
2965m
Col de la Fache
2664m
Gran Facha / Grande Fache
3005m
Pic Arraillous
2704m
Refuge Wallon
1865m
PLA-DE-LA-GOLE
Gave-du-Marcadau
Río Aguas Limpias

Fache on your left. ▸ Keep the lakes (2514m) on your left-hand side and climb E on a steep slope to the

Early in the season large amounts of snow could cause some difficulties near the Lacs de la Fache.

5.40 Col de la Fache (2664m), a pass on the French-Spanish border that gives access to the Vallée du Marcadau (signpost). Descend E on an obvious path that is marked with cairns. Notice two lakes (also called Lacs de la Fache) on your right-hand side at some distance and pass a third lake (2291m) on its south side. Cross a stream after passing this tiny lake and go down in a series of long zigzags to the Pla de Loubosso, in which you'll meet the Ruisseau (stream) du Port du Marcadau. Just before a footbridge the path forks (signpost); turn left, cross one footbridge, then another, then turn left and walk NE to the Pla de la Gole. Cross another footbridge on the Gave des Batans and arrive at the

7.45 Refuge Wallon (1865m). Owned by the FFCAM, the hut is being renovated and enlarged at the time of writing. Reopening is planned for the 2022 season, check www.refuge-marcadau.csvss.fr/en/the-refuge for the latest updates and reservations. Bivouac is allowed on a designated area on the plateau. This is a beautiful place to stay for the night, but you won't be alone!

Refugio de Respomuso at the Embalse de Respomuso (Variant 2)

SUMMIT 1

Grande Fache (3005m) from Refuge Wallon

Start	Refuge Wallon (Day 14/15)
Distance	11km
Total ascent/descent	1110m
Grade	F+
Time	6hr 30min (3hr 30min to reach the top)

Should you decide to take Variant 2, which leads to Refuge Wallon via the Col de la Fache, then climbing the Grande Fache, one of the 212 Pyrenean summits that exceed 3000m, en route is well worth the extra effort. From Col de la Fache it's 1hr to the top and you could be down again in 45min. Thanks to its height and its situation on the French-Spanish border, the Grande Fache (Gran Facha in Spanish) offers superb views, in particular of the Balaïtous (3144m), the Picos del Infierno (3082m), the Pic du Midi d'Ossau (2884m), the Vignemale (3298m) and, of course, the enchanting Vallée du Marcadau. The climb is steep but not difficult. Should there be climbers above you, watch out for stonefall. Haute Route walkers who have followed the main route to Wallon could consider taking a day off in order to climb the Grande Fache. The route description starts at Refuge Wallon.

For map of the route from Refuge Wallon to Col de la Fache, see Variant 2.

0.00 Refuge Wallon (1865m). ◄ From the hut, turn right and soon cross the Gave des Batans by a footbridge. Climb NW on an obvious path and cross two more footbridges. Immediately after the second footbridge the path forks; turn right, ignoring the path that goes S towards the Port du Marcadau. The path now climbs in a number of long zigzags and then goes WSW. Cross a stream near a tiny tarn (2291m) on your right and notice a few lakes a little distance away on the left on your way up. Continue to climb W on a rather steep scree slope and arrive without any difficulties at the

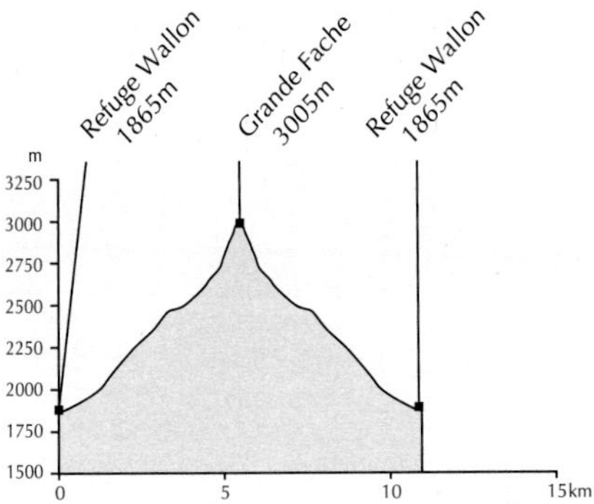

2.40 Col de la Fache (2664m). Turn left to leave the pass, climbing S to gain the steep frontier ridge that leads to the Grande Fache. There are sufficient cairns on this western ridge to guide you; here and there some easy scrambling is required. Stay a little on the right (W) of the ridge and gain a secondary summit (Pointe Lagardère, 2990m), then go down a few metres and climb to the summit of the

3.30 Grande Fache (3005m). Take the same route back to Refuge Wallon.

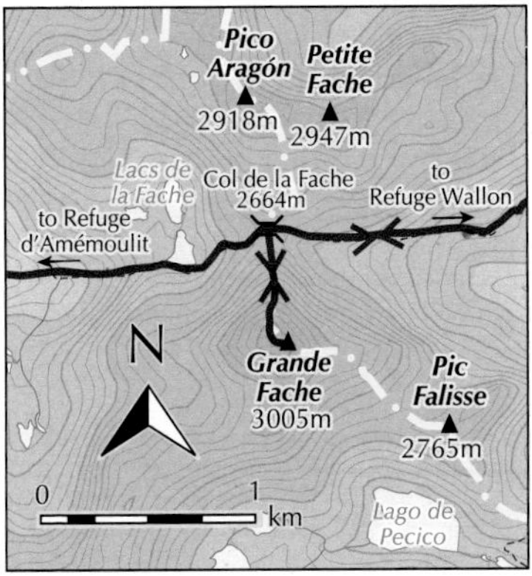

DAY 15

Refuge Wallon to Refuge de Bayssellance

Start	Refuge Wallon
Distance	13.5km
Total ascent	1510m
Total descent	720m
Grade	2
Time	7hr 20min
Map	Rando Editions Mapa Excursionista, 1:50,000, no 12: Gavarnie–Ordesa
Route	Via the Col d'Arratille (2528m), the Col des Mulets (2591m) and the Hourquette d'Ossoue (2734m)
Note	Ice axe and crampons may be useful if hiking early in the season

On a beautiful day this is a surprisingly easy walk without any real obstacles, although early in the season there may be some steep snow near the Lac du Col d'Arratille, beyond Col des Mulets and near the Hourquette d'Ossoue. A little care is needed on the rough terrain on the steep east side of Col des Mulets.

0.00 Refuge Wallon. From the refuge, go down gently E on a path for a few minutes to a junction near the place where the Gave d'Arratille meets the Gave des Batans (1810m, together they form the Gave du Marcadau). A signpost indicates the junction; turn right and cross the Gave des Batans by a footbridge, then cross the Gave d'Arratille by a footbridge a little further and follow the stream as you climb, initially between pine trees and later on a grassy slope.

The path bends away from the stream and you climb ESE to reach a slope with polished rocks where the water coming from Lac d'Arratille finds its way. Soon the path, marked with cairns, climbs in zigzags and then more

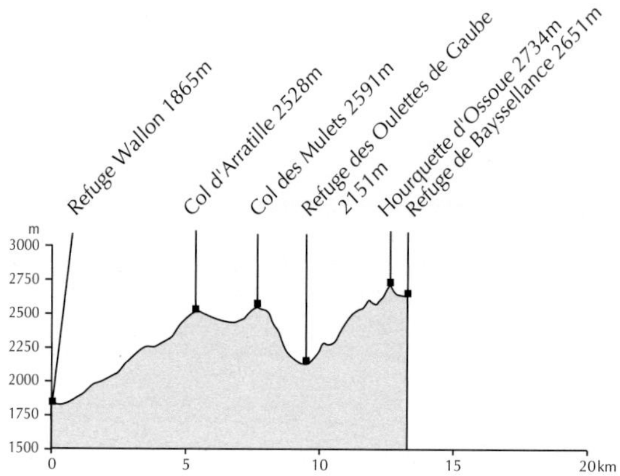

gradually S. Cross the Gave d'Arratille by a footbridge and soon reach the

1.35 Lac d'Arratille (2247m). Walk S, staying a few metres above the western shore of the lake. From the south side of the lake follow a well-marked path that climbs rather steeply SSE. During the ascent the path bends a little to the right and climbs S to the **Lac du Col d'Arratille** (2501m). ▶ Keep the lake below on your right-hand side and continue to the

Early in the summer season there are often short but steep snowfields next to the lake. Crampons and ice axe may be needed.

2.45 Col d'Arratille (2528m), on the French-Spanish border. What follows is a short walk in the upper section of the Valle de Ara, in Spain. Descend on an obvious path and, at 2450m, walk NE on a more or less level path on the rocky southern slopes of Pic Alphonse Meillon. Finally climb steeply SE to again reach the border and the

4.00 Col des Mulets (2591m), which gives access to the Vallée de Gaube. Descend steeply on the east side of the pass, following paint flashes. Below the pass there is normally a large snowfield (except late summer), but if you follow the waymarks it can be avoided. After the steep section, go down in zigzags on a slope covered with stones to a bivouac area on the east side of a large

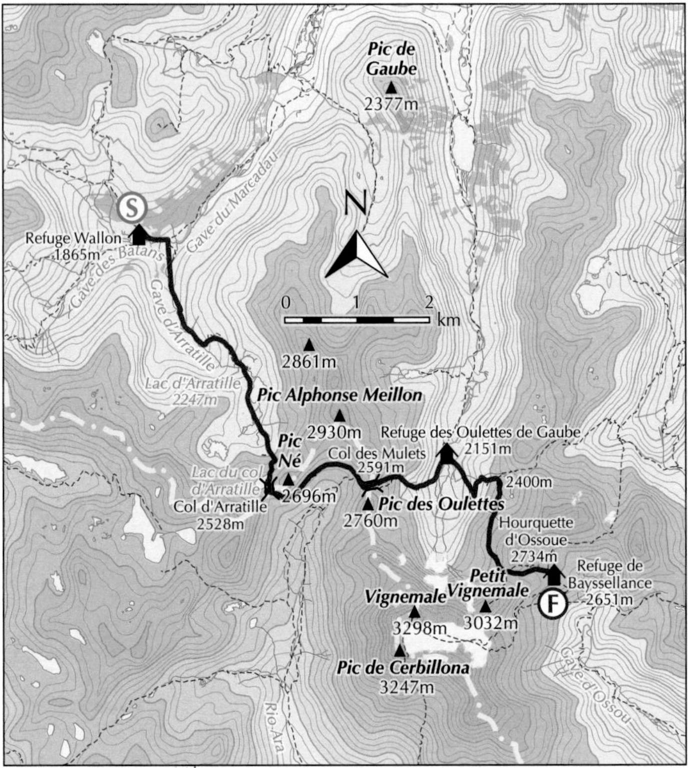

bowl, out of which slowly runs the meltwater from the north face of the Vignemale. Continue to the

5.00 Refuge des Oulettes de Gaube (2151m), situated on a bluff and looking towards the famous north face of the Vignemale (3298m; highest of the French Pyrenean summits). The hut belongs to the FFCAM, has 80 places and is manned from mid February until the end of September, tel 09 88 18 41 46 or 07 68 35 78 65. You'll meet the white-and-red marks of the GR10 at the refuge. There also is a bivouac area with a view that has no equal in the Pyrenees.

Curious isard near the Hourquette d'Ossoue

The Haute Route now follows the GR10 all the way to Gavarnie. Take the obvious path that climbs initially SW and then E in zigzags to a junction that's indicated by a signpost (**2400m**). Ignore the path that climbs steeply E towards the Col d'Arraillé and instead climb gently S. The final metres of the climb to Hourquette d'Ossoue are steep and go through loose scree. In early summer you will encounter some snowfields, but even then, this climb isn't difficult. Reach the summit of the

7.00 Hourquette d'Ossoue (2734m).

To climb the Petit Vignemale

One of the summits of the Vignemale's north face, the Petit Vignemale (3032m), can easily be reached from the Hourquette d'Ossoue in less than 1hr. Just climb the ridge S, staying a little to the left of it, to the top. There are excellent views, especially of the Vallée de Gaube, the Glacier d'Ossoue and the summits of the Cirque de Gavarnie.

To continue to Refuge de Bayssellance, descend E on the east side of Hourquette d'Ossoue and walk through a barren landscape to the

7.20 Refuge de Bayssellance (2651m), the highest manned mountain hut in the Pyrenees. ◀ Another FFCAM refuge, this one is manned from June until the end of September, 58 places, tel 09 74 77 66 52. It boasts wide views onto the summits of the Cirque de Gavarnie. There are plenty of bivouac spots near the refuge, but all are on a rather hard surface. A great base camp for a climb to the top of the Vignemale!

The ascent of Vignemale starts from the refuge and takes 5hr 30min (return) – see 'Summit 2'.

SUMMIT 2

Vignemale (3298m) from Refuge de Bayssellance

Start	Refuge de Bayssellance (Day 15/16)
Distance	7km
Total ascent/descent	930m
Grade	F+
Time	5hr 30min; allow 3hr for the ascent
Note	The route involves hiking on a glacier; check the conditions prior to setting out. Ice axe and crampons required.
Warning	Beware rockfall below the summit

The Vignemale is the highest mountain in the French Pyrenees. It's an iconic peak with two very famous faces: the north face is a beautiful and impressive grey limestone cirque; and the east side is home to the Pyrenees' second largest glacier, the Glacier d'Ossoue. In the immediate surroundings are a number of valleys that are among the most beautiful in the entire Pyrenees: Vallée d'Ossoue, Vallée de Gaube and Valle del Ara.

The climb to the top of the Vignemale requires some preparation but is nevertheless a very doable adventure. Crampons and ice axe are needed. Check the state of the glacier at the Refuge de Bayssellance beforehand. Until mid July there are usually no crevasses, but that can change quickly later in summer. Crevasses mainly appear on the lower, steepest part of the glacier, south of the Petit Vignemale. Luckily, there is a safe way over smooth rocks to avoid this potentially dangerous part. The final climb to the top is a steep scramble on a slope full of loose rock. There is a risk of stonefall and concentration is required for your own safety and that of others.

There are two options for the return route: you can either retrace your steps or take a looping route back to the main path via Pic de Cerbillona and Pic Central. Finally, a very early start (at the break of dawn) gives you the best snow conditions and avoids crowds on the final scramble. If you decide on such an early start, it is advised to familiarise yourself with the first stage of the route, from the refuge to the bottom of the glacier, on the day before your climb.

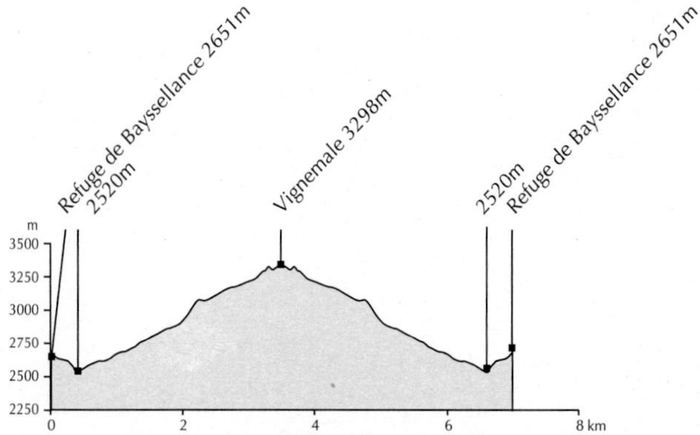

HENRY RUSSELL AND THE VIGNEMALE

Thanks to the Pyrenean enthusiast and eccentric pioneer Henry Russell, the Vignemale has become a mountain of mythical proportions. Count Russell (1834–1909), who was born in Toulouse to a French mother and an Irish father, spent a lot of his time in the Pyrenees. He made a significant number of new climbs (the Pic Carlit, for example) and wrote several books and articles, but he was most famous for his passionate devotion to one single mountain: the Vignemale. He climbed the mountain 33 times and spent some 150 nights on its slopes.

Russell bivouacked in the open at first, but eventually he had a total of seven grottoes carved in the rocks. On the GR10 down to Gavarnie you will notice the three Grottes Bellevue at 2400m, where the Glacier d'Ossoue ended in the late 19th century! Near the Col de Cerbillona (3195m) there are the three Grottes Russell (now well above the glacier, back then easily reachable in summertime). The middle cave was Russell's own residence and is named Villa Russell. This cave had a metal door and a woodstove. Nowadays the glacier is much lower but there is a rope that allows a courageous hiker to climb up and go inside. The cave close by on the left is the Grotte des Guides, and the one a little higher on the right is called the Grotte des Dames and was built in the event a lady should arrive. Finally, only 18 metres below the summit lies a cave built for just Russell himself, Le Paradis.

From inside Villa Russell

Russell celebrated the Vignemale in a way that is perhaps hard to understand nowadays: he received friends, held dinner parties, celebrated a mass, built a huge 3m-high cairn on the summit (as a result the Vignemale exceeded 3300m) and spent many days and nights on the summit or slopes of the mountain (the last time he stayed for 16 days). In Gavarnie, just outside the village, along the road to Gèdre, you'll find a statue of Russell, which only few visitors notice.

0.00 Refuge de Bayssellance (2651m) From the refuge, descend SE for about 15min on the obvious path that

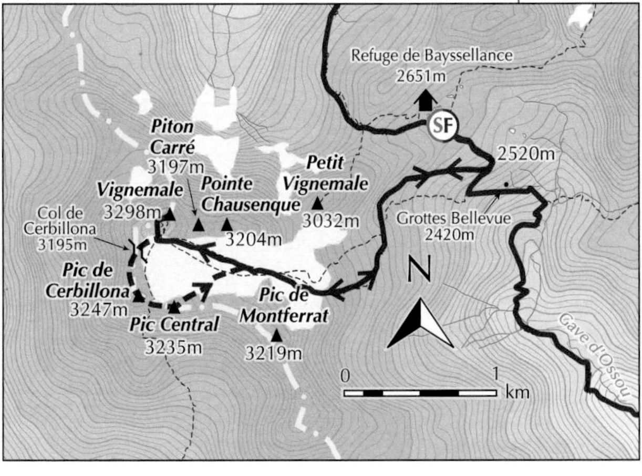

On Vignemale, overlooking the Soum d'Aspe, the Ossoue glacier, the whole Ossoue valley and the Cirque de Gavarnie

drops towards Gavarnie until you notice at around **2520m** a small path on your right. Turn right and follow this more or less level path next to a steep rocky slope. Walk SW towards the glacier, but don't go onto it, as there might be crevasses. Climb SSW on rocks, with the glacier on your right, occasionally crossing snow between the flattened rocks. A few cairns guide you W to a short, steep climb on snow, and soon you'll find yourself overlooking the wide, long glacier.

Climb more gently on an obvious track, pass the beautiful Brèche de Gaube (a gap offering great views) on your right and continue to the place below the Vignemale peak where the final scramble to the top begins. ◂ There are some cairns that will lead you to the summit of the

Take extreme care to avoid stonefall on your way up (and down).

3.00 Vignemale (3298m). Retrace your steps to return to the **Refuge de Bayssellance**.

Alternative descent route

From the top, go back to the glacier and then turn right and follow a track that leads to the **Col de Cerbillona** (3195m), a broad saddle that offers superb views to the west. ◂ Follow the ridge S and gain without any problems the **Pic de Cerbillona** (3247m), after which the ridge makes a turn left. Go down E a little and after a short climb reach the **Pic Central** (3235m), then leave the ridge

Just before arriving at the col there are the three Grottes Russell well above the glacier.

and go down NE to the glacier. Continue NE to the main track on the glacier and return to **Refuge de Bayssellance**.

DAY 16

Refuge de Bayssellance to Gavarnie

Start	Refuge de Bayssellance
Distance	17.5km
Total ascent	510m
Total descent	1795m
Grade	2
Time	5hr 20min
Map	Rando Editions Mapa Excursionista, 1:50,000, no 12: Gavarnie–Ordesa
Route	Via Barrage d'Ossoue (1843m)

The Haute Route follows the GR10 all the way to Gavarnie. This is an easy walk on a well-worn path, with no route-finding difficulties under normal conditions.

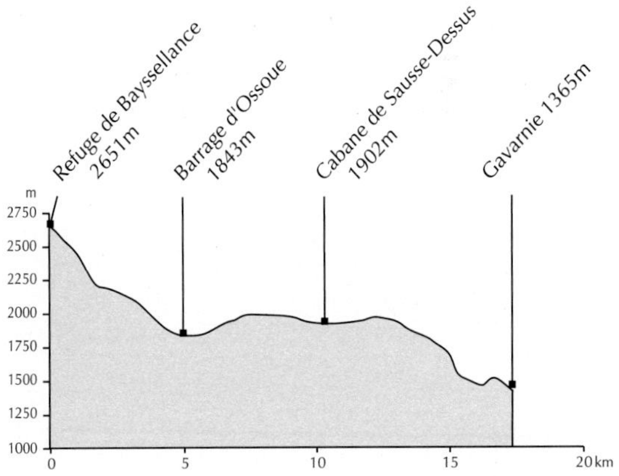

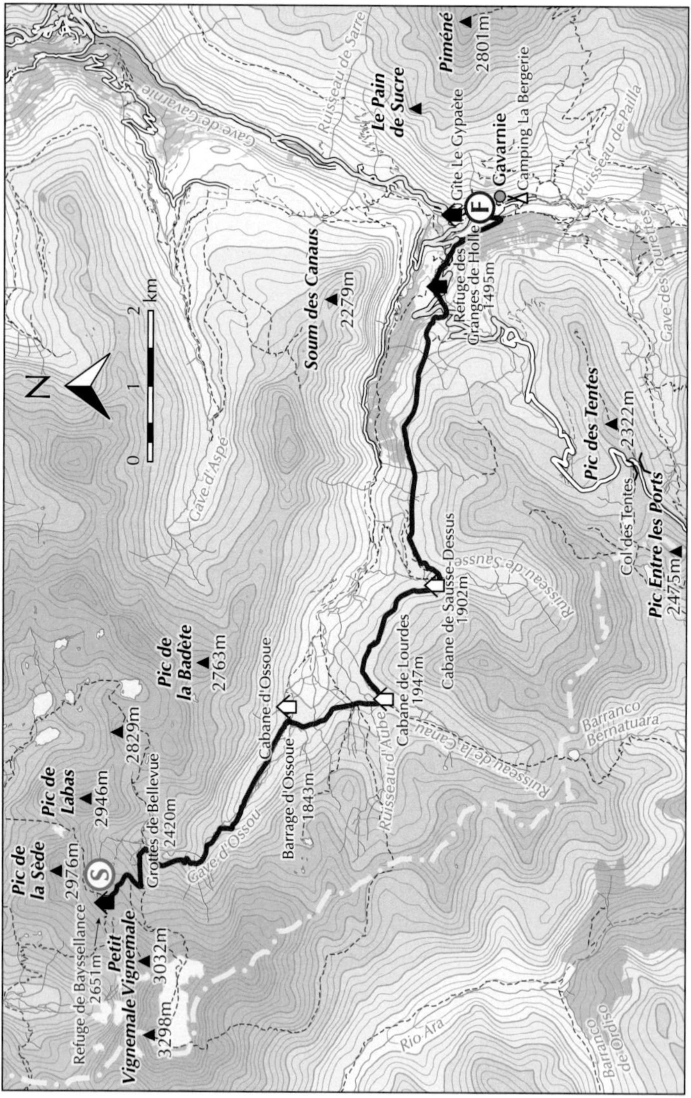

N
0
1
2
km
S
F
Pic de la Sède
2976m
Pic de Labas
2946m
2829m
Grottes de Bellevue
2420m
Refuge de Bayssellance
2651m
Petit Vignemale
3032m
Vignemale
3298m
Pic de la Badète
2763m
Cabane d'Ossoue
Gave d'Ossoue
Barrage d'Ossoue
1843m
Ruisseau d'Aube
Cabane de Lourdes
1947m
Ruisseau de la Canau
Cabane de Sausse-Dessus
1902m
Ruisseau de Sausse
Barranco Bernatuara
Rio Ara
Barranco de Ordiso
Soum des Canaus
2279m
Gave d'Aspé
Refuge des Granges de Holle
1495m
Gîte Le Gypaète
Gavarnie
Camping La Bergerie
Le Pain de Sucre
Piméné
2801m
Ruisseau de Sarre
Gave de Gavarnie
Ruisseau de Pailla
Gave des Tourettes
Pic des Tentes
2322m
Col des Tentes
Pic Entre les Ports
2475m

Descending from Refuge de Bayssellance to Barrage d'Ossoue

0.00 Refuge de Bayssellance. From the refuge, descend mainly SE on a well-worn path until you see the **Grottes de Bellevue** (2420m) on your left-hand side. Past the grottoes the path makes a curve to the right; descend S in zigzags to a bowl in which a few streams, coming from the Glacier d'Ossoue, have to be crossed. After a short ascent go down again to another bowl, in which a further few streams are crossed. Continue the descent along a steep rocky slope with the Gave d'Ossoue on your left-hand side until you reach the west side of a large plateau. Cross the Ossoue stream by a footbridge and walk E to the dam on the east side of

2.00 Barrage d'Ossoue (1843m), where bivouac is possible on a designated area to your left, and there is a simple *cabane* that offers primitive emergency shelter. Cross a footbridge a few metres below the dam and climb gently SSE through grass towards

2.35 Cabane de Lourdes (1947m). Keeping the *cabane* a little distance away on your right, cross the Canau stream by a footbridge. The GR10 now follows an almost level path that makes a large curve and reaches

3.20 Cabane de Sausse-Dessus (1902m), a basic shelter. Cross a stream just before the hut and cross the main stream by a footbridge. Walk on a more or less level path for some time, and then past a small concrete building (on your left, below) the path undulates.

Go through a gate after a short descent and climb gently. Pass an old *cabane* on the right, and a drinking trough for cattle, and follow the GR10 marks very carefully as the path is not always evident and makes a few sharp turns in a grassy area. Finally, follow the path that goes down to the road (D923, 1640m) that links Gavarnie with the Col des Tentes.

Cross the road and take the path (a shortcut) that descends steeply to rejoin the road. Take another shortcut and arrive at **Refuge des Granges de Holle** (1495m) on the left side of the road (tel 05 62 92 48 77, hut owned by the FFCAM, open all year except in November, meals available). Pass the refuge, cross a bridge, then cross a large parking area and arrive back on the road. Cross the road and continue SE to the end of the parking area on the other side of the road. Follow a path that starts here and continues generally SE. After 1km you will notice the village Gavarnie below on your left. Turn sharply left onto a small path and left again when you reach another path. Very soon you find Gavarnie's graveyeard and church on your left and you arrive at the centre of

5.20 Gavarnie (1365m). Turn right at the next junction (supermarket) and walk through the village, heading towards the Cirque de Gavarnie. To continue to the campsite, keep walking for 600 metres, cross the Gave de Gavarnie and reach the entrance to the **Camping La Bergerie**. ◂ For Gîte Le Gypaète, don't turn right at the supermarket, but continue to the tourism office and follow the street behind the building for about 100m. For practical information on Gavarnie see the introduction to this section.

The ascent of Le Taillon starts from the campsite and takes 10hr (return) – see 'Summit 3'.

SUMMIT 3

Le Taillon (3144m) from Gavarnie

Start	Camping La Bergerie (Day 16/17)
Distance	20km
Total ascent/descent	1950m
Grade	F
Time	10hr; allow 5hr 55min to reach the summit

Le Taillon is the most westerly summit of the Cirque de Gavarnie. Like all summits of the cirque it exceeds 3000m, but despite its altitude the ascent presents no significant difficulties in good weather. The route to Le Taillon is scenically spectacular and contains many highlights, such as the Grande Cascade, the famous Brèche de Roland (a gap in the Cirque de Gavarnie) and the views from the Plateau de Bellevue on the Cirque de Gavarnie. This walk can be accomplished in one day, but you may opt to make it a two-day excursion by spending the night at Refuge des Sarradets (also called Refuge de la Brèche de Roland, reservations essential) or by bivouacking on the way back.

0.00 Camping La Bergerie (1365m). From the campsite, walk S on the dirt road with the Gave de Gavarnie on your right-hand side. Eventually you will arrive at the

1.00 Hotellerie du Cirque (1570m, large building with a tavern). Cross the Gave de Gavarnie by a footbridge about 100 metres past the *hotellerie*, then follow a track SW that climbs a little and leads to the base of the cirque. Eventually you will find cairns that lead you to **L'Échelle des Sarradets**. ▶ Large red-and-yellow marks keep you on the right track.

This natural staircase leads to impressive views of the Grande Cascade, one of Europe's highest waterfalls.

At around 2000m the path bends to the left and you climb steeply SW. The route curves around the south slopes of Pic des Sarradets and you climb W through a chaotic landscape full of rocky terraces. The route is well

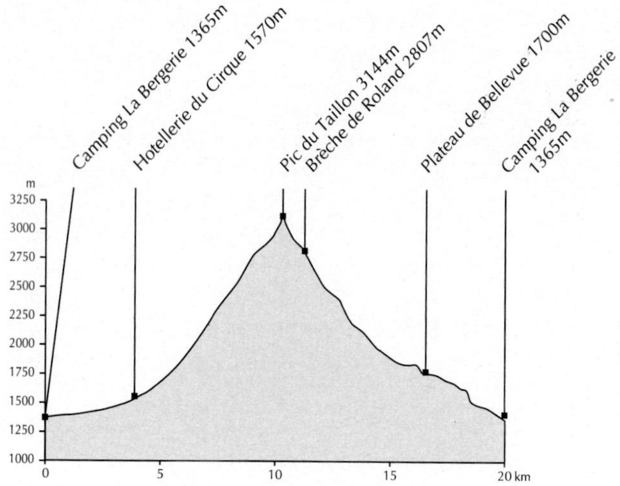

marked with cairns and some ancient red marks. Find your way without difficulty to

4.00 Refuge des Sarradets (2587m), a very popular mountain hut in a stunning setting, beautifully situated below the Brèche de Roland. Owned by the FFCAM, 57 places, open from mid-June until the end of September, tel 06 83 38 13 24. From here, climb on a steep slope full of stones and scree towards the Brèche de Roland and arrive on a plateau from where the Brèche presents itself in all its glory. Then climb on an obvious path through snow to the

4.45 Brèche de Roland (2807m). Don't go down on the Spanish side but turn right and follow a track W along the vertical walls of the Cirque de Gavarnie. Soon Le Doigt (the finger), a small rock pillar, comes in view. Go to this pillar, walk around it on its north (French) side and follow the obvious path W on the east ridge of Le Taillon until you finally arrive at the summit of the

5.55 Pic du Taillon (3144m). Enjoy the colourful views and return on the same track to

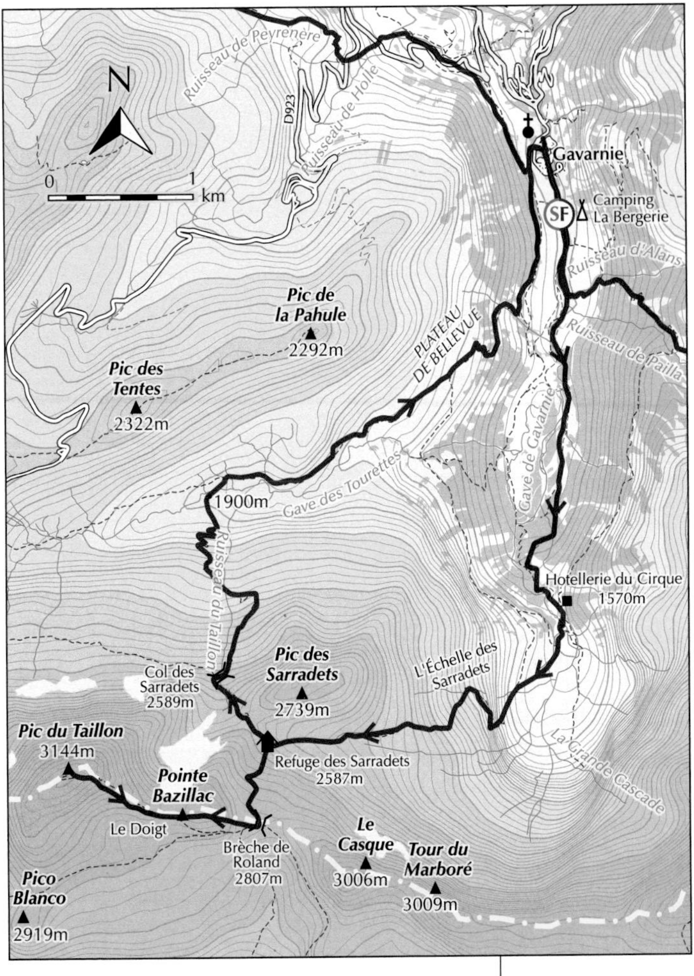

7.25 Refuge des Sarradets. On the way back to Gavarnie you take a different route: follow the path NW that leads to the **Col des Sarradets** (2589m), which affords a classic view of the Cirque de Gavarnie and the refuge,

View from the top of L'Échelle des Sarradets

and a nice view of Le Taillon, its glacier and Le Doigt. Descend steeply in a rocky area and carefully cross the meltwater of the glacier (follow the marks). Soon the path forks (signpost); turn right, cross the meltwater once again, and descend steeply N on a scree slope.

After a long zigzag the stream is crossed once more on a kind of balcony, and then a series of zigzags bring you finally to the floor of the Vallée de Pouey Aspé (**1900m**). Cross a stream and reach a junction; turn right and walk ENE on a lovely track above the valley that descends gently and offers excellent views of the valley. Arrive at a junction at the

9.00 Plateau de Bellevue (1700m), with superb views of the Cirque de Gavarnie. Don't turn right but follow the path towards Gavarnie, which continues NE and soon descends in zigzags. Continue N after the zigzags, then descend once more in zigzags and finally walk N to the centre of

10.00 Gavarnie (1365m). Turn right at the junction with the supermarket, cross the Gave de Gavarnie 600 metres further on and reach **Camping La Bergerie**.

SECTION 3: GAVARNIE TO SALARDÚ

Lac de Barroude and the Barroude wall (Day 18)

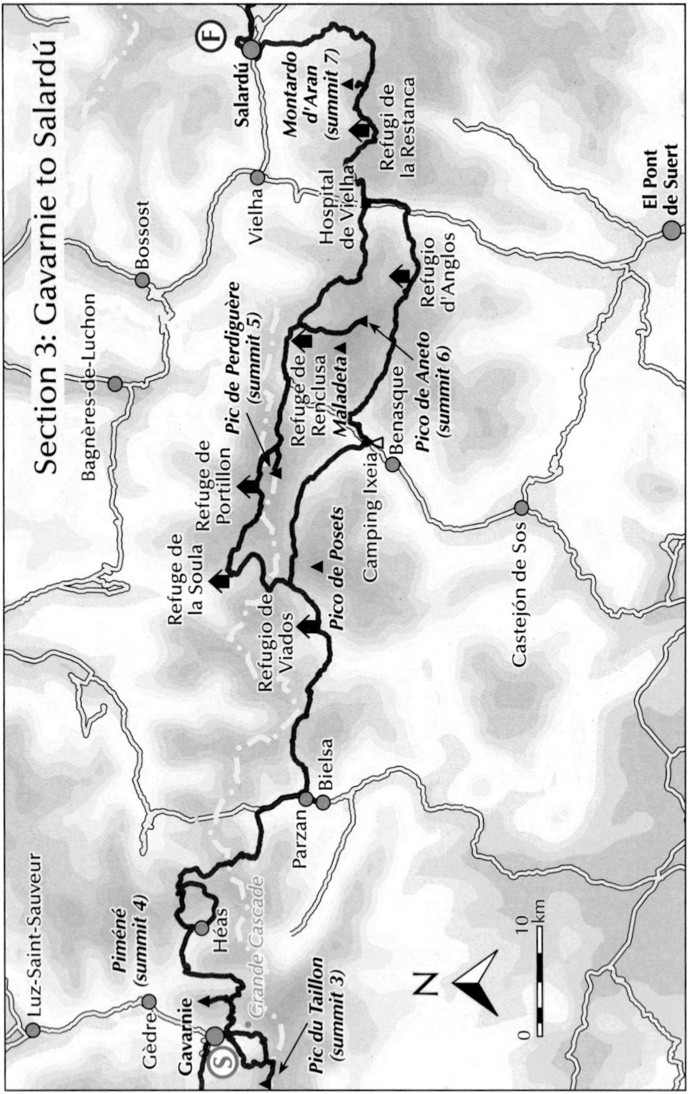
Section 3: Gavarnie to Salardú
Bagnères-de-Luchon
Bossost
Vielha
Salardú
F
Montardo d'Aran (summit 7)
Refugi de la Restanca
Hospital de Vielha
Refugio d'Anglos
El Pont de Suert
Pic de Perdiguère (summit 5)
Refuge de Portillon
Refuge de la Soula
Refuge de Renclusa
Maladeta
Pico de Aneto (summit 6)
Benasque
Camping Ixeia
Castejón de Sos
Refugio de Viados
Pico de Posets
Bielsa
Parzan
Luz-Saint-Sauveur
Piméné (summit 4)
Héas
Grande Cascade
Gèdre
Gavarnie
S
Pic du Taillon (summit 3)
N
0
10
km

Refuge des Espuguettes is dwarfed by the western side of the Cirque de Gavarnie (Day 17)

THE HARD OR THE EASY WAY TO SALARDÚ?

The second section showed you the highlights of the Parc National des Pyrénées. If everything goes according to plan, you'll leave the national park for good on the second day of the third section. However, you might want to postpone your farewell, as the second stage is long and demanding and the Barroude lakes, together with the massive Barroude wall, make a fabulous place to pitch a tent for the night. When taking the exciting alternative route (Variant 3) to Hourquette de Héas, a stay at the Barroude lakes is definitely recommended, although very energetic hikers could make it to Parzán in one day.

The walk from Gavarnie to Salardú presents impressive landscapes which are at times tricky to navigate. The Viados–La Soula–Portillon–Renclusa–Hospital de Vielha trail is full of challenges: you have to face steep slopes full of scree and rocks, large snowfields and some remains of glaciers, as well as lots of sections without a path and a number of high passes. The Col Inférieur de Literole (2983m) and the Coll de Mulleres (2924m) are the two highest passes of the entire Haute Route. Crampons and ice axe are often needed here until late July. You will walk through intimidating landscapes, like the Portillon region – an alpine wilderness with numerous 3000m summits, covered with snowfields and remains of former glaciers, enormous boulderfields and a number of high lakes, often with ice floating in them.

There is an alternative to the main route: a three-day variant (Variant 4) that can serve as an escape route in bad weather. It is also a safe option for those who don't want to carry crampons and ice axe. This is the GR11 trail from Refugio de Viados to Hospital de Vielha.

On both trails there is the option to have a rest day in a convenient place: halfway on the Pyrenean Haute Route you are close to Benasque, a small town with campsites, shops, restaurants and a post office.

There are many highlights during this third section of the Haute Route – the view from Viados of the Posets' west face; the Portillon region dominated by a dozen 3000m summits; the magnificent Ibon Blanc de Literola, mostly covered with ice; the beautifully shaped Lac du Milieu and Lac des Isclots filled with green water; and, of course, the snow-covered northern slopes of the Maladeta massif, with Aneto (3404m), the highest summit of the Pyrenees. It's certainly worth fitting a summit climb in by making a longer day or by taking a day off.

In this section the ascents of four classic summits are described: Piméné (2801m, Day 17), Pic Perdiguère (3222m, Day 21), Pico de Aneto (3404m, Day 22) and the Montardo (2826m, Day 25).

VAL D'ARAN

Val d'Aran is remarkable for being Spanish territory despite the fact that its rivers flow to the Atlantic Ocean. After the Middle Ages, France and Spain agreed to draw their borders depending on which direction the water flows; in most places this is indeed the case, but Val d'Aran is clearly an exception as the Garonne has its origin here.

Val d'Aran used to be a rather isolated valley, due to its location between high mountain ranges (Maladeta, Besiberri, Encantats, Beret). For most of the year it was cut off completely when the high access roads became impassable. The inhabitants of the valley lived in small communities, each with its own Romanesque church. The valley developed its own character and even its own language. In the course of the 20th century, the isolation of the Val d'Aran came to an end with the opening of the Vielha tunnel (1948) and several roads. Nowadays, the popular ski resort of Baqueira-Beret, one of the largest in the Pyrenees, and the Aigüestortes national park attract a lot of tourists. Val d'Aran has become a valley with great contrasts between old and new: in the villages there is often a picturesque old centre surrounded by new buildings that serve mass tourism. Salardú is a good example, but other villages have changed beyond recognition over the years. However, when you walk to Pla de Beret, don't forget to look back; from a distance Val d'Aran, with the snow-covered Maladeta massif in the background, still looks very attractive.

PRACTICAL INFORMATION

Public transport to Gavarnie

Take the Eurostar to Paris Gare du Nord, then the subway to Gare Montparnasse and from there take the TGV (high-speed train) to Lourdes. From Lourdes go by bus to Gavarnie. Note that in summer there is only one morning bus to Gavarnie; see http://summer.gavarnie.com for the schedule.

Facilities in Gavarnie

Facilities in the village include the Office du Tourisme, the Maison du Parc National, a small but decent supermarket, a basic campsite, a picnic spot (next to the church), a cash dispenser, hotels, restaurants, bars and souvenir shops. The campsite is reached by walking down Gavarnie's main street for 600 metres and crossing the Gave de Gavarnie by a bridge. It's highly recommended to make a reservation, as this is a very popular campsite.

Facilities in Salardú

This old village, situated in the eastern section of the Val d'Aran, has a lovely village centre around the Plaça Major, with a Romanesque church. On the Plaça Major you'll find Refugi Rosta – a simple hotel and certainly a fine place to stay for walkers. There are small rooms and a dormitory, a good kitchen and an excellent breakfast. Open from late June until late September, 55 places, tel 973 645 308, fax 973 645 814.

However, the most logical place for walkers to spend the night might be the Aran Hostel, situated in the east

Refugi de la Restanca and its beautiful surroundings (Day 24)

part of Salardú. A large *refugi* owned by the CEC (Centre Excursionista de Catalunya) with small dormitories (4–5 people) as well as double rooms, good meals available, 112 places. Tel 648 528 196.

The village has a bank (with cash dispenser), supermarket, food shop, small tourist office next to the shop, hotels, restaurants, bars and a public swimming pool. There are no campsites; the nearest is Era Yerla in the village of Arties, about 3km west of Salardú.

Public transport from Salardú

From Salardú there is a local bus to Vielha, 14 times daily. From Vielha there is a long-distance bus to Barcelona. Both lines are operated by the same company; see www.alsa.com for the schedule. There are no options to reach the French side of the Pyrenees by public transport from Salardú.

Variants

Variant 3 is a very challenging option that presents a more difficult but also more interesting climb to Hourquette de Héas (Day 18). For independent trekkers who don't wish to stay at the Refuge de la Soula at the end of Day 20, there is an easy shortcut to Lac de Caillauas. The main route from Refugio de Viados (Day 20) to Hospital de Vielha (Day 23) includes snowfields and very steep slopes and should certainly be avoided in poor conditions: Variant 4 offers an easier three-day alternative route, following the GR11, for those wishing to avoid these obstacles.

Classic summits

Piméné (2801m) can be climbed from Refuge des Espuguettes (Day 17). Pic Perdiguère (3222m) can be climbed from Portal de Remune (Day 22). Pico de Aneto (3404m), the highest peak in the Pyrenees, can be climbed from Refugio de la Renclusa, which is reached at the end of Day 22. Montardo d'Aran (2826m) can be climbed from Coll de Crestada (Day 25).

Food and fuel

In Parzán (Day 18) you can buy food from one of the supermarkets. Most hikers will also go into Benasque (Day 21, 9km) to replenish their supplies. If you're short on food when you reach Hospital de Vielha, you could hitch-hike to Vielha (12km). Vielha is also easily reached from Salardú (Day 24, 10km), at the end of this section. Gas canisters and liquid fuel can be obtained in Benasque and Vielha.

Maps

Rando Editions Mapa Excursionista, 1:50,000: No 22: Pica d'Estats–Aneto; No 23: Aneto–Posets; No 12: Gavarnie–Ordesa

Accomodation: contact details

All numbers and other information on accommodation on the Haute Route are also given in the route description.

- Gavarnie: Gîte Le Gypaète, tel 05 62 92 40 61; Camping La Bergerie – tel 05 62 92 48 41
- Day 17: Auberge de la Munia – tel 05 62 92 48 39
- Day 18: Hostal La Fuen – tel 628 38 36 79
- Day 19: Refugio de Viados – tel 974 341 613
- Day 20: Refuge de la Soula – tel 05 62 40 23 41
- Day 21: Refuge du Portillon – tel 05 61 79 38 15
- Day 22: Refugio de la Renclusa – tel 974 344 646
- Day 23: Refugi de Conangles – tel 696 649 871
- Day 24: Refugi de la Restanca – tel 608 036 559
- Salardú: Aran Hostel – tel 648 528 196; Refugi Rosta – tel 973 645 308; Camping Era Yerla (in Arties) – tel 973 641 602
- Variant, Day 1: Camping Ixeia (camping and cabins) – tel 974 552 129
- Variant, Day 2: Refugio d'Anglos **(unmanned, no meals)**

DAY 17

Gavarnie to Héas

Start	Gavarnie
Distance	18km
Total ascent	1285m
Total descent	1150m
Grade	2
Time	6hr 45min
Map	Rando Editions Mapa Excursionista, 1:50,000, no 12: Gavarnie–Ordesa
Route	Via the Hourquette d'Alans (2430m)

An easy walk on well-worn paths, with no route-finding difficulties under normal weather conditions. The final part is on road. The route provides fine views of the Cirque de Gavarnie and a passing acquaintance with a lesser-known cirque – the Cirque d'Estaubé.

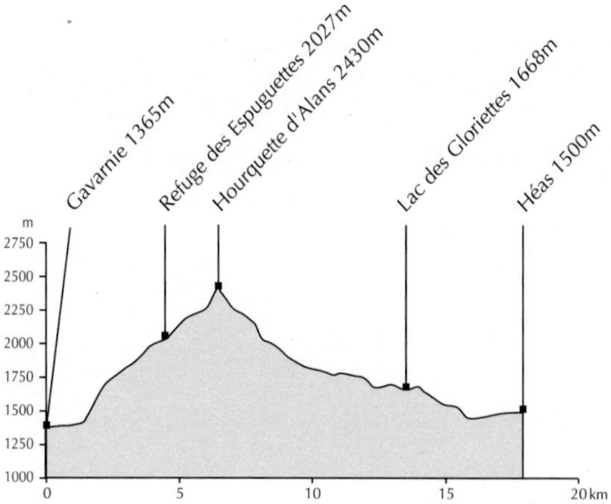

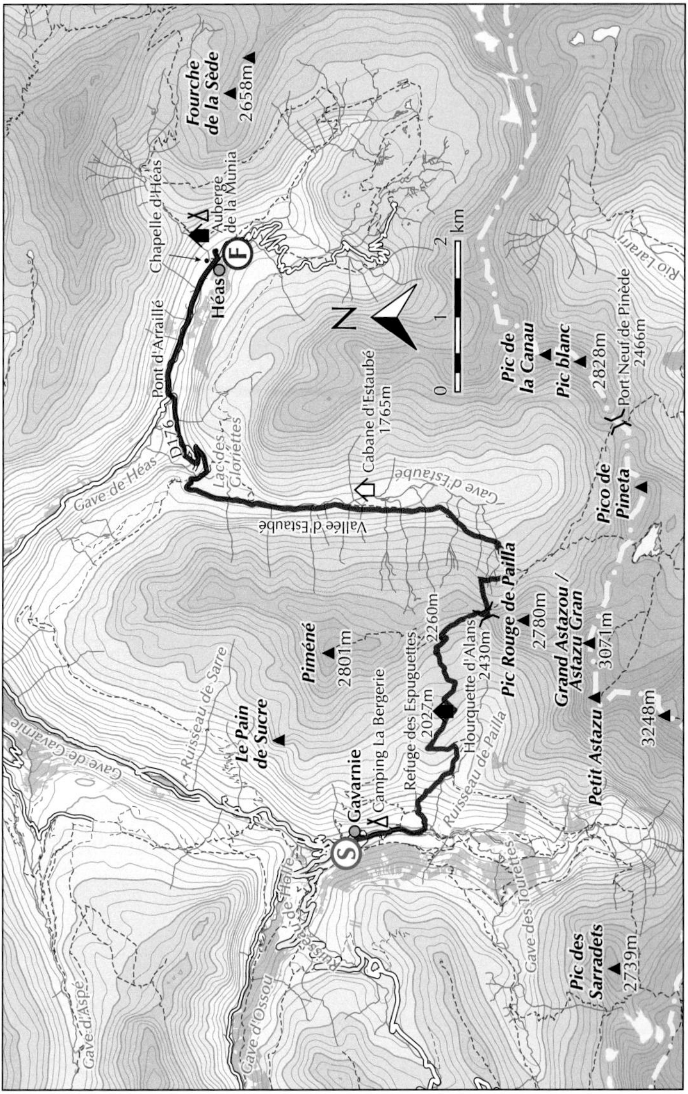
Fourche de la Sède
2658m
Chapelle d'Héas
Auberge de la Munia
Héas
F
Pont d'Arraillé
D176
Gave de Héas
Lac des Gloriettes
Cabane d'Estaubé
1765m
Gave d'Estaubé
Vallée d'Estaubé
N
0
1
2
km
Pic de la Canau
Pic blanc
2828m
Port Neuf de Pinède
2466m
Rio Lararri
Pico de Pineta
Pic Rouge de Pailla
2780m
Grand Astazou / Astazu Gran
3071m
Hourquette d'Alans
2430m
2260m
Refuge des Espuguettes
2027m
Piméné
2801m
Le Pain de Sucre
Ruisseau de Sarre
Gave de Gavarnie
Gavarnie
S
Camping La Bergerie
Ruisseau de Pailla
Petit Astazu
3248m
Gave des Tourettes
Pic des Sarradets
2739m
Ruisseau de Holle
Gave d'Ossoue
Gave d'Aspé

0.00 Gavarnie (1365m). Walk S down the main street for 600 metres and then cross a bridge over the Gave de Gavarnie. Pass the entrance to the campsite, which is situated right across the bridge, and follow the dirt road S on the east side of the river. Ignore a path coming from the left and then turn left after about 500 metres, just before a building (signpost), and climb an obvious track SE that soon enters the Arribama forest.

Climb in zigzags to a junction near the border of the Parc National, just outside the forest. Turn left before you reach a signpost and ascend in an open field towards the Refuge des Espuguettes, which is now visible. It's possible to climb in a straight line ENE to the refuge, but the track (marked with a few cairns) climbs more gently, turns N and then ESE to arrive at the

2.00 Refuge des Espuguettes (2027m), hut owned by the Parc National des Pyrénées, 60 places, meals available, manned from June until September, tel 05 62 92 40 63. ◀ From here there are fine views of the Cirque de Gavarnie and the famous Brèche de Roland.

The ascent of Piméné starts from the refuge and takes 4hr 15min (return) – see 'Summit 4'.

To continue, climb generally E in zigzags on a well-worn path until the path forks at **2260m**. Ignore the path

The Cirque d'Estaubé is less famous than its neighbour in Gavarnie but is still a popular place

that climbs to the Piméné (2801m, the route to the summit is described at the end of this walk) and climb SE to the

3.15 Hourquette d'Alans (2430m), which gives access to the Vallée d'Estaubé. Descend in short zigzags on the east side of the col (ignore a path on your right-hand side after a few zigzags) on an obvious path until the path forks at about 2160m in the centre of the Cirque d'Estaubé. Ignore the path that goes SE to the Port Neuf de Pinède and instead go NE down to the floor of the Vallée d'Estaubé. Stay left of the Gave d'Estaubé, leave the Parc National, and go gently down to the

5.30 Lac des Gloriettes (1668m). Pass the dammed lake along its western shore, ignore the path that branches off to the left (to the Granges de Coumély) and cross the dam. Turn left and go down to a small parking area below the dam, then go NE down a small road (D176) to the **Pont de l'Arraillé** (1459m), where you'll meet the D922. Cross the stream, turn right (large Parc National information board) and walk SE for 2.2km on the road, which climbs a few metres, to the hamlet of

6.45 Héas (1500m). In Héas it's possible to spend the night at the Auberge de la Munia hostel, 10 places, excellent meals available, ordering bread is possible, tel 05 62 92 48 39, www.aubergedelamunia.com. There is a charming campsite called Le Cairn next to the hostel. Héas has no shops, just a few houses and a chapel (worth visiting).

SUMMIT 4

Piméné (2801m) from Refuge des Espuguettes

Start	Refuge des Espuguettes (Day 17)
Distance	8.5km
Total ascent/descent	760m
Grade	F
Time	4hr 15min; allow 2hr 15min to the summit

The Piméné isn't particularly high, but its place on the ridge separating the Vallée de Gavarnie from the Vallée d'Estaubé allows the courageous hiker top-class views onto the cirques of both Gavarnie and Estaubé; the Monte Perdido (3355m) in the Ordesa National Park; the summits of the Cirque de Troumouse; the long, stretched valley of Gavarnie; the Pic Long (3192m) and other peaks in the Néouvielle region. Above all you can draw a straight line through the Vallée d'Ossoue towards the glacier-draped east face of the Vignemale (3298m).

The climb is very straightforward, although the final section is rather steep and requires a little care.

0.00 Refuge des Espuguettes (2027m). Follow the Haute Route trail towards the Hourquette d'Alans until the path forks (**2260m**). Turn left and climb on a clear path in a number of long zigzags to the

1.25 Col du Piméné (2522m), then follow a track through scree on the east side of the ridge and go around the Petit Piméné (2667m). Gain the ridge once again north of the Petit Piméné and climb steeply N until you finally reach the summit of the

2.15 Piméné (2801m). Follow the same route back to the refuge.

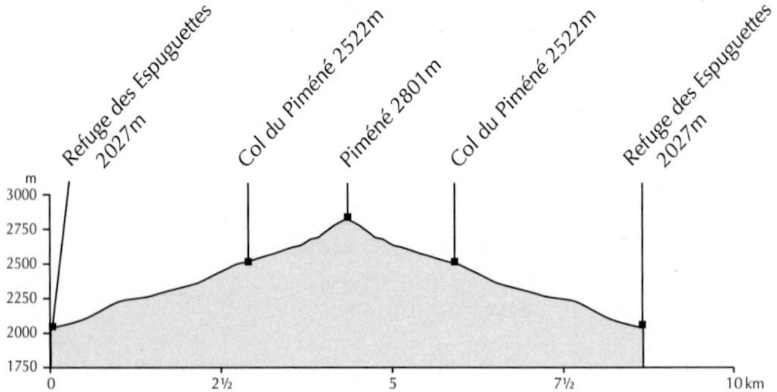

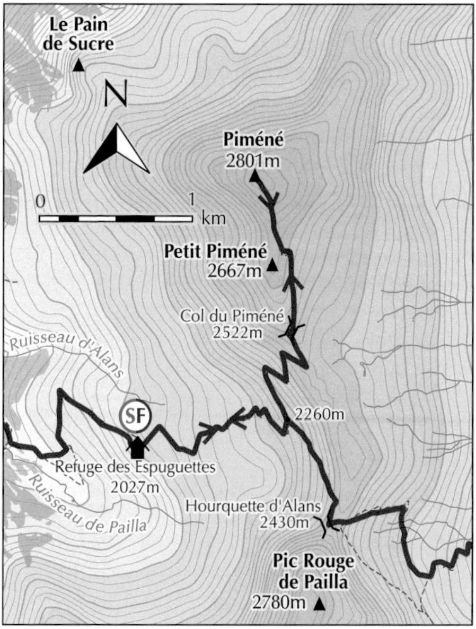

DAY 18

Héas to Parzán

Start	Héas
Distance	27.5km
Total ascent	1725m
Total descent	2125m
Grade	3
Time	10hr
Map	Rando Editions Mapa Excursionista, 1:50,000, no 12: Gavarnie–Ordesa
Route	Via the Hourquette de Héas (2608m), the Hourquette de Chermentas (2439m) and the Port de Barroude (2534m)
Note	Steep snowfields may be encountered in early summer; ice axe and crampons recommended

A very long walk with several challenges. The route to Hourquette de Héas is steep and not easily found. On the other side of the Hourquette steep snowfields may challenge you in early summer. But altogether it's a splendid walk, the last (partly) within the boundaries of the Parc National. Considering its length, you might want to divide it in two; the Barroude lakes are a magical place to spend the night and admire the sunrise.

Variant 3 offers a challenging high-level alternative route to Hourquette de Héas and adds an extra hour to the walk time.

0.00 Héas. ◄ Walk SE from Auberge de la Munia and soon find a signpost at the left of the road. Turn left and follow the path that climbs SE through the Vallon de Touyères to arrive after a minute at a junction. Here turn left and climb gently NNE, then follow numerous zigzags on an obvious path. Notice a water point with a footbridge on your left at 1750m and climb, always staying on the right of the stream, to a small plateau in which the Ruisseau de l'Aguila flows. Ignore another footbridge (1880m) and on the other side of the stream you'll find the

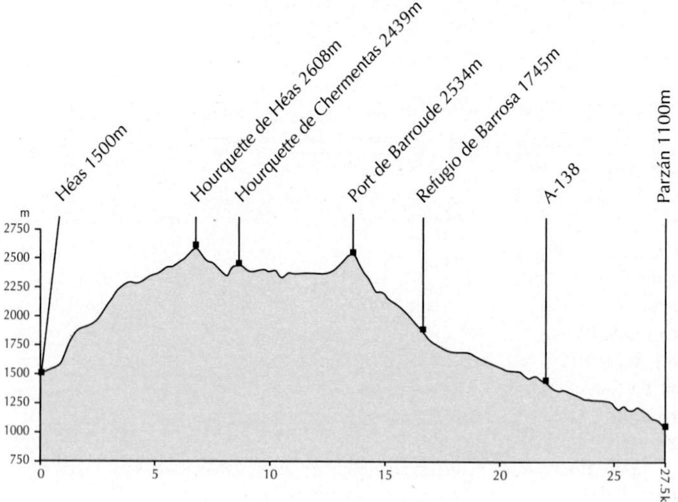

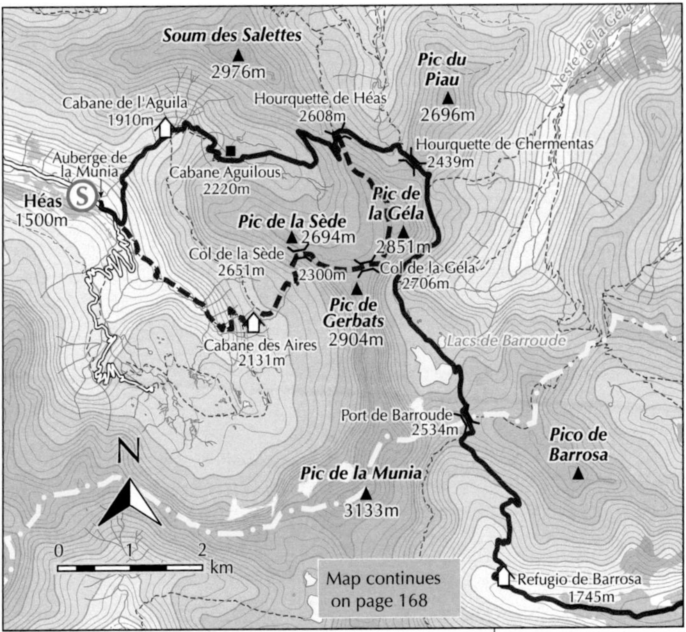

1.15 Cabane de l'Aguila (1910m), a basic but useful shelter with six places. Keep the stream on your left-hand side and pass the little Oratoire de Sainte-Famille (water source). The path enters the Parc National, makes a turn to the right and climbs E a little way from the Aguillous stream (fine views of the distant Vignemale). It climbs in a number of zigzags to meet this stream on a small plateau. Notice **Cabane Aguilous** (2220m, a shepherds' hut, closed to hikers) on the other side of the stream. ▶ Cross the Ruisseau d'Aguillous (last water source until the Lacs de Barroude) and climb E towards the ridge that hides the Hourquette de Héas. The path makes a number of large zigzags and finally reaches the

In good weather, the huge cairn on the Hourquette de Héas is visible from this *cabane*.

3.45 Hourquette de Héas (2608m), a well-hidden pass on the Crête (ridge) des Aguillous. Descend carefully NE on the steep east side of the col. At 2450m the path

Overlooking the Vallée de Badet from the Hourquette de Héas

forks; don't turn left but continue to go down to approximately 2300m and then climb E to the

4.15 Hourquette de Chermentas (2439m), where Refuge de Barroude is indicated. Descend in zigzags on the east side of the pass for a short while and then climb

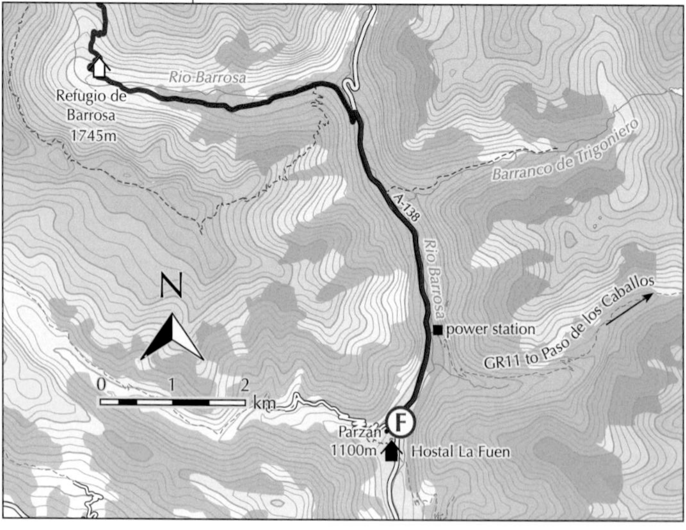

Sunrise at Lacs de Barroude

along the impressive rock faces of the Pic d'Aguillous (2851m). The path bends around the Pic d'Aguillous and reaches a junction (notice Pic de Gerbats on your right); don't turn left but climb gently SE on an obvious path along the large Barroude wall to arrive at the

5.45 Lacs de Barroude (2373m). The refuge that used to sit on a bluff above the largest of the two lakes was destroyed by fire in 2014. There are plans to build a new refuge here in the future. Bivouac is possible near the lake, and there are two small emergency shelters (both have two places) where the refuge used to be. To continue, follow the path that leads to the east side of the lake, cross a stream and climb S on a path that brings you to the

6.30 Port de Barroude (2534m), on the French-Spanish border. Descend on the south side of the large pass to the floor of the Valle de Barrosa; there is a signpost that indicates the path (white-and-yellow marks). After descending in a number of zigzags the descent eases somewhat and you go down SE. The path eventually bends to the right and descends S to the floor of the valley.

Cross a stream, notice the unmanned **Refugio de Barrosa** (1745m, solid hut, 10 places, tables, chairs) on your right and finally reach the main stream in the valley, the Rio Barrosa. Cross the stream (around 1700m; stepping-stones may be submerged after heavy rainfall but the crossing should not present much difficulty), turn left and follow an obvious path E with the stream on your left-hand side, then after crossing several minor streams the path eventually turns into a dirt road, which you follow down E to the

9.00 A-138 (1410m), the road that links de Valle de Bielsa (Spain) with the Vallée d'Aure (France) through the Bielsa tunnel. Turn right and walk SSE on the gently descending road for 5km. Notice on your way to Parzán an ancient customs house (1290m) and a **power station** (1200m), and notice the dirt road that leads to the Lago de Urdiceto (tomorrow's walk) after 3.5km. There are several good places for a bivouac along this dirt road. Don't turn right to the hamlet of Parzán, but walk on the A-138 to

10.00 Hostal La Fuen (hotel/bar/restaurant, 1100m), on the west side of the road, tel 628 383 679 (a convenient but not especially attractive place to spend the night). A little before Hostal La Fuen there are several supermarkets.

VARIANT 3

Parzán via the high route to Hourquette de Héas

Start	Héas (Day 17/18)
Finish	Parzán (Day 18/19)
Distance	28.5km (8.5km to Hourquette de Héas)
Total ascent	1970m
Total descent	2370m
Grade	3
Time	11hr
Route	Via the Col de la Sède and the Col de la Géla
Notes	Good visibility required; check conditions before setting out. Snowfields may be encountered in early summer; crampons and ice axe recommended. For map, see Day 18.

A very challenging variant which presents a more difficult but also more interesting climb to Hourquette de Héas. There are magnificent views over the Cirque de Troumouse (which remains out of sight on the main route) from Col de la Sède and equally amazing views of the Lacs de Barroude from Col de la Géla. The route is mostly unwaymarked and in early summer crampons and ice axe may be needed. Good visibility is a must. This variant makes the already long route to Parzán an hour longer; for hikers who have already decided to bivouac at the Lacs de Barroude it is definitely an alternative to consider.

0.00 Héas (1500m) Walk SE from Auberge de la Munia and soon find a signpost at the left of the road. At the junction, ignore the path to Cabane d'Aguila and continue on the path SE towards Cabane des Aires. At 1850m continue on several zigzags, ignore the path to the Vierge de Troumouse and arrive at

1.45 Cabane des Aires (2131m, hut sometimes in use by a herder, five places) Climb (no path, no waymarks) gently NE over grass left of a riverbed until you reach the bottom of the steep, rocky climb to Col de la Sède. Climb N on a natural staircase of sorts until you reach a place (around 2600m) where you can continue climbing gently E to

Col de la Sède offers amazing views of the Cirque de Troumouse

There are magnificent views of the Cirque de Troumouse and, in the distance, the Ossoue glacier and the Vignemale.

3.25 Col de la Sède (2651m, large cairn). ◀ Continue on the NE side of the col, descend to 2600m and then continue E, possibly crossing a large snowfield, to

4.00 Col de la Géla (2706m), with fantastic views of the Barroude wall and lakes. Continue N horizontally, next to Pic de la Géla, until you join the ridge. Then continue NW on the ridge to

4.40 Hourquette de Héas (2608m). From here follow the route to **Parzán** described in Day 18.

DAY 19

Parzán to Refugio de Viados

Start	Parzán
Distance	21km
Total ascent	1675m
Total descent	1015m
Grade	2
Time	7hr 15min
Map	Rando Editions Mapa Excursionista, 1:50,000, no 23: Aneto–Posets
Route	Via the Paso de los Caballos (2314m)

Today the Haute Route follows the GR11 all day, so there are no route-finding difficulties. First you face a rather boring, long climb on a dirt road (11km), to the Paso de los Caballos. An early start is highly advised here to avoid hiking in the hottest part of the day. The second half of the walk leads through much more interesting landscapes, and the end of the day is perfect: a superb view from Refugio de Viados of the impressive west face of Pico de Posets (3375m), the second highest summit in the Pyrenees.

0.00 Parzán. Climb N on the A-138 and turn right after 1.5km, before the Barrosa power station. Cross the **Rio Barrosa** and climb SE, then ENE on a dirt road, keeping the **Barranco de Urdiceto** below on your right-hand

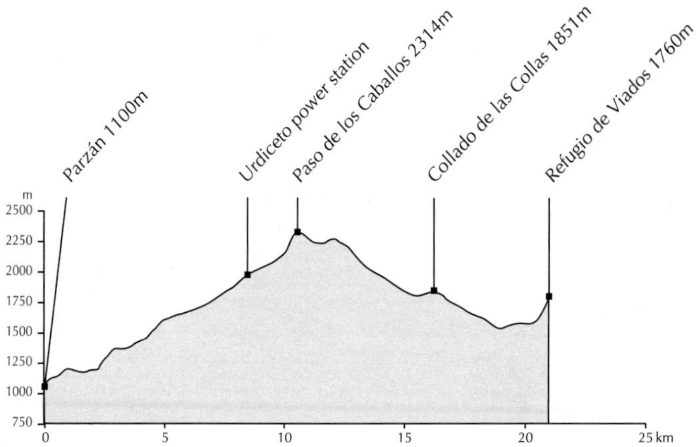

side. About 1km up this road there's a good place for a bivouac (water available) on the right side of the road.

Follow a path that shortcuts a section of the dirt road before reaching the **Urdiceto power station** and continue climbing the dirt road for about 1km. (There are some more fine places for a bivouac on your right below, next to a stream.) Take a track on the right side of the dirt road (2137m), just before the dirt road climbs steeply in zigzags, and then arrive on the road again. Turn right and walk a few metres to the

3.30 Paso de los Caballos (2314m). Now leave the dirt road (which climbs to the Lago de Urdiceto), turn left and walk on a level track to a *cabana* (good emergency shelter). Make a short descent and climb E to a ridge. At the highest point (2286m) the long descent to Valle de Gistain begins; initially the path goes down gently, but then the route makes a sharp turn to the left and goes down more steeply. Go down to the valley through which the Barranco de Montarruegos runs.

Cross the stream (2000m) and follow the path SE that bends away from the stream and goes down a little between pine trees. Cross a marshy area and arrive in an

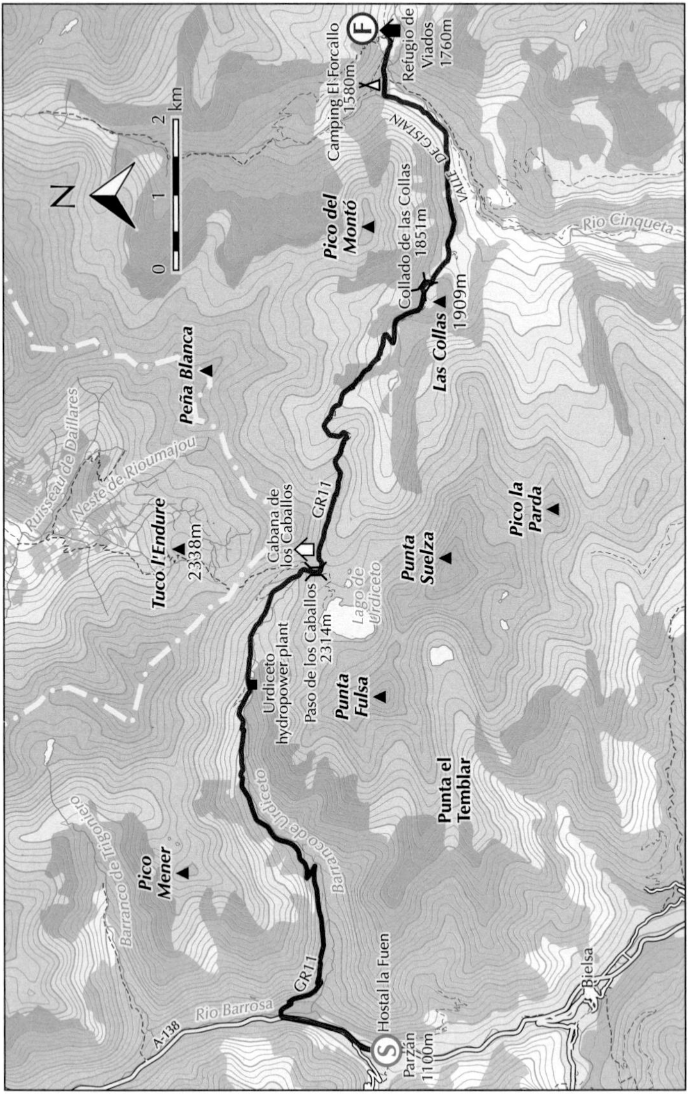
N
0
1
2 km
Camping El Forcallo
1580m
Refugio de
Viados
1760m
F
VALLE DE GISTAIN
Rio Cinqueta
Pico del
Montó
Collado de las Collas
1851m
Las Collas
1909m
Peña Blanca
Ruisseau de Daillares
Neste de Rioumajou
Tuco l'Endure
2338m
Cabana de
los Caballos
GR11
Paso de los Caballos
2314m
Lago de
Urdiceto
Punta
Suelza
Pico la
Parda
Urdiceto
hydropower plant
Punta
Fulsa
Punta el
Temblar
Barranco de Urdiceto
Barranco de Trigoniero
Pico
Mener
GR11
Rio Barrosa
A-138
Hostal la Fuen
S
Parzán
1100m
Bielsa

Cabana de los Caballos offers fine views to the west side of the Posets

open landscape with a primitive *cabana* on a hill on your right, and then follow a dirt road. Soon take a shortcut left of the road; this leads to the road again, then you cross a stream, take another shortcut on the left side of the road and climb to the

5.15 Collado de las Collas (1851m), between pine trees. Follow the dirt road up for a few minutes to a signpost, then turn right and make a number of shortcuts (signed for GR11). Follow the road again, go through a gate and notice a *cabana* on your right; leave the road on your left (signpost) and after another shortcut arrive again on the road. Turn left, climb a few metres and pass a small house (1720m), then descend E to a junction in the **Valle de Gistain** (1540m, signpost GR11).

Turn left and climb very gently NE for 1.3km (towards Camping Forcallo) on a dirt road, keeping the Rio Cinqueta that runs through the valley on your right-hand side. After the building belonging to the Campamento Virgin Blanca (a holiday camp for children) and north of the place where the Rio Cinqueta de la Pez and the Rio Cinqueta de Añescruzes meet (and thus form the Rio Cinqueta), cross the Rio Cinqueta de la Pez and arrive at

6.45 Camping El Forcallo (1580m), a small campsite with good facilities, bar, meals sometimes available if ordered well in advance, open July and August. Leave the dirt road past the campsite and take a shortcut to arrive at the dirt road again. Take another, much longer shortcut, notice a barn on your right and climb to the dirt road once more. Cross the dirt road and climb between pine trees to the back of

7.15 Refugio de Viados (1760m); private hut. Manned from mid June until the last week of September, 70 places, meals available. Reservation necessary, tel 974 341 613. Bivouac is not allowed near the hut. The hut has a pleasant atmosphere and offers great views of the Posets' west face.

DAY 20

Refugio de Viados to Refuge de la Soula

Start	Refugio de Viados
Distance	13km
Total ascent	1055m
Total descent	1125m
Grade	3
Time	6hr 30min
Map	Rando Editions Mapa Excursionista, 1:50,000, no. 23: Aneto–Posets
Route	Via the Port d'Aygues Tortes (2683m, also called Col Supérieur d'Aygues Tortes)

After an easy start on the GR11, there is a long section without path or waymarks. The climb to the Port d'Aygues Tortes is not difficult under normal summer conditions. After a steep descent on the French side of the pass, an easy walk through the Vallon d'Aygues Tortes leads to Refuge de la Soula. If you have no reason to descend to the Refuge de la Soula you can opt for the shortcut, which takes a more direct route to Lac de Caillauas (Day 21). Also look ahead at the next two days, which include several high passes; there's a three-day alternative (Variant 4) that avoids these obstacles. The choice needs to be made shortly after leaving Refugio de Viados.

The Granjas de Viados are well-conserved barns that date to a time when more people lived and worked in the Pyrenees

0.00 Refugio de Viados. ▸ Go down a few metres in front of the *refugio*, cross a stream and take the GR11 trail that climbs gently E along the Bordas de Viados (meadows with a number of barns, the Granjas de Viados). The track soon turns into a path and arrives at a junction (signpost); ignore the path to Collado de Eriste on your right and

Variant 4 offers an easier three-day alternative route from Refugio de Viados to Hospital de Vielha, following the GR11.

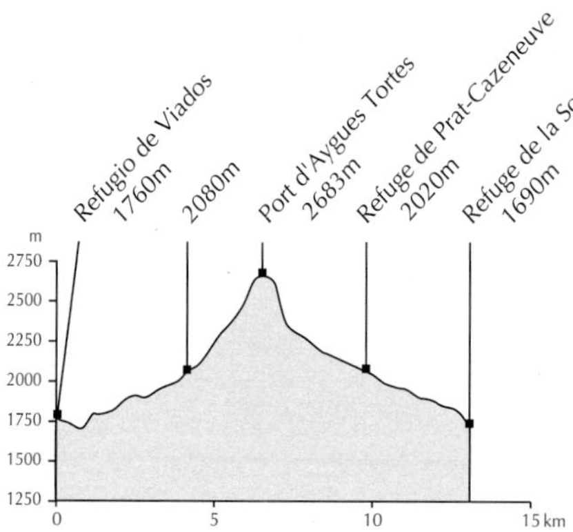

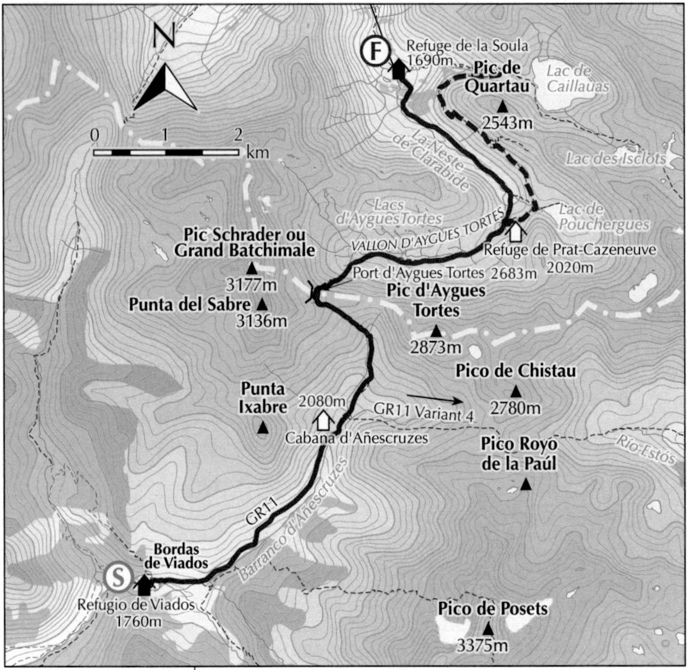

go NE, following the path that turns to the valley of the **Barranco de Añescruzes**.

Stay left of the stream and climb gently NE, staying high above the stream. A little care is needed when crossing a few small ravines. Notice a *cabana* on your left above, and further on notice the **Cabana de Añescruzes** (a good shelter) on a bluff ahead of you. Go around this bluff on the right with the stream below in a deep gully and go down a few metres to the place where

1.30 three streams meet and thus form the Barranco de Añescruzes (2080m, signpost). Notice an old, low *cabana* on your left, cross the stream coming from the west, then the one coming from the north (taking care after heavy rain), and leave the GR11 (unless you want to take the three-day variant – see 'Variant 4'). From now until the Port d'Aygues Tortes there is a faint path with only a few cairns to guide you.

Climb NNE on a grassy slope with the stream on your left-hand side. Beyond a small cascade in the stream and a section of rocks you arrive at a small plateau; keep the stream on your left-hand side and turn left at the northern end of the plateau. Follow the cairns, staying close to the stream, and climb steeply NW through scree. After passing a tiny tarn, arrive at the

3.25 Port d'Aygues Tortes (2683m) on the French-Spanish border. Take time to find a path that goes NNE: at first it's very faint but the way ahead soon becomes clear. Descend in zigzags through scree on a very steep slope until you reach the floor of the Vallon d'Aygues Tortes (2290m), then go down beyond a small dam in the stream. Continue on a faint path close to the stream and keep going down to arrive at a small plateau with

4.50 Refuge de Prat-Cazeneuve (2020m), an unmanned, comfortable hut (10 places, tables, mattresses).

Shortcut to Lac de Caillauas

If you don't need to descend to Refuge de la Soula, Lac de Caillauas on the next stage can be reached in 1hr

Clouds fill the valley while the high route to Lac de Caillauas still enjoys sunshine

by leaving the main route here. From Refuge de Prat-Cazeneuve continue N, keeping the Ruisseau d'Aygues Tortes on your left-hand side, and turn right at a junction about 80 metres beyond the hut. Continue on an almost level path to **Lac de Pouchergues**. Turn left before reaching the lake (which remains out of sight) and continue NW.

You are now entering an abandoned mining site.

Walk under overhanging rocks, continue NW and pass the entrance to an old mine. ◂ Go under a series of metal arches and walk through the ruins of a building; open a green door and go through a small building. Almost immediately after a closed mine entrance with a railway, turn right and ascend. Soon, at 2140m, you join the path coming from Refuge de la Soula and continue to **Lac de Caillauas** (2160m). See Day 21 for the route description from here.

To go to Refuge de la Soula, continue N from Refuge de Prat-Cazeneuve, keeping the Ruisseau d'Aygues Tortes on your left-hand side. Ignore a path that branches off to the right. Notice a small cascade in the stream, cross another stream and walk NW through the narrow valley of the Neste (river) de Clarabide, surrounded by impressive steep slopes. Keep the Neste de Clarabide on your left-hand side and follow a trail that goes up and down, cross several small plateaux and finally go down between pine trees to

6.30 Refuge de la Soula (1690m), next to a power station. A hut with 60 places, manned from June until the end of September, tel 05 62 99 68 40, mob 06 16 85 68 66. Bivouac is possible nearby. Given the proximity of the power station, this is not the most attractive place to spend the night!

DAY 21

Refuge de la Soula to Refuge du Portillon

Start	Refuge de la Soula
Distance	11km
Total ascent	1500m
Total descent	620m
Grade	E
Time	6hr 15min
Map	Rando Editions Mapa Excursionista, 1:50,000, no 23: Aneto–Posets
Route	Via the Col des Gourgs-Blancs (2877m) and the Tusse de Montarqué (2889m)
Note	Steep snowfields may be encountered even in summer; crampons and ice axe advised
Warning	The terrain on this section of the route is particularly challenging. Good weather conditions are vital.

Snowfields, steep scree slopes, some sections on boulders and a few high passes make today's walk a tough one. The final section is difficult and highly inadvisable in bad weather. Otherwise, it's an exciting walk. It leads to an impressive and remarkable alpine landscape with numerous 3000m summits.

0.00 Refuge de la Soula. Ascend NE from the refuge on a well-worn path. Pass a *cabane* and climb towards a narrow valley. The path bends a little to the right and climbs in numerous zigzags SE above the left of the stream coming from the Lac de Caillauas. Near the end of the climb to the lake, the path forks: keep left and climb to the north side of the dam of the

1.30 Lac de Caillauas (2160m). Cross the dam and climb steeply above the south side of the lake among alpenrose and billberries on a small path, keeping well above the water level. Beyond the lake you'll arrive at a small valley; continue SE, cross the stream coming down

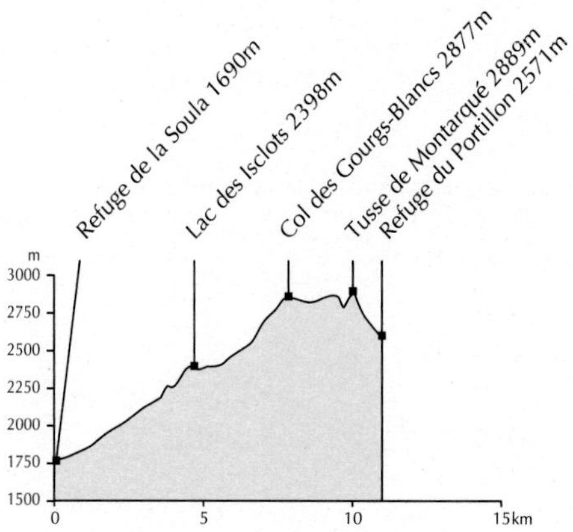

from the Lac des Isclots (you might get wet feet after heavy rainfall) and climb on a path marked with cairns that bends away from the stream to arrive at the

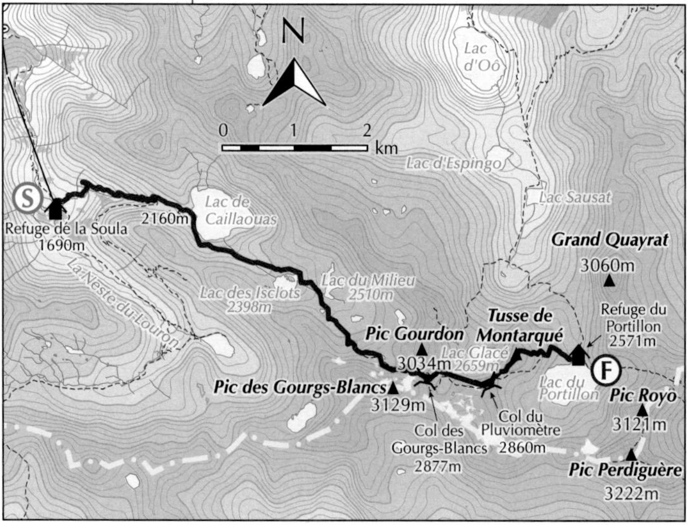

2.30 Lac des Isclots (2398m; isclots means 'tiny islands'). ▶ An excellent place to bivouac. To continue, walk along the northern shore of the lake and climb on an obvious path SE to the

The lake is filled with icy water coming from the glacier of the Gourgs-Blancs; the water has a remarkable soft green colour.

2.55 Lac du Milieu (2510m). Cross a stream just before the lake and walk along the south shore. Beyond the lake, climb SE on a boulderfield and arrive at a tiny plateau with big rocks and some grass. Now climb SE on a very steep scree slope (the route is well cairned) towards the glacier of the Gourgs-Blancs, which is normally covered with snow. ▶ Stay on the right side of the glacier, closer to the Pic des Gourgs-Blancs, and climb gently through snow, ice and scree to the

Due to the enormous number of rocks on the ice, this glacier looks rather intimidating.

4.10 Col des Gourgs-Blancs (2877m), a large pass between the Pic des Gourgs-Blancs (3129m) and Pic Gourdon (3034m). The steep east side of the pass could be covered with snow, but in August there is probably only a small snowfield just below the col. Go down steeply E, and when you reach a flat part there is a small valley leading down to Lac Glacé du Port d'Oô on your left. Don't go down here, but ascend SE following cairns. Climb on boulders to arrive at the

Lac Glacé in the high Portillon region

5.00 Col du Pluviomètre (2860m), so called because of the rain gauge a few metres above the pass (it's worth very carefully approaching the rim to have a look at the Lac Glacé de Port d'Oô which lies below). Descend carefully NE on boulders to another pass (2795m) and then climb, aided by a faint track and a few cairns, to the

5.30 Tusse de Montarqué (2889m). The summit is, in fact, a large plateau. Walk N on this plateau and find an obvious path that descends E. This rough path, marked with cairns, eventually reaches the

6.15 Refuge du Portillon (2571m, also called Refuge Jean-Arlaud), a modern hut situated near the dam of Lac du Portillon, 80 places, meals available, manned from May until October, tel 05 61 79 38 15. The hut is owned by the FFCAM. Bivouac is possible a little distance from the hut, but the rocky terrain is not ideal for camping. Better bivouac places can be found next to Ibon Blanc de Literola, 1½–2hr into tomorrow's route.

DAY 22

Refuge du Portillon to Refugio de la Renclusa

Start	Refuge de Portillon
Distance	16km
Total ascent	1050m
Total descent	1480m
Grade	E
Time	7hr
Map	Rando Editions Mapa Excursionista, 1:50,000, no 23: Aneto–Posets
Route	Via the Col Inférieur de Literole (2983m)
Note	Snowfields will be encountered even in summer; crampons and ice axe are recommended
Warning	The terrain on parts of this stage is particularly demanding and should only be undertaken by experienced mountain walkers, preferably in good weather conditions.

Rough alpine landscapes, snowfields and the highest pass of the whole traverse make this a difficult stage. Only experienced hikers should walk from Portillon to Valle de Benasque. In poor visibility route-finding could be an issue, especially in the uncompromising landscapes between Col Inférieur de Literole and Portal de Remune. The east side of the Col Inférieur de Literole is steep and always covered with snow. Even in summer an ice axe and crampons may be necessary. Near the end of the stage there is the option of taking a bus to the touristic little town of Benasque, where you can buy food – and since it has a relaxed campsite and many other options, you might consider having a rest day there.

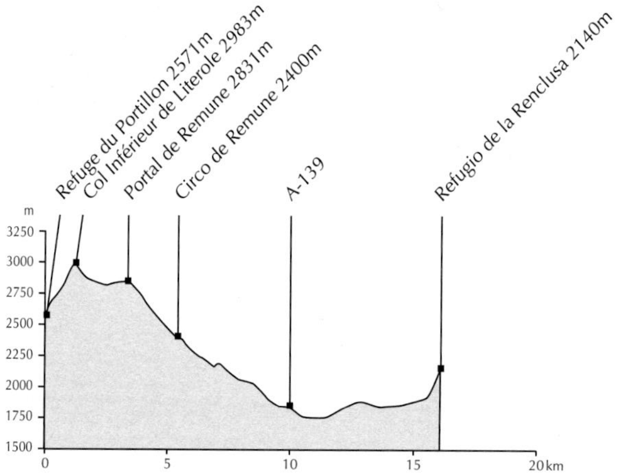

0.00 Refuge du Portillon. From the hut, cross the dam, turn right and walk a few minutes along the lake. Turn left and climb steeply E on a small track marked with cairns. Don't be tempted to go over the central field of rocks; instead, turn sharply left (this turn is easily missed) and continue climbing on a clear path. Keep a tiny tarn on your left, and at 2780m the path disappears into a boulderfield. Cross the boulderfield and climb on scree and snow to the

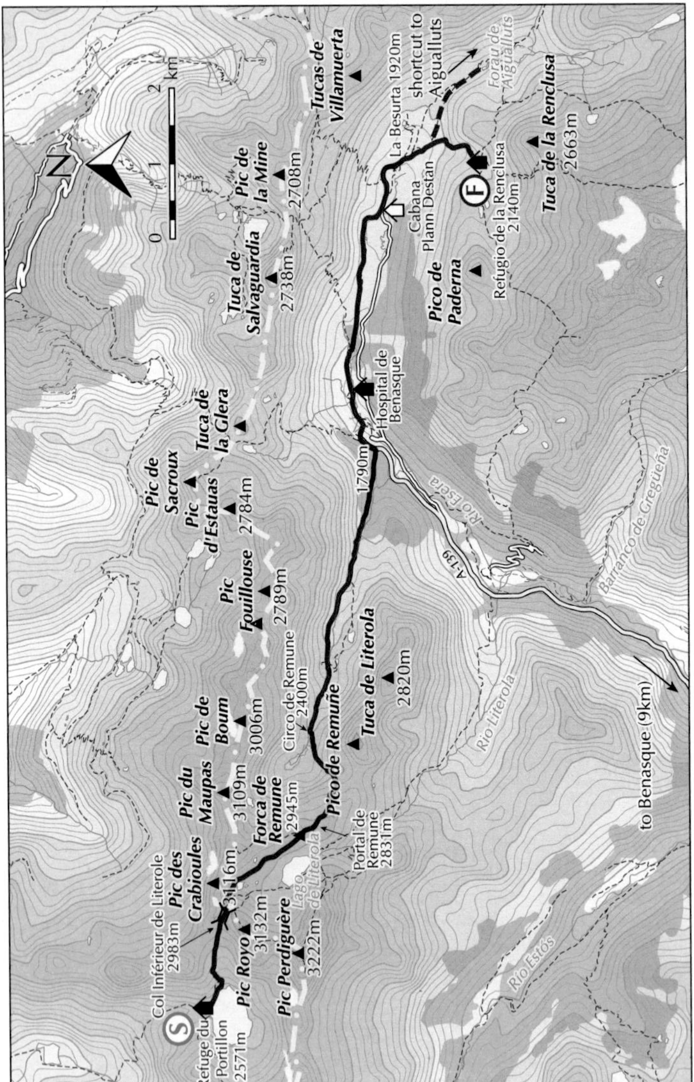
N
0
1
2
km
S
Refuge du Portillon 2571m
Col Inférieur de Literole 2983m
Pic des Crabioules 3116m
Pic Royo 3132m
Pic Perdiguère 3222m
Lago de Literola
Pic du Maupas 3109m
Forca de Remune 2945m
Portal de Remune 2831m
Pic de Boum 3006m
Circo de Remune 2400m
Pico de Remuñe
Tuca de Literola 2820m
Pic Fouillouse 2789m
Pic d'Estauas 2784m
Pic de Sacroux
Tuca de la Glera
1790m
Hospital de Benasque
Tuca de Salvaguardia 2738m
Pic de la Mine 2708m
Tucas de Villamuerta
Cabana Plann Destan
La Besurta 1920m
shortcut to Aigualluts
Forau de Aigualluts
F
Refugio de la Renclusa 2140m
Tuca de la Renclusa 2663m
Pico de Paderna
Río Esera
A-139
Barranco de Gregüeña
Río Literola
Río Estós
to Benasque (9km)

Hikers making their way down from the Col Inférieur de Literole

1.15 Col Inférieur de Literole (2983m), on the French-Spanish border. ▸ Descend carefully on the steep east side of the pass, which is likely to be covered with snow. Staying well above the large Ibon Blanc de Literola, climb on rocks and snowfields to the ridge that separates the Valle de Remune from the Valle de Literola. Continue walking SE on rocks and snowfields, skirting the Forca de Remune (2945m), to arrive at a large pass: the

This is the highest pass of the entire Haute Route.

2.15 Portal de Remune (2831m). ▸ This pass is so wide you might not recognise it as a pass! Descend E, following cairns, through a chaotic granite wilderness in the direction of the Pico de Remune. At an altitude of 2625m the Haute Route bends to the left: descend N, initially on boulders and later on a steep scree slope, follow the red dots and arrive at the floor of the Valle de Remune in the

The ascent of Pic Perdiguère starts from here and takes 2hr 45min (return) – see 'Summit 5'.

3.00 Circo de Remune (2400m, stream). Turn right and follow the right bank of the stream, which initially flows through a narrow gorge surrounded by steep rocky slopes. Carefully cross a few boulders and then cross the stream. The Valle de Remune then opens out and you descend gently ESE on an obvious path that follows the left bank of the main stream.

Cross a small plateau with a tiny lake at 2256m, then at 1930m you'll reach a plateau, shortly before entering a pine forest. The track now bends away for good from the main stream. Go down in the forest until you arrive at the

4.45 A-139, the road coming from Benasque (1790m), which ends here. Turn left and follow the road until you're about 70 metres from its end, then turn right, spot a few buildings on your right below and descend in the Valle de Esera on a vague path.

Cross two side-streams of Rio Esera and go NE on a path through the valley with the Rio Esera on your right-hand side. Cross two more side-streams, this time by footbridges, and arrive close to **Hospital de Benasque** (1760m), a large building, hotel/bar/restaurant serving good meals, open all year, tel 608 536 053. ◂

It's possible to get a bus to Benasque from here; see 'Optional rest day' below.

Stay left of Rio Esera and follow a path with green markers. Cross another sidestream by a wooden bridge, fork right at a junction (signpost to La Besurta) and climb in zigzags on a path that enters a pine forest.

The path climbs gently in the small forest and the landscape soon opens. Pass a narrow plateau on the left and soon arrive at a much larger plateau: Plan d'Estan (1865m, indicated). Keep the plateau on your right and turn right at a junction (signpost). A few minutes later you'll reach the small road that runs through the Valle de Esera.

Turn left, notice Cabane Plann Destan (basic, sleeps 2–3) on your right after 100 metres (there is a path, starting just past the cabane, that leads to the place where the road ends, so if you want, you can avoid the tarmac) and climb the small road for around 10min to

6.00 La Besurta (1920m), where the road ends. ◂ There is a bar selling food. Pass the bar, cross a side-stream and climb S between pine trees on a well-worn path, then cross a stream and soon arrive at a junction.

Six buses a day connect La Besurta with Benasque, should you wish to spend a rest day there (see below).

Shortcut bypassing Refugio de la Renclusa
For walkers who don't want to climb the Aneto and prefer to spend the night in a tent, it makes no sense to go to Refugio de la Renclusa. Turn left at the junction and follow tomorrow's route to the large plateau of Aiguallut. There are some good bivouac sites to be found on the east side of the plateau.

To continue to the refuge, turn right at the junction and climb in zigzags to

7.00 Refugio de la Renclusa (2140m, CEC-owned hut), a logical base for the climb to the highest summit of the Pyrenees: Pico de Aneto (3404m). 110 places, reservation essential, overcrowded in August, meals available, manned from the end of June to the end of September, tel 974 344 646. ▶

The ascent of Pico de Aneto starts from here and takes 7hr 30min (return) – see 'Summit 6'.

OPTIONAL REST DAY IN BENASQUE

Whether to take a break from hiking or not is entirely up to you, but Valle de Benasque is in many ways an ideal place for a day of rest. It's halfway on the Pyrenean Haute Route, Benasque is a place where you can buy anything you need, and Camping Ixeia is an inspiring, quiet place to rest after your efforts and deal with practical issues such as washing clothes. It is often worth having a break from your hiking routine; you get a chance to recharge your batteries and can start again with a refreshed mind and body.

Getting to Benasque from Hospital de Benasque or La Besurta
There's a bus service (from July until mid September) from Hospital de Benasque and La Besurta to Benasque (same bus, see Day 22). The bus goes six times a day and leaves La Besurta at 6am, 10am, 1.30pm, 5pm, 7pm and 9pm. You can get off the bus close to Camping Ixeia or in Benasque. Check the most recent bus schedule at http://turismobenasque.com.

Facilities in Benasque
Benasque is a compact, cosy town with a tourist office, several supermarkets, a pharmacy, shops selling local specialities, outdoor shops, a post office (Mon–Fri 8.30am–2.30pm, Sat 9.30am–1.30pm), hotels, restaurants, bars, etc. Some shops and most restaurants respect the siesta and will be closed between 2 and 4 or 5pm. About 3km north of Benasque there are several campsites. If you're sure Coll de Mulleres (French: Col de Molières)

Benasque is a fine place for a rest day in the middle of the Haute Route

(Day 23) is snow-free, you could send your crampons and ice axe home from here.

Camping Ixeia

Small cabins and a refuge allow you to sleep inside here too. The site is beautifully located on the banks of the Rio Esera, it's quiet, there are places to pitch the tent in the shade, good sanitary facilities, maps available from the reception, and internet access. It's located 3km north of the village of Benasque. The owner knows the wide area very well, so you can ask him all your hiking questions, including those concerning the ascent of the Aneto.

Getting back to the Haute Route

If you're hiking from Refuge de la Renclusa to Hospital de Vielha, you can take the same bus service that you arrived on, in the opposite direction. The bus will take you to La Besurta, from where it's a 20min walk to Refuge de la Renclusa, the starting point for Day 23. If you are instead following the GR11 as per Variant 4, then simply walk to the end of Camping Ixeia's driveway, where you join the GR11 path. Turn left and continue the description of Day 2 of the variant route.

SUMMIT 5

Pic Perdiguère (3222m) from Portal de Remune

Start	Portal de Remune (Day 22)
Distance	4km
Total ascent/descent	460m
Grade	F+
Time	2hr 45min; allow 1hr 45min to reach the summit of Pic Perdiguère

Pic Perdiguère is the highest of all the summits in the Cirque du Portillon and therefore makes an obvious goal. Thanks to its altitude and its position on the French-Spanish border, the summit offers superb views: Lac du Portillon, all the summits that form the Cirque du Portillon, Pico de Posets, Pic Schrader (3177m, in the west) and the Maladeta massif. It's a steep climb that offers no real difficulties. Practically the whole route goes over rocks, so keep focussed at all times. There are a few good bivouac places (stone windbreaks) in-between Portal de Remune and the outflow of Ibón Blanco de Literola, making it possible to climb this mountain in the early morning while leaving your tent and gear below.

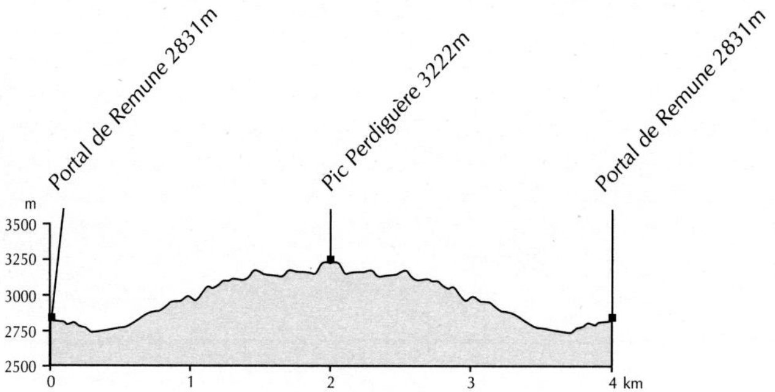

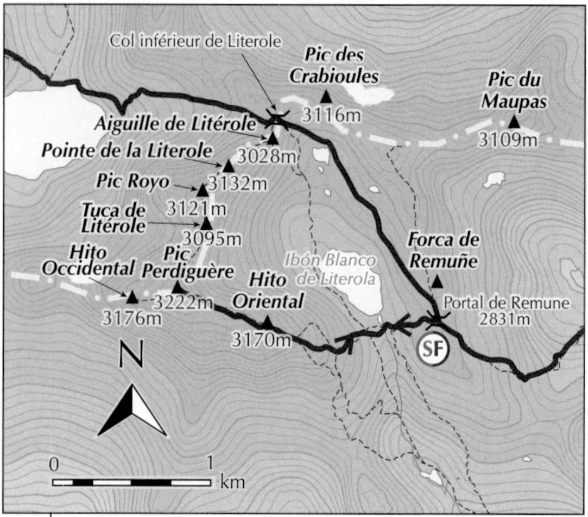

A bivouac at Ibón Blanco de Literola allows for an early start to Pic Perdiguère (3222m, second peak from the left)

0.00 Portal de Remune (2831m). Descend W towards the outflow of Ibón Blanco de Literola, at the end of the lake. The first part of the outflow is usually covered with snow. Carefully cross the snow at a safe distance from the lake and climb WSW over rocks until you reach a height of 2890m, following a few cairns. Soon you'll be walking only on rocks and boulders. From 2890m, follow the

cairns WNW to a first peak at 3170m: the **Hito Oriental**. Continue for another 15min to the

1.45 Pic Perdiguère (3222m), where you find a stone windbreak. Follow the same route back down to Portal de Remune.

SUMMIT 6

Pico de Aneto (3404m) from Refugio de la Renclusa

Start	Refugio de la Renclusa (Day 22/23)
Distance	11km
Total ascent/descent	1255m
Grade	F+
Time	7hr 30min; allow 4hr for the ascent
Note	The route involves walking on a glacier; ice axe and crampons are essential
Warning	Parts of the route are very exposed, requiring a high degree of caution.

Pico de Aneto is the highest mountain in the Pyrenees, attracting large numbers of hikers each summer. Make a very early start (about an hour before dawn) to get good snow conditions on your way to the top.

This climb contains no major difficulties, but it has to be taken seriously. There is a rough climb to Portillon Superior, with a lot of boulders to tackle, and a long stretch over snow on the Aneto glacier (crampons and ice axe needed). Close to the summit, the Puente de Mahoma has to be crossed: a quite narrow ridge of about 30 metres. The passage is not at all technically difficult, but at a few points it's very exposed.

0.00 Refugio de la Renclusa (2140m). From the refuge climb S on a path that is marked with an abundance of cairns. At times there might seem to be more than one path, but it doesn't matter which you follow; to ensure that you go in the right direction, keep the Portillon ridge

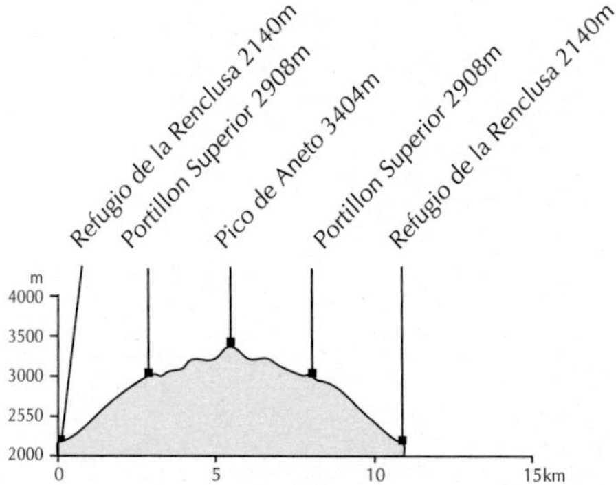

on your left-hand side and climb SSW to an obvious gap in the Portillon ridge:

2.00 Portillon Superior (2908m). Go through the gap, go down a few metres and climb SSE on boulders and/or snowfields to reach the Aneto glacier (in early summer covered with snow; later in summer some parts

On the way to the Aneto peak (3404m)

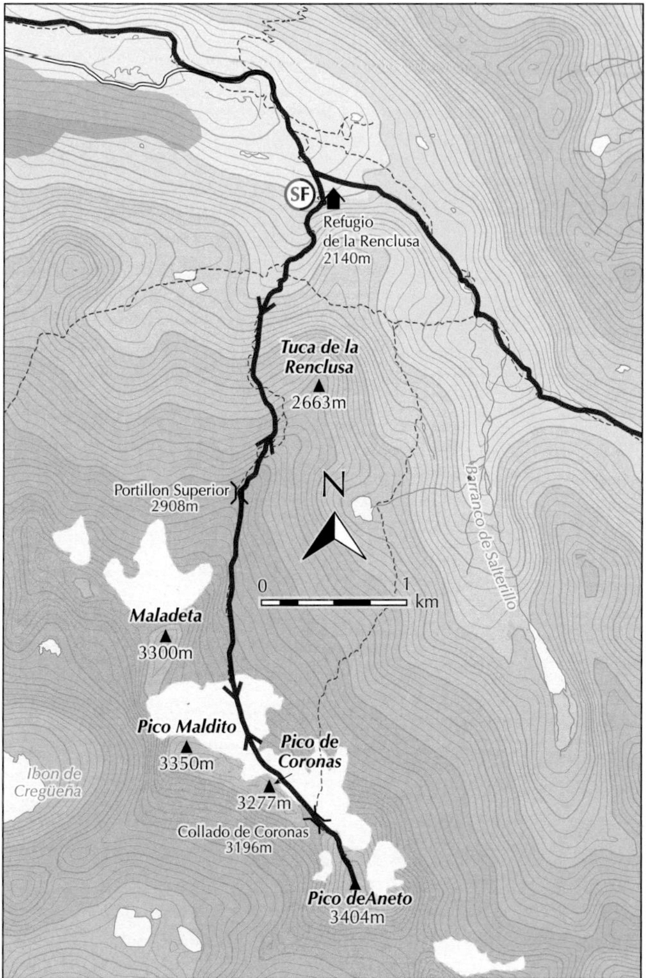

of the glacier are snow-free). Keep climbing in the same direction (in late summer, when there's only a small amount of snow on the glacier, the safest way is to climb

SSW in the direction of Pico Maldito (3350m) and then to walk SE, close to the ridge, until you arrive at the Collado de Coronas), continuing on an obvious track to arrive close to the

3.15 Collado de Coronas (3196m). Keep the pass to your right and climb a steep snow-slope until the climb eases somewhat. Take off your crampons when you reach the rocks, and continue on until you arrive at the Puente de Mahoma, very close to the summit. Carefully scramble over this narrow ridge and finally walk to the summit of the

4.00 Pico de Aneto (3404m), where you'll find a large cross. Follow the same track back to Refugio de la Renclusa.

DAY 23

Refugio de la Renclusa to Hospital de Vielha

Start	Refugio de la Renclusa
Distance	15km
Total ascent	1060m
Total descent	1575m
Grade	E
Time	7hr 45min
Map	Rando Editions Mapa Excursionista, 1:50,000, no 23: Aneto–Posets
Route	Via the Coll de Mulleres (2928m)
Warning	This stage involves extremely steep terrain and should only be attempted in good weather. In early summer ice axe and crampons are recommended.

A magnificent stage that skirts the north side of the Maladeta massif and enters the Catalan Pyrenees. The crossing of the Coll de Mulleres should be attempted only in good weather conditions. The first metres on the east side of the pass are extremely steep. Great care is needed on this initial stage of the descent. The manned Refugi de Conangles is 20min from the stage end.

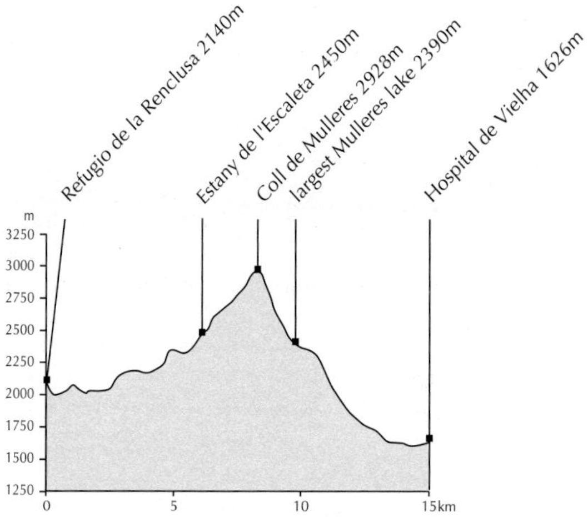

0.00 Refugio de la Renclusa. From the refuge, retrace your steps from the end of Day 22 to the junction (1980m). ▸ Turn right and follow a path that arrives at a level area, then turn right again and walk SE on an obvious path to the **Forau de Aiguallut** (also called the Trou de Toro), a deep hole into which the melting water flowing down from the Aneto glacier disappears. Pass the Forau de Aiguallut and a fine waterfall (good view of the snow-covered summit of Aneto) and arrive on a large grassy plateau, the

Hikers who took the shortcut omitting Refugio de la Renclusa should follow the route description from here.

1.00 Plan d'Aiguallut (2050m). Cross the plateau SE until you reach a stream coming down from a higher level: the Barranco de Escaleta. Cross the stream and climb in a few zigzags to the Valleta de Escaleta, then cross this valley also SE and walk towards the remarkable twin peaks of Pico Forcanada, which you can't overlook. At the end of the valley, the climb becomes steeper. The path, well marked with cairns, reaches a tarn (2320m); keep the tarn on your left-hand side and climb to another lake that you keep on your right-hand side. Climb steeply on rocks to the

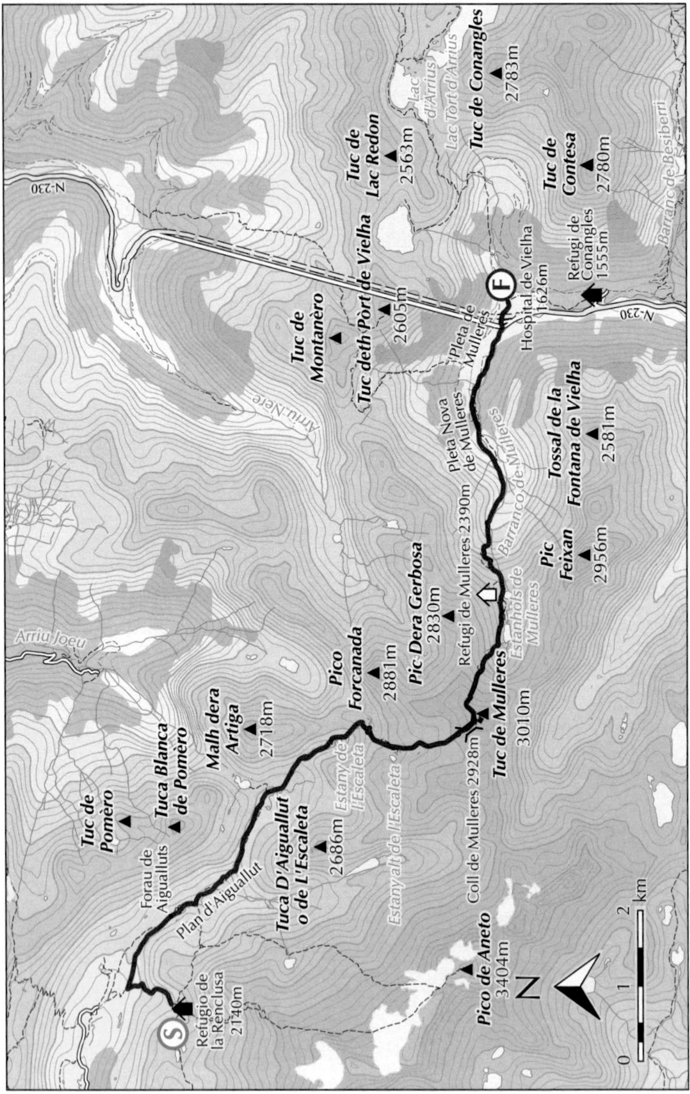
S
Refugio de la Renclusa 2140m
Plan d'Aiguallut
Forau de Aiguallut
Tuc de Pomèro
Tuca Blanca de Pomèro
Malh dera Artiga 2718m
Tuca D'Aiguallut o de L'Escaleta 2686m
Estany de l'Escaleta
Estany alt de l'Escaleta
Pico Forcanada 2881m
Pic Dera Gerbosa 2830m
Arriu Joeu
Coll de Mulleres 2928m
Tuc de Mulleres 3010m
Pico de Aneto 3404m
Refugi de Mulleres 2390m
Estanhols de Mulleres
Pic Feixan 2956m
Barranco de Mulleres
Tossal de la Fontana de Vielha 2581m
Pleta Nova de Mulleres
Pleta de Mulleres
Arriu Nere
Tuc de Montanèro
Tuc deth Pòrt de Vielha 2605m
F
Hospital de Vielha 1626m
Refugi de Conangles 1555m
N-230
N-230
Tuc de Contesa 2780m
Barranc de Besiberri
Tuc de Lac Redon 2563m
Lac d'Arrius
Lac Tort d'Arrius
Tuc de Conangles 2783m
N
0 1 2 km

2.45 Estany de l'Escaleta (2450m). Cross the outflow and climb steeply SSW on a slope that's covered with loose boulders. This steep section, which is well cairned and not difficult, ends at about 2600m. Notice another lake (Estany alt de l'Escaleta, 2619m, good places to pitch a tent) on your right and carefully observe the summits south of you. Locate the **Tuc de Mulleres** (3010m) and walk, initially on polished boulders, S towards a large pass north of the summit. Make sure you do not climb too high, which would make you pass the Tuc de Mulleres. The Haute Route, marked with a few cairns, bends to the left and arrives at

4.20 Coll de Mulleres (2928m, also called Col de Molières).

To climb the Tuc de Mulleres (3010m)

The Tuc de Mulleres can easily be climbed from the Coll de Mulleres. Climb S on boulders to the summit; it takes about 15min to get to the top, where you'll find a huge

On the summit of the Tuc de Mulleres (3010m)

cairn. There are excellent views of the Maladeta massif, the Besiberri ridge in the east and the Valle de Mulleres.

In early summer there could be snow close to the pass, which makes the descent rather precarious.

Descend carefully on the east side of Coll de Mulleres. Don't go down directly E, as this is extremely steep. Instead, carefully scramble down more gradually N. The first metres require great care, but soon you'll have a wider platform to stand on. ◂ Descend SE over rocks to arrive above the

5.35 largest Mulleres lake (Estanhols de Mulleres in Spanish, 2390m). Keep the lake at a distance and follow cairns that pass the next two lakes. NE of the last lake you'll see **Refugi de Mulleres** (2390m, unmanned hut, comfortable beds, nine places) above. Beyond the last lake the route bends to the left and leaves the stream that cascades into the valley below. Go down in zigzags to the floor of this very rough valley and cross the valley E, staying left of the stream which here and there disappears.

Beyond the valley, the path descends steeply for a few metres close to the cascading stream (1855m). The descent then eases and you go down to the **Pleta Nova de Mulleres**, a flat grassy and marshy area. Keep on the left side of the plateau and go down through a forest, in which you pass a beautiful waterfall. Finally, still on the left bank of the stream, walk on a broad track through the **Pleta de Mulleres** (a flat area, possible to bivouac) to the southern snout of the Vielha tunnel. Cross the road and walk to the

7.45 Hospital de Vielha (1626m), where there are number of buildings but no accomodation. If you climb a little, you'll find fine places to bivouac, with a full view on your descent from the Coll de Mulleres. The nearest place to sleep inside is Refugi de Conangles, about 20min away (see Variant 4, Day 3).

DAY 24

Hospital de Vielha to Refugi de la Restanca

Start	Hospital de Vielha
Distance	13.5km
Total ascent	1125m
Total descent	740m
Grade	2
Time	7hr 15min
Map	Rando Editions Mapa Excursionista, 1:50,000, no 22: Pica d'Estats–Aneto
Route	Via the Port de Rius (2320m) and Colhada de Lac de Mar (2487m)

A tough walk without any major obstacles. Care is needed on the eroded, steep east side of Colhada de Lac de Mar. The Haute Route follows the GR11 track to Lac de Rius.

0.00 Hospital de Vielha. Past the courtyard (in-between two large buildings) and a drinking trough for cattle you'll

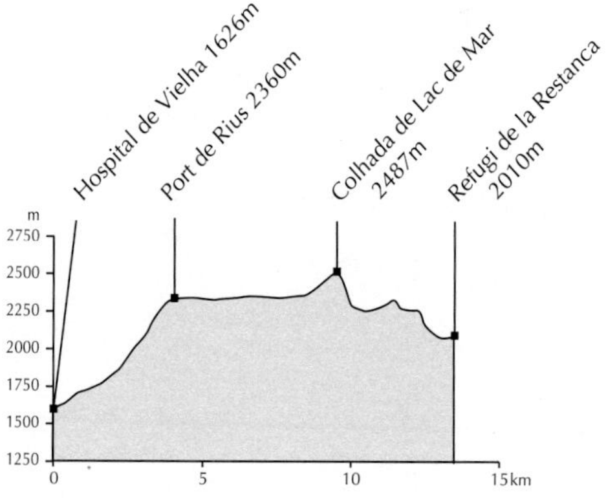

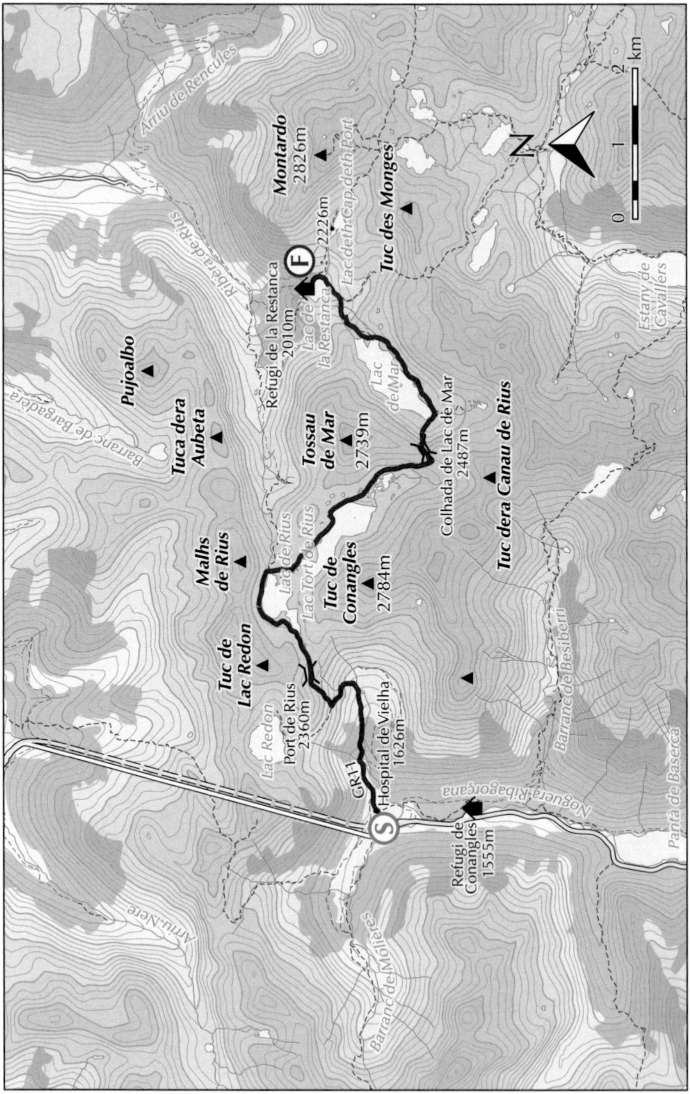
Arriu de Rencules
Montardo
2826m
2226m
Lac deth Cap deth Port
Tuc des Monges
F
Refugi de la Restanca
2010m
Lac de la Restanca
Ribera de Rius
Pujoalbo
Barranc de Bargadera
Tuca dera Aubeta
Tossau de Mar
2739m
Lac de Mar
Colhada de Lac de Mar
2487m
Tuc dera Canau de Rius
Estany de Cavallers
Malhs de Rius
Lac de Rius
Lac Tort de Rius
Tuc de Conangles
2784m
Tuc de Lac Redon
Port de Rius
2360m
Lac Redon
Hospital de Vielha
1626m
GR11
S
Noguera Ribagorçana
Refugi de Conangles
1555m
Barranc de Besiberri
Pantà de Baserca
Arriu Nere
Barranc de Molières
N
0
1
2 km

Lac de Rius is a wonderful place for a break

find a signpost indicating the GR11 track to the Port de Rius. Follow the GR signs and arrive at a dirt road; walk E on this road and turn left just before the bridge over the Barranc de Conangles. Cross the stream coming from Lac Redon and climb E through a mixed forest (oak, beech, pine) to arrive at an open field, then climb N in zigzags. The obvious path bends eventually a little to the west. At a junction, ignore the path that goes to Lac Redon (2140m), turn right and climb NE to the

2.15 Port de Rius (2360m). Keep walking NE and pass the large Lac de Rius along its northern shore. As soon as the lake is passed, leave the GR11 by turning right and following a line of cairns that leads S to **Lac Tort de Rius**. Keep this very long lake on your right-hand side on a route that goes up and down on rocky terrain. Beyond the lake, pass another lake (excellent places for a bivouac) and climb on a vague track SE to

4.15 Colhada de Lac de Mar (2487m). Go down in zigzags to the beautiful **Lac de Mar** on a very steep slope. Turn right and walk to the east side of the lake, then walk NE along its shore. This will take some time because of the many rocks that have to be crossed.

Lac de Mar, one of the most beautiful lakes in the whole Pyrenean range

At the northeast side of the lake pass a small tarn on your right and you'll arrive at a path with yellow waymarks. Descend NE in zigzags on this path to reach a small grassy plateau. Cross a side-stream and then another stream and turn left. The path soon forks, and it makes little difference which route you choose. Go down to a stream, cross it and go down steeply between pine trees to the east side of **Lac de la Restanca**. Walk along the eastern shore of the lake to the

7.15 Refugi de la Restanca (2010m), a hut near the dam, 80 places, manned from mid June to the end of September, owned by the FEEC (Federació d'Entitats Excursionistes de Catalunya), often crowded, meals available, tel 608 036 559, or for reservations call the Central del Refugis: tel 973 641 681. Bivouac is not allowed near the lake or the *refugi*. If you continue along tomorrow's track for 45min you'll find some very fine places to bivouac near Lac deth Cap deth Port.

DAY 25

Refugi de la Restanca to Salardú

Start	Refugi de la Restanca
Distance	20.5km
Total ascent	795m
Total descent	1535m
Grade	2
Time	7hr 15min
Map	Rando Editions Mapa Excursionista, 1:50,000, no 22: Pica d'Estats–Aneto
Route	Via the Col de Crestada (2468m) and the Port de Caldes (2570m)

In good weather conditions this is an easy walk on well-worn paths, forest tracks and roads. The Haute Route follows the GR11 to Refugi de Colomers. The walk includes a brief visit to the Aigüestortes national park, which may well inspire further exploration.

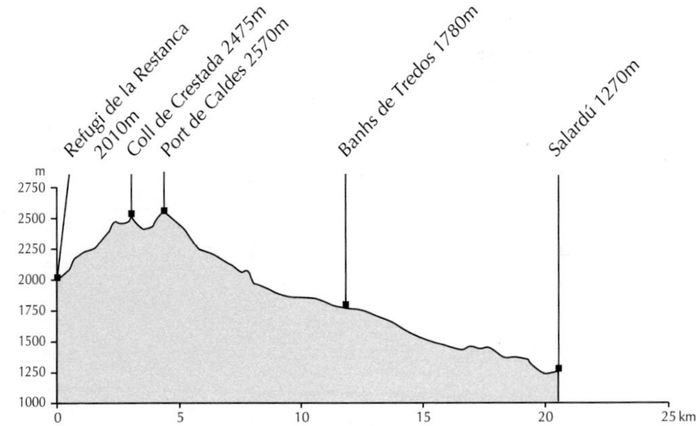

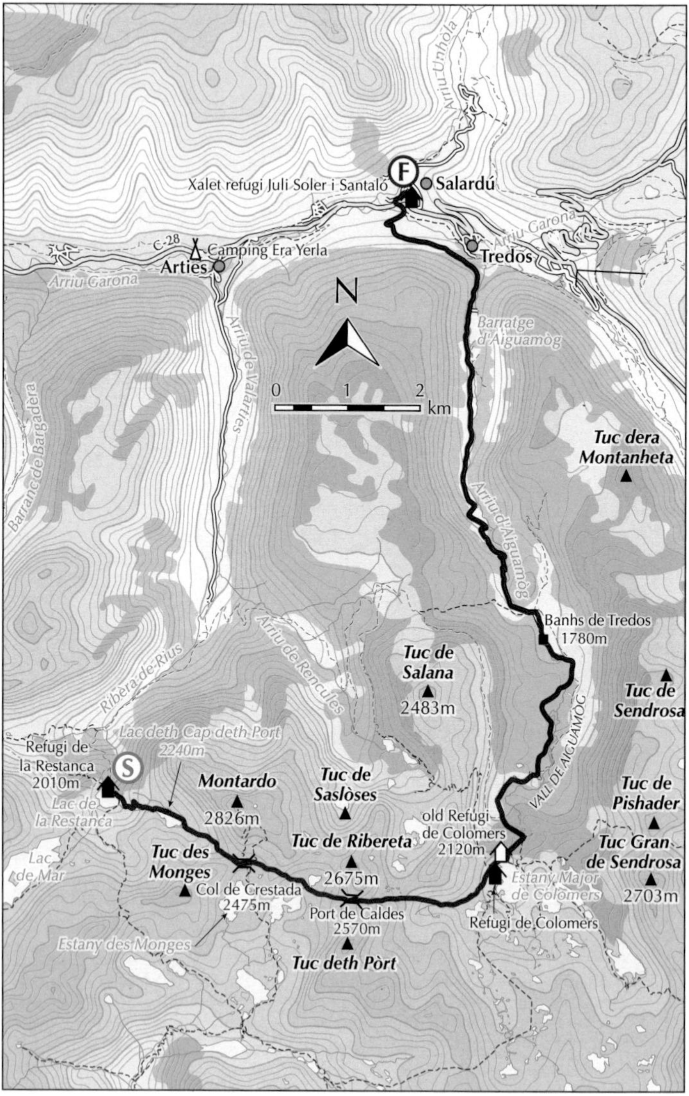
F
Xalet refugi Juli Soler i Santaló
Salardú
Arriu Unhòla
Arriu Garona
C-28
Camping Era Yerla
Arties
Arriu Garona
Tredos
N
0
1
2
km
Barratge d'Aiguamòg
Arriu de Valarties
Barranc de Bargadera
Tuc dera Montanheta
Arriu d'Aiguamòg
Banhs de Tredos 1780m
Ribera de Rius
Arriu de Rencules
Tuc de Salana 2483m
Tuc de Sendrosa
VALL DE AIGUAMÒG
Lac deth Cap deth Port 2240m
Refugi de la Restanca 2010m
S
Montardo 2826m
Tuc de Saslòses
Tuc de Pishader
Lac de la Restanca
old Refúgi de Colomers 2120m
Lac de Mar
Tuc des Monges
Tuc de Ribereta 2675m
Tuc Gran de Sendrosa 2703m
Col de Crestada 2475m
Estany Major de Colomers
Port de Caldes 2570m
Refúgi de Colomers
Estany des Monges
Tuc deth Pòrt

A late-evening hiker on the route between Refugi de la Restanca and Lac deth Cap deth Port

0.00 Refugi de la Restanca. From the refuge, follow the GR11 which climbs SE in zigzags and reaches a stream. Climb steeply along the stream, keeping it on your right-hand side, to arrive at the lovely **Lac deth Cap deth Port** (2240m). Cross the small dam and pass the lake along its northern shore, then climb SE on a beautiful, wild slope covered with rocks and boulders, following the GR11 marks that lead to the

1.30 Coll de Crestada (2475m, also called Coll de Goellicrestada), situated on the border of the Parc Nacional de Aigüestortes i Estany de Sant Maurici. ▸ Go down in the park on the east side of the pass for a short while. Keeping the sensational **Estany des Monges** (2410m) to your right, climb to an unnamed pass on a narrow ridge that offers fine views of the two Mangades lakes. A steep descent leads to a path in-between the two lakes; cross a stream, gain height E and arrive at the

The ascent of Montardo d'Aran starts from here and takes 2hr (return) – see 'Summit 7'.

2.30 Port de Caldes (2570m, national park signpost), on the border of the national park, which you now leave. Descend E, notice a tarn some distance to the right and one on the left, and go down SE in zigzags until you reach a stream. Follow this stream, staying close to it

Lakes and high passes characterise the Aigüestortes national park

and keeping it on your right-hand side. Eventually the stream turns left; cross the stream to avoid a few boulders obstructing the path, cross it again and walk NE to a junction above Estany Major de Colomers.

Don't turn right (this path goes down to the new Colomers refuge – 60 places, manned from June to the end of September, meals available, owned by the FEEC, reservation obligatory: tel 902 734 164, www.lacentralderefugis.com (bookings) or 973 641 681, www.refugicolomers.com (general contact)). Instead walk above the lake, ignore a GR11 variant that branches off to the left, and continue to the

3.45 old Refugi de Colomers building (2120m). ◂ Leave the GR11 (which crosses the dam) and descend N beneath the dam between pine trees. Go down to the floor of the valley, where you'll meet a stream; follow the left bank of the stream to an open field. Turn left and walk N on a boardwalk through this level field. Notice a small lake on your right and, past the lake, go down steeply in zigzags until you arrive at a road (1980m).

This former *refugi*, which has been closed since 2008, overlooks the dammed Estany Major de Colomers.

Turn right and descend gently on this road through the **Vall de Aiguamòg**, taking shortcuts where possible. After about 20min, notice a path on the left that goes to Bahns de Tredos (Camin dera Montanheta). Turn left, enter the pine forest and follow the path which goes up and down. ▶

Numerous wooden constructions have been made to enable hikers to walk through this enchanting but marshy wood without getting wet feet.

Beyond a pass, go down a few metres to a bridge on the main stream (a fine place to relax), cross it and arrive a few moments later near a *cabane* and a cattlegrid, back at the road. Don't follow the road but go down a path left of the road (with a beautiful waterfall on your left-hand side), then follow the right bank of the main stream. Eventually the path becomes almost level. On emerging from the forest you'll arrive at the

5.45 Banhs de Tredos (1780m), hotel/bar/restaurant, tel 973 253 003. Pass the building to the right and turn left past a parking area. Cross the stream and descend, generally N, on a small road through the Vall de Aiguamòg. Pass **Barratge d'Aiguamòg** after about 5km and keep following the road for another 2.5km until you reach a roundabout in

7.15 Salardú (1270m). Practical information about Salardú is given in the introduction to this section. From the roundabout, Refugi Rosta is to your left and the Aran hostel is to your right. The nearest campsite is Era Yerla, in the nearby village of Arties (3km west of Salardú), tel 973 641 602.

SUMMIT 7

Montardo d'Aran (2826m) from the Coll de Crestada

Start	Coll de Crestada (Day 25)
Distance	2.5km
Total ascent/descent	280m
Grade	F
Time	2hr; allow 1hr 10min for the ascent

Just like the Piméné, it's not the altitude or the shape of Montardo d'Aran that makes this mountain so special – it is the superb views from the summit, which attract numerous walkers each summer. The dawn view from here is one of the finest experiences a Pyrenean hiker can have, taking in all the summits of the Aigüestortes region, the Besiberri massif, long views north to the Val d'Aran and the frontier ridge, the Maladeta massif and numerous lakes such as the Lac de la Restanca and Lac de Mar. The ascent of the Montardo presents no difficulties.

0.00 Coll de Crestada (2475m, also called Coll de Goellicrestada), situated on the border of the Parc Nacional de Aigüestortes i Estany de Sant

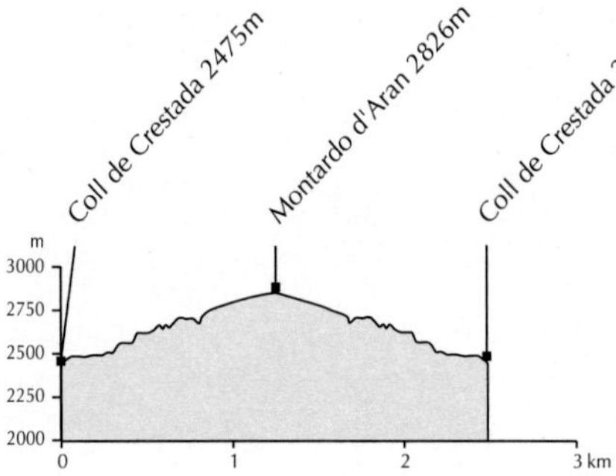

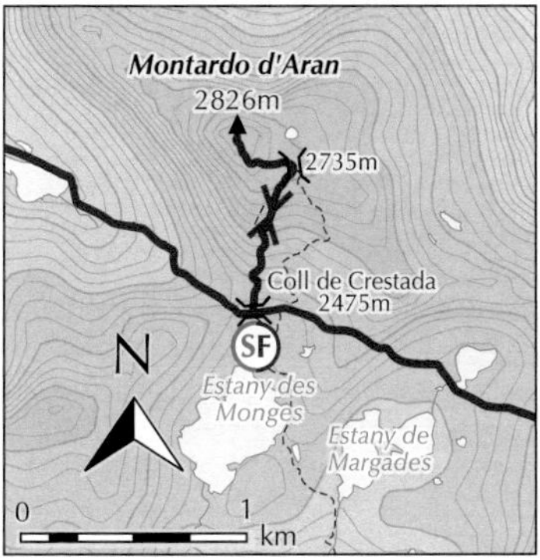

Maurici. Go down in the park on the east side of the pass for 100 metres to arrive at a junction (signpost) where the ascent of the Montardo d'Aran begins. Follow a path (marked with cairns) that climbs N in numerous short zig-zags until you reach a ridge; cross the ridge, turn left and walk on a more or less level path towards a **pass** (2735m). Turn left and climb steeply but without difficulty to reach the summit of the

1.10 Montardo d'Aran (2826m). Follow the same track back to the Haute Route trail.

Climbing to Montardo d'Aran in the early morning sun

VARIANT 4

Three days on the GR11 from Refugio de Viados to Hospital de Vielha

Start	Refugio de Viados (Day 19/20)
Finish	Hospital de Vielha (Day 23/24)
Distance	53km
Total ascent	3595m
Total descent	3730m
Grade	2
Time	3 days

This variant is a less challenging route to Hospital de Vielha, avoiding the very high passes and rough terrain encountered on the main route. Should a thunderstorm be forecast for Day 22 and/or Day 23, it is highly recommended that you should choose this variant.

DAY 1

Refugio de Viados to Camping Ixeia

Start	Refugio de Viados
Distance	21km
Total ascent	1150m
Total descent	1625m
Grade	2
Time	8hr 10min
Map	Rando Editions Mapa Excursionista, 1: 50,000, no 23: Aneto–Posets
Route	Via the Puerto de Gistain (2572m)
Note	Snowfields may be encountered in early summer

An easy but long walk to the Valle de Benasque. The navigation is very easy on well-worn paths with GR marks. In early summer snowfields on both sides of the Puerto de Gistain could cover the track.

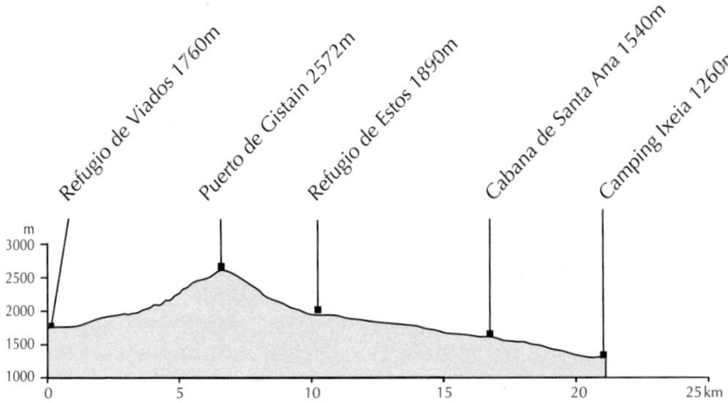

0.00 Refugio de Viados. Go down a few metres in front of the *refugio*, cross a stream and take the GR11 trail that climbs gently E past the Granjas de Viados (a number of barns). The track soon turns into a path and arrives at a

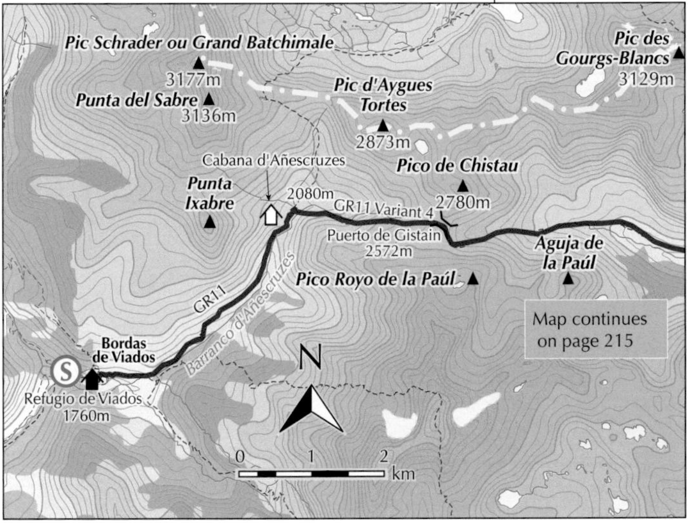

junction (signpost); ignore the path to Collado de Eriste on your right and go NE, following the path that turns to the valley of the Barranco d'Añescruzes.

Stay left of the stream and climb NE gently, staying high above the stream. A little care is needed when crossing a few small ravines. Notice a *cabana* on your left above, and further on notice the Cabana de Añescruzes (a good shelter) on a bluff ahead of you. Go around this bluff on the right with the stream below in a deep gully and descend a few metres to

1.30 the place where three streams meet (2080m, signpost). Cross the stream coming from the west and then the one coming from the north, then continue following the GR11 signs and cross the Barranc de Gistain. Climb E (rather steeply at first and eventually more gently) on an obvious track to the

3.10 Puerto de Gistain (2572m), which gives access to the Valle de Estos. From here follow the path as it makes a turn S to the right before descending E through the rough upper section of the Valle de Estos. Descend the right side of the Valle de Estos through scree to the floor of the valley, cross a stream three times and go down to a confluence of two streams. Cross the left stream and from here on stay left of the stream. Walk through the valley on an obvious path that bends away a little from the Rio de Estos and leads to

5.15 Refugio de Estos (1890m), well hidden until the last moment, a hut with 145 places, manned all year, owned by the FAM (Federación Aragonesa de Montañismo), tel 974 344 515. Meals are available, but walkers can also cook their own meal in the kitchen. This is a nice, cosy, modern refuge. Bivouac is not allowed near the hut.

Go SE down an obvious path, staying left of the Rio de Estos. Eventually cross the Palanca del Turmo (footbridge on the Rio de Estos) and follow the path over a level area to arrive in an open field at **Cabana del Turmo** (1750m). Pass the *cabana* on the right side, cross a pasture, climb a few metres and descend gently on a dirt road, ignoring a path that branches off to the left.

The road crosses a secondary stream; follow the road and arrive at another stream that can be crossed by a footbridge, and continue to descend gently SE through the Valle de Estos. Cross another stream, gain a little height and cross the Rio de Batisielles. Ignore the path

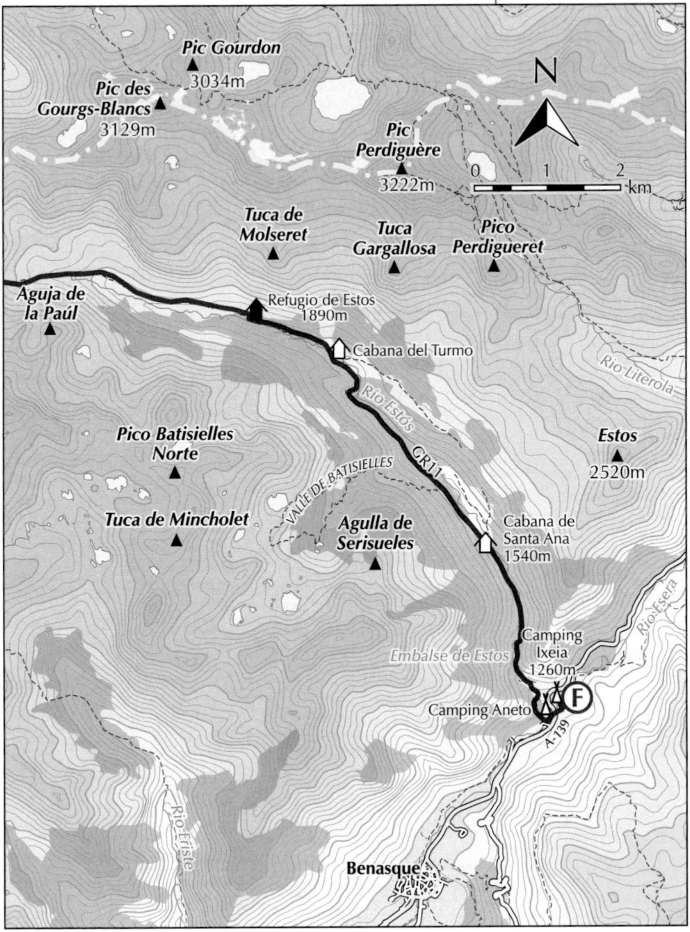

that climbs W to the Valle de Batisielles (signpost) and follow the dirt road.

Pass **Cabana de Santa Ana** (1540m, unmanned hut, on your right-hand side) and gain the left bank of the Rio de Estos by crossing the Palanca de Aiguacari (1450m). Continuing the descent, pass the **Embalse de Estos** (1350m), turn right at a signpost and go down a path to a parking area. Turn right at the next signpost, follow an asphalt road for a short while, then turn right again and follow a small path.

Cross the beautiful Puento de San Jaime, turn left, pass the back of Camping Aneto, and continue along the Rio Esera, walking under a bride that carries the A-139 road. Leave the Rio Esera and reach a dirt road, turn left, cross a small stream by a footbridge and finally follow the signs to the campsite and go down to

The owner of the campsite knows the wide area very well, so you can ask him all your hiking questions, including those concerning the ascent of the Aneto.

8.10 Camping Ixeia (1260m, tel 974 552 129), a campsite with small cabins and a refuge allowing you to sleep inside here too. The site is beautifully located on the banks of the Rio Esera; it's quiet, with places to pitch the tent in the shade, good sanitary facilities, maps available from the reception, and internet access. It's 3km north of the village of Benasque. ◂

DAY 2

Camping Ixeia to Refugio d'Anglos

Start	Camping Ixeia
Distance	22.5km
Total ascent	2125m
Total descent	1165m
Grade	2
Time	8hr 30min
Map	Rando Editions Mapa Excursionista, 1: 50,000, no 23: Aneto–Posets
Route	Via Refugio de Coronas
Note	There may be snow on the trail in early summer

A beautiful and dramatic route through rough alpine landscapes punctuated with numerous tarns and lakes. No major difficulties in high summer. In early summer the track could be covered with snow near Collado de Ballibierna and the Collet dels Estanyets. Care is needed on the rough terrain and some steep slopes. The stage ends at an unmanned hut so you will need to bring food.

0.00 Camping Ixeia. Walk up the campsite's driveway to the GR11, turn left and follow the dirt road. Cross a stream and walk NE towards the dam of the Embalse del Paso Nuevo. The dirt road doesn't go all the way to the dam but makes a surprising turn to the right; it's possible to follow the road, but it's better to take a shortcut left of the road. Follow the GR11 waymarks and climb steeply between trees and shrubs until you again arrive on the dirt road.

Turn left, walk along the dammed lake and continue to a junction, where a signpost indicates the GR11 track through the Valle de Ballibierna. Turn right here and climb

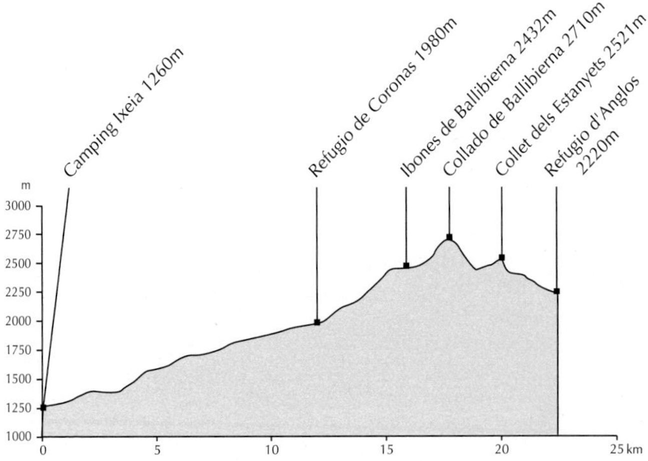

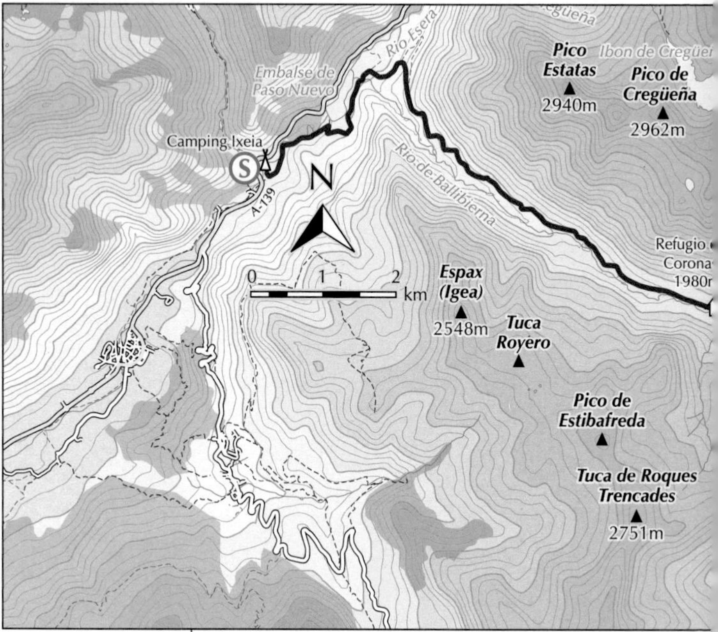

gently on a dirt road. Before entering the Ballibierna valley the dirt road climbs NE and SE, making a large hairpin bend (it's possible to take a shortcut, but this path can easily be overlooked) in a pine forest. Walk through the valley, with the Rio de Ballibierna on your right-hand side far below. Continue for 6km and arrive at the

3.30 Refugio de Coronas (1980m), a solid but unmanned hut with 14 places, at the point where the dirt road finally ends. Cross a stream just before the hut and follow a broad stone path that climbs initially NE on the left side of the Rio de Ballibierna. Ignore the path that climbs N to the Lagos de Coronas and climb SE on a path that gradually becomes smaller. Arrive at a large open field where the Barranco de Llosas gently runs – the Pleta de Llosas – and cross the stream as soon as you arrive on the plateau, then climb SE along the highest pine trees.

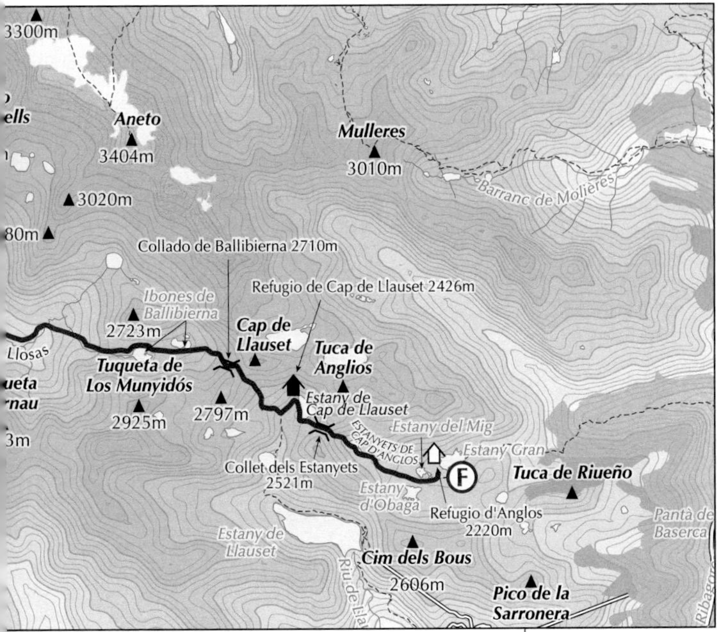

Reach two streams, cross the left one and climb to the first of the

5.00 Ibones de Ballibierna (2432m). Climb a little and pass the lake along its northern shore, at first close to the water and then high above the water level. Follow the GR11 waymarks on giant boulders as you pass the lake, then pass close to a steep rocky slope, where a little care is needed, and climb E on boulders to the highest of the Ibones de Ballibierna (2484m, fine places for a bivouac). Pass the lake along its south side and climb steeply E on a rocky slope to the

6.25 Collado de Ballibierna (2710m, a narrow gap in a ridge). Go down on the steep east side of the pass on rocks and scree (possibly on some snowfields) until the route bends a little to the right to avoid a rocky section. Then go down SE between boulders and on grass

The four Estanyets de Cap d'Anglos, seen from Collet dels Estanyets

to the upper section of a tiny valley where the path forks (2594m, signpost); turn left here and go down to the next junction (2419m).

Ignore the GR11 variant that goes S to the large Estany de Llauset, turn left and walk to a stream. Cross the stream, climb with the stream on your left-hand side and soon arrive at the **Estany de Cap de Llauset**. At the northern end of the lake, at a very short distance from the GR11, is the modern **Refugio de Cap de Llauset** (hut with 86 places, open all year, owned by the FAM, meals available, tel 972 120 400). Continue S along the lake's southern shore and after a short climb reach the

7.35 Collet dels Estanyets (2521m). Go down on the very steep east slope (full of scree and rocks) from the pass (snowfields in early summer could make this descent precarious) to the **Estanyets de Cap d'Anglos**, seen ahead of you. Pass the first two lakes along their southern shores, the third along its northern shore, and the fourth again along its southern shore. Descend on an obvious path to the Estanys d'Anglos (2249m), a few lakes situated in a large flat area. ▶ Go in-between **Estany d'Obaga** and **Estany del Mig**, cross a stream and turn left. Cross another stream and climb a few metres to

There are plenty of beautiful spots for a bivouac here.

8.30 Refugio d'Anglos (2220m): unmanned, basic hut, 14 places.

Refugio d'Anglos

DAY 3

Refugio de Anglos to Hospital de Vielha

Start	Refugio d'Anglos
Distance	9.5km
Total ascent	320m
Total descent	940m
Grade	2
Time	3hr 20min
Map	Rando Editions Mapa Excursionista, 1:50,000, no 23: Aneto–Posets
Route	Via Rio Salenques and the N-230

0.00 Refugio d'Anglos. From the hut, continue on the GR11 along the southern and eastern shore of Estany Gran, the largest Anglos lake. Descend gently E on the right bank of the Barranc d'Anglos, through alpenrose and pine trees, until the path makes a turn left and goes down steeply NE, initially on a scree slope. Enter a forest and continue to descend very steeply to the floor of the Valle de Salenques, then turn right and follow the right bank of the Rio Salenques. Soon you will arrive at a

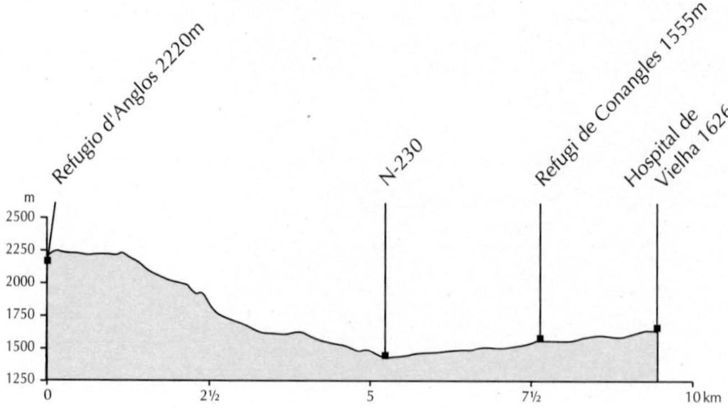

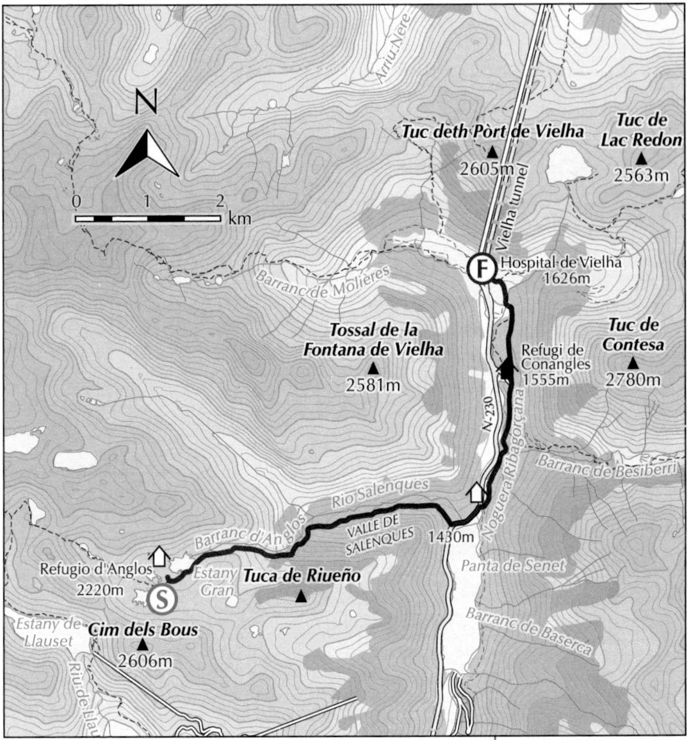

junction and signpost; keep following the stream, cross a few minor streams and arrive at the

1.50 N-230 (1430m). Turn left, cross the Pont de Salenques and follow the road. Past a basic shelter on the right side of the road, and north of the Panta de Senet (lake), leave the road and turn right. Cross a bridge over the stream that runs to the lake, arrive at a dirt road, turn left and climb N for a short while. The road turns into a path which approaches the stream running through the valley. Keep the stream on your left-hand side and walk to **Barranc de Besiberri**, a side-stream coming from the east.

Climb a few metres along the stream and cross it by a footbridge. Here the path becomes faint; go down through grass to the main stream and arrive at a dirt road. Turn right, enter a forest and follow the dirt road to a junction, then rather than turning right, keep walking N on a road that climbs very gently. Notice a picnic area on your left; beyond this area you'll arrive at a small tarmac road. Turn right, pass a fountain and soon the road forks: turn left to arrive at

3.00 Refugi de Conangles (1555m), property of the Conselh Generau d'Aran, hut with 36 beds, meals service but no kitchen for walkers who want to cook their own meal. There's a nice atmosphere in the hut; tel 0619 847 077.

If continuing to Hospital de Vielha, return to the place where the road forks, turn left and follow the dirt road that climbs gently. Leave the forest and cross two streams (the second by a footbridge), then turn right and follow a vague track left of the stream. At a junction where the *refugi* is indicated, turn left and walk in five minutes to the

3.20 Hospital de Vielha (1626m) – a number of buildings but no accomodation. If you climb a little N (no path) you'll find fine places to bivouac with good views. The nearest place to sleep inside is Refugi de Conangles. ◂

For the continuation of the Pyrenean Haute Route, see Day 24.

The GR11 variant to Hospital de Vielha provides an easy-to-follow alternative to the main route

SECTION 4: SALARDÚ TO L'HOSPITALET-PRÈS-L'ANDORRE

Estany de Baciver (Day 26)

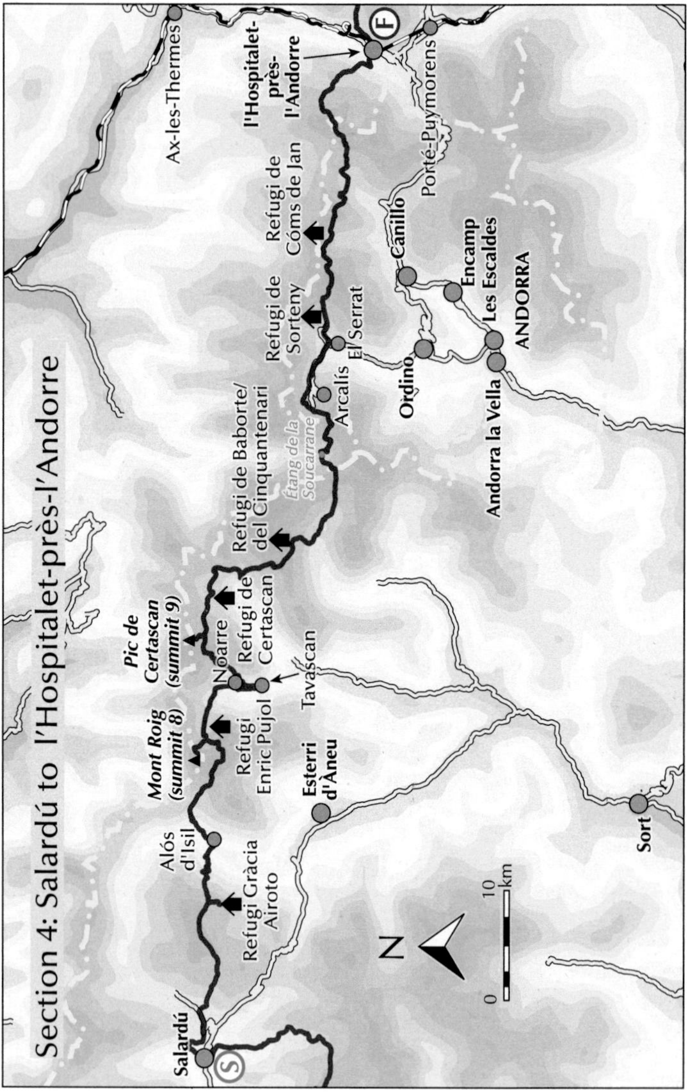
Section 4: Salardú to l'Hospitalet-près-l'Andorre
Salardú
Refugi Gràcia Aïroto
Alós d'Isil
Mont Roig (summit 8)
Refugi Enric Pujol
Esterri d'Àneu
Pic de Certascan (summit 9)
Noarre
Refugi de Certascan
Tavascan
Refugi de Baborte/ del Cinquantenari
Étang de la Soucarrane
Arcalís
Refugi de Sorteny
El Serrat
Refugi de Cóms de Jan
Ax-les-Thermes
l'Hospitalet-près-l'Andorre
Porté-Puymorens
Canillo
Ordino
Encamp
Les Escaldes
Andorra la Vella
ANDORRA
Sort
N
0
10
km

NINE DAYS THROUGH A MOUNTAIN WILDERNESS

One of the bounties of the PHR is to get away from the clutter of everyday life, into a world of mountains, lakes and hiking paths. At the same time, civilisation is never really far away, giving hikers the opportunity to have a reasonably light backpack and stock up on supplies regularly. Until now, many of these places have been on the route itself. Part four of the Haute Route, however, leads you through a hardly inhabited area of the Pyrenees with very few villages and no shops at all. Most hikers will choose to walk, hitchhike or catch a bus to some of the villages in the valleys near the Haute Route in order to buy food. The small village of Tavascan (Variant 5) is especially worth a visit.

In some ways, this fourth section is the hardest of all. There are much fewer manned huts than previously, the walks are long and tough, you will meet just a few fellow hikers on the way and the absence of markings on several parts of this route further adds to its wild character. Your map-reading and orientation skills will occasionally be put to the test in order to stay on course in this mountain wilderness.

However, it might also turn out be the most rewarding section of all. When you manage to overcome all the challenges on the way, you'll have a sense of accomplishment that will stay with you for a long time.

It's definitely worth climbing one or both of the classic summits described in this section – Mont Roig and Pic de Certascan.

PRACTICAL INFORMATION

Public transport to Salardú

The Haute Route can only be reached by public transport from Spain at this point. From Barcelona, take a long-distance bus to Vielha. Once in Vielha you can take a local bus to Salardú. Both buses are operated by the same company; check www.alsa.com for the schedules.

Facilities in Salardú

Salardú has a simple hotel, a large *refugi*, a bank (with cash dispenser), supermarket, food shop, small tourist office, restaurants, bars and a public swimming pool. There are no campsites (there is one in the village of Arties, about 3km west of Salardú).

Facilities in l'Hospitalet-près-l'Andorre

This border village is nothing close to romantic but for various reasons it is still interesting. Firstly, l'Hospitalet can easily be reached by public transport. Secondly, there is a basic campsite north of the village, a tiny food shop, a post office, a cash dispenser, a hotel and a gîte d'étape (open all year except November, tel 05 61 05 23 14, meals available, free wi-fi, gas canisters for sale). And above

View to Val d'Aran

all, l'Hospitalet-près-l'Andorre lies at 1436m – not a bad altitude to start a walk in the Pyrenean mountains.

Public transport from l'Hospitalet-près-l'Andorre

Trains from Latour-de-Carol to Paris (Gare Austerlitz) stop at l'Hospitalet-près-l'Andorre.

Variants

Should you wish to resupply, Variant 5 offers an alternative route to Noarre (Day 29) via Tavascan, where there are shops and restaurants.

Classic summits

Mont Roig (2868m) can be climbed from Refugi Enric Pujol, which is reached at the end of Day 28. Pic de Certascan (2853m) can be climbed from Coll de Certascan (Day 29).

Food, drink and fuel

In this section, most services are off-route. On Day 29 you can descend to the village of Tavascan, where you'll find restaurants, a small food shop and an outdoor shop that sells gas cartridges. On Day 32 you can go to the supermarket on the road between El Serrat and La Massena.

Maps

Rando Editions Mapa Excursionista, no 22, 1:50,000: Pica d'Estats–Aneto; Rando Editions Mapa Excursionista, no 21: Andorra–Cadi.

Accomodation: contact details

All numbers and other information on accommodation on the Haute Route are also given in the route description.

- Salardú: Aran Hostel – tel 648 528 196; Refugi Rosta – tel 973 645 308; Camping Era Yerla (3km from Salardú) – tel 973 641 602
- Day 26: Refugi Gràcia Airoto **(unmanned, no meals)**
- Day 27: Refugi d'Alós – tel unknown at time of publishing
- Day 28: Refugi Enric Pujol **(unmanned, no meals)**
- Day 29: Refugi de Certascan – tel 647 961 946
- Day 30: Refugi del Cinquantenari **(unmanned, no meals)**
- Day 31: No accommodation. Alternative: continue to El Serrat (see Day 32) where there is a choice of hotels
- Day 32: Refugi de Sorteny – tel 846 446
- Day 33: Refugi de Cabana Sorda **(unmanned, no meals)**
- L'Hospitalet-près-l'Andorre: Gîte l'Hospitalité – tel 06 74 87 05 05

DAY 26

Salardú to
Refugi Gràcia Airotò

Start	Salardú
Distance	17km
Total ascent	1540m
Total descent	610m
Grade	3
Time	7hr 35min
Map	Rando Editions Mapa Excursionista, 1:50,000, no 22: Pica d'Estats–Aneto
Route	Via the Tuc de Marimanya (2662m) and the Coll d'Airoto (2510m)

A very demanding route, including some stretches without path or waymarks, as well as rough terrain, a steep climb and a large section of boulders. The first part of the walk offers superb views of the Maladeta massif. The stage ends at an unmanned hut so you will need to bring food.

0.00 Salardú. Follow the road that goes to the village of Bagergue until you reach the junction where a road branches off to the small hamlet of Unya, which is nicely situated on a bluff. Turn left, cross the Riu Unyola by a bridge (water point) and turn right immediately. Past the last houses you'll find a broad track that climbs gently NE (you'll follow the white-and-red marks of this path to the Plan de Beret). Follow this track, cross the stream once again and climb along pastures and stone walls to the village of

0.45 Bagergue (1419m). Pass the church and enter the village. Walk to the main street (the one from Salardú) that runs through the village, turn left and climb this road for a short while until you reach an electricity pylon. Walk under the cables and turn right (signpost), ignore a private road on your right and walk between trees. Cross

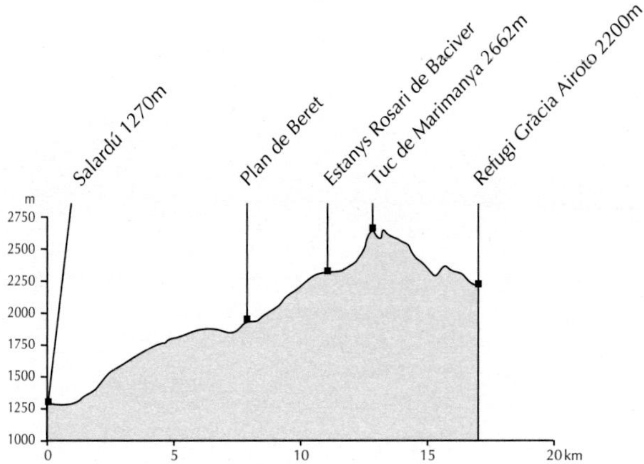

a stream and soon climb ESE in a few zigzags to a dirt road (1588m).

Turn right and walk S on this gently ascending road. Ignore a dirt road that branches off to the right and walk E now until you arrive at the road that goes to the Plan de Beret (signpost). Cross this road and follow a dirt road NE, staying a little below the road you've just crossed. Ignore a path coming from the right. The dirt road climbs and finally reaches a large flat area:

2.20 the Plan de Beret. The route forks near a *cabana*; turn left, keep the *cabana* on your right-hand side (1890m) and continue to a road that leads to Parking Orri in the ski resort of **Baqueira-Beret**. Turn right and follow the level road to the large parking area. Walk under a ski lift and go right past a chalet-style building with a stone chimney (1819m). (For a short while there is no track.) Walk SSE straight ahead and soon you'll find an obvious path on the right side of two small peaks. Climb for about 500 metres; at 1950m turn right and follow a path with cairns to a tiny but obvious pass. Behind the pass you'll find the

3.30 Estany de Baciver (2078m). Keep left of the dam and follow the shoreline of the lake, cross several small

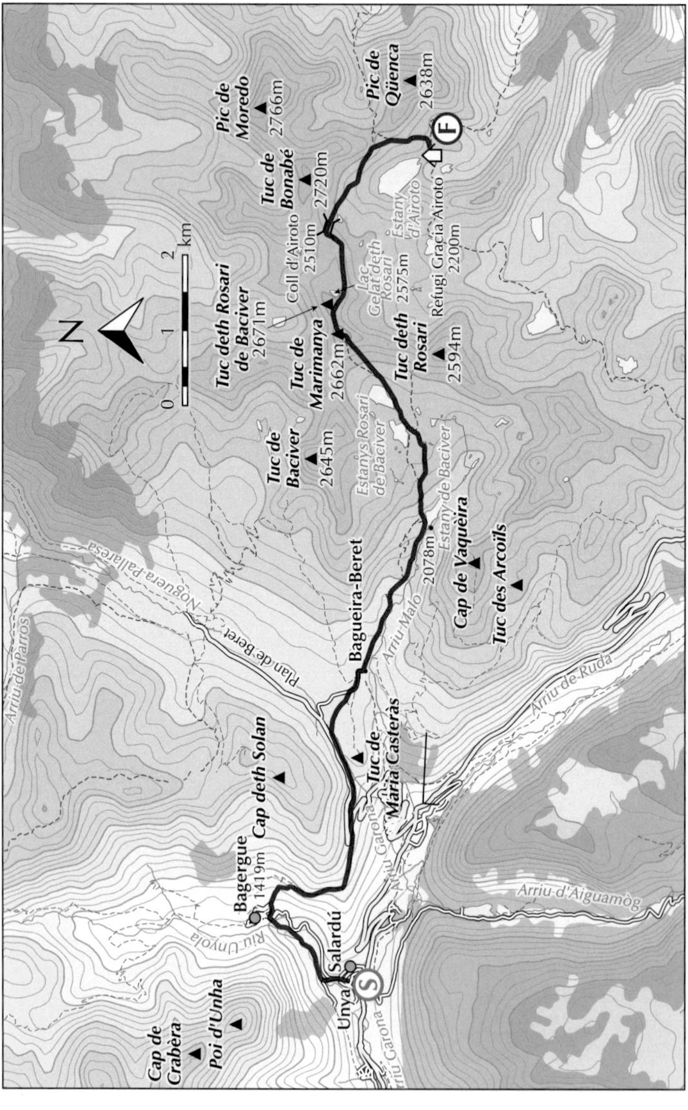
Pic de Moredo
2766m
Pic de Qüenca
2638m
F
Tuc de Bonabé
2720m
Coll d'Airoto
2510m
Estany d'Airoto
Refugi Gràcia Airoto
2200m
Lac Gelat deth Rosari
2575m
Tuc deth Rosari de Baciver
2671m
Tuc de Marimanya
2662m
Tuc deth Rosari
2594m
N
0
1
2
km
Tuc de Baciver
2645m
Estanys Rosari de Baciver
Estany de Baciver
2078m
Cap de Vaquèira
Tuc des Arcoils
Noguera Pallaresa
Plan de Beret
Baqueira-Beret
Arriu Malo
Arriu de Ruda
Arriu de Parros
Cap deth Solan
Tuc de Maria Casteràs
Arriu Garona
Arriu d'Aiguamòg
Bagergue
1419m
Riu Unyola
Salardú
S
Unya
Garona
Arriu Garona
Cap de Crabèra
Poi d'Unha

The Tuc de Marimanya offers extensive views

streams (coming from the Estanys Rosari de Baciver) and climb NE with the main stream on your left-hand side. Cross the stream twice and you soon arrive at the first of the two large **Estanys Rosari de Baciver** (2311m).

Walk along the lake, keeping it on your left-hand side, and do the same with the second lake (2318m). ▸ Both lakes are situated in an immense plateau, where horses and cows are often grazing. Suitable places for a bivouac are not hard to find. Already at the first lake you will find yellow markers that lead all the way up to Tuc de Marimanya.

Fill up on water as this is your last source for a while!

As you are walking past the second lake, look straight ahead NE and notice two peaks very close to one another: aim for these peaks. Walk on grass until the rocky base of the climb (2434m) and then ascend on rocks on a very steep slope. Climb to the highest point, the

5.15 Tuc de Marimanya (2662m), which offers excellent views, especially of the Estanys Rosari de Baciver and the Maladeta massif in the distance. Descend E on a ridge and then climb on the same ridge to a place just before the Tuc deth Rosari de Baciver (2671m), where a path leaves the main ridge and turns SE to go around Lac Gelat deth Rosari (2575m) on a ridge well above the lake. Follow this ridge, which soon turns N and NE. Stay close to the edge for the best views and gradually descend to

Refugi Gràcia Airoto

6.00 Coll d'Airoto (2510m). Go SE down a steep slope towards the N shore of a tiny tarn below the col. Don't go all the way to the tarn but head down towards the large Estany d'Airoto, initially through grass and later on giant boulders. Pass the northern shore of the large lake, staying 150–200m above the water level, still walking on boulders. NE of the lake, climb steeply through grass until you meet a rather vague track that's marked with cairns. If you're carrying a tent, you could continue on tomorrow's route immediately and turn left. Otherwise, turn right and go down with the lake a little distance on your right, to reach

There are plenty of billberries between the refuge and Estany d'Airoto.

7.35 Refugi Gràcia Airoto (2200m), an unmanned hut of the UEC (Unió Excursionista de Catalunya), south of the Estany d'Airoto. This is a basic shelter in which six walkers can sleep, in an idyllic spot. Water point. ◂

DAY 27

Refugi Gràcia Airoto to Alós d'Isil

Start	Refugi Gràcia Airoto
Distance	8km
Total ascent	260m
Total descent	1190m
Grade	2
Time	3hr 30min
Map	Rando Editions Mapa Excursionista, 1:50,000, no 22: Pica d'Estats–Aneto
Route	Via the Coll del Clot de Moredo (2429m) and the Bordes de Moredo (1680m)

A short stage that brings you to the hamlet of Alós d'Isil. There are no shops in the hamlet, but there is a comfortable refuge. Energetic walkers will continue on tomorrow's track and pitch the tent somewhere suitable.

0.00 Refugi Gràcia Airoto. From the hut, return to the junction above the Estany d'Airoto, turn right and continue to climb to the **Collado del Clot de Moredo** (2429m). Go down on the east side of the pass to a tiny tarn called **La Basseta**, walk along the southern shore of the lake (fine places for a bivouac here) and then climb a few metres to

1.20 a minor pass at 2228m. From here continue the descent in a narrow valley with the white limestone walls of the Pic de Qüenca on your right. At an altitude of about 2100m you'll meet the Barranc de Moredo; stay left of the stream and go down to a dirt road, the Pista de Moredo (1990m). From here you can clearly see the Bordes de Moredo (a number of farmhouses). Follow the dirt road that winds down or, alternatively, a series of optional shortcuts that descend more directly, cutting across the road several times. The shortcuts start at 1970m, on the right side of the Pista de Moreda. These

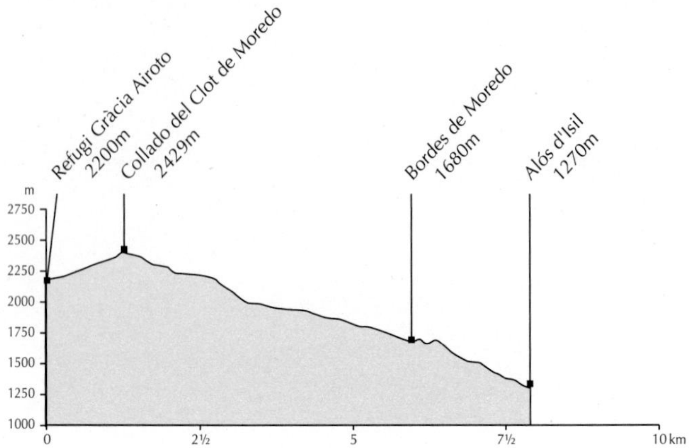

shortcuts are cairned but nevertheless not always easy to follow. Whichever option you take, at 1770m you leave the Pista de Moredo to go down to a smaller dirtroad leading to Bordes de Moredo. Turn left upon reaching the dirtroad, cross a concrete bridge and reach

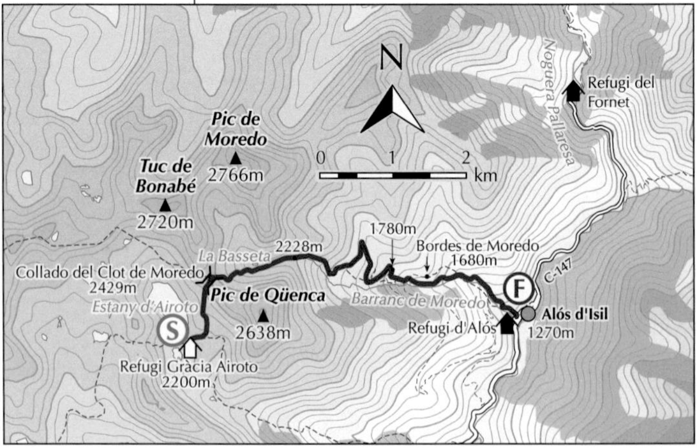

Bordes de Moredo, a tiny hamlet on the way down to Alós d'Isil

2.20 a place 100m before Bordes de Moredo (1700m). Turn right, leaving the dirtroad, and walk SE to an opening in an old stone wall. Go through the opening and continue E on a faint trail. Soon the trail becomes much clearer and yellow markers guide you along the left bank of Barranc de Moredo. The path first follows the river closely and then keeps higher before going down in a few switchbacks to the river again. Turn right when you are close to the village and walk into

3.30 Alós d'Isil (1270m, church). The Refugi d'Alós, 200m SW of the church, is the only facility in the village. In the summer of 2023, the refuge was manned again after having functioned as an unmanned refuge for many years. At the time of writing, it is known that the local municipality wants to keep it manned in the future, but it is yet unclear who the wardens will be. Information like a telephone number for reservations and the opening times are still unclear and those you will need to look up yourself. The *refugi* is a comfortable hut and has a dining room and a single dormitory for 20 hikers.

If you prefer a bivouac, the best thing to do is to continue on tomorrow's route. There are some fine places to be found close to the Noguera Pallaresa in the first half-hour of the walk.

DAY 28

Alós d'Isil to Refugi Enric Pujol

Start	Alós d'Isil
Distance	12km
Total ascent	1535m
Total descent	515m
Grade	2
Time	7hr 25min
Map	Rando Editions Mapa Excursionista, 1:50,000, no 22: Pica d'Estats–Aneto
Route	Via the Coll de la Cornella (2485m), the Coll de Curios (2455m) and the Coll de Calberante (2610m)

Three passes have to be crossed in this tough stage. Due to the rough terrain, poor waymarking and the absence of a path here and there, it will take concentration to stay on course. Care is needed on the very steep east side of the Coll de la Cornella. On the final descent to Refugi Enric Pujol you'll walk over beautifully polished granite – a reminder of the immense glaciers that once covered this area. The refuge is unmanned so you will need to bring food.

0.00 Alós d'Isil. Return to the church, leave it on your left-hand side and walk NE through the hamlet. Reach the C-147 and turn left. Follow this tarmac road which climbs gently with the Noguera Pallaresa on its right-hand side. After 35min, leave the road and go down to the **Pont de la Pina** (1315m, bridge) on the river. Cross the bridge and climb on a dirt road that winds up in a few zigzags.

Soon you'll notice a barn on your right; follow the grassy road to two other barns at 1450m. The dirt road ends at the buildings. Walk between the buildings, continue through grass for a few metres and turn right. Enter a forest and follow a clear track that climbs steeply until you're well above the Barranc de Comamala. From

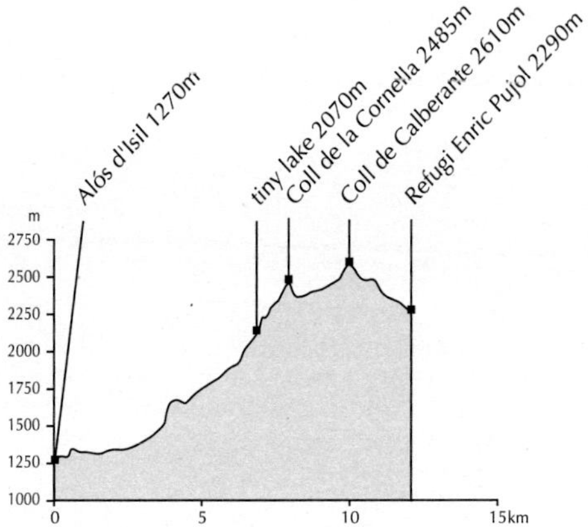

1600m the track climbs much more gently and crosses several minor streams.

After leaving the forest, walk SE through a more or less open valley and stay left at a little distance from the Comamala stream. Climb steeply and arrive at a marshy plateau; cross the plateau and climb a little on a faint path to the end of the valley (about 1900m). Cross a minor stream and then cross the left of three streams, then climb S in zigzags with a beautiful cascade on your right-hand side between alpenrose, heather and lots of billberries to arrive to a

3.30 tiny lake at 2070m – a fine place to bivouac. Leave the lake on your right and climb E towards the Coll de la Cornella, passing two false cols. You'll reach the first at 2190m. Ignore the cairns that branch off to the right and keep climbing very steeply on a rough slope in the same direction to the second false col (2340m). The route, marked with cairns, makes several turns to avoid rocks as far as possible and then climbs steeply through scree to the

4.45 Coll de la Cornella (2485m), a small gap in the ridge southwest of Mont Roig (also called Mont Rouch). ▸ Descend carefully on an extremely steep

Take a moment to look at the route to Coll de Curios from here.

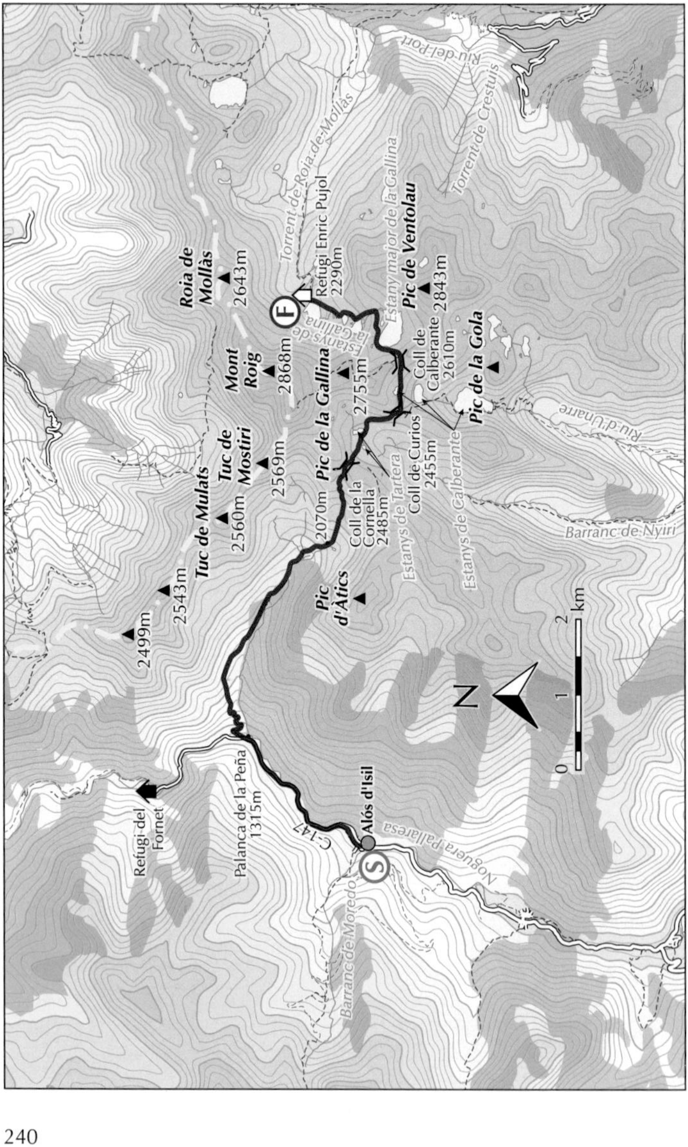
Roia de Mollàs
2643m
Mont Roig
2868m
Tuc de Mostiri
2569m
Tuc de Mulats
2560m
2543m
2499m
F
Refugi Enric Pujol
2290m
Torrent de Roia de Mollàs
Riu del Port
Torrent de Crestuis
Estany major de la Gallina
Estanys de la Gallina
Pic de Ventolau
2843m
Pic de la Gallina
2755m
Coll de Calberante
2610m
Pic de la Gola
Riu d'Unarre
Coll de Curios
2455m
Coll de la Cornella
2485m
2070m
Estanys de Tartera
Estanys de Calberante
Barranc de Nyiri
Pic d'Àtics
N
0
1
2
km
Refugi del Fornet
Palanca de la Peña
1315m
Alós d'Isil
C-147
S
Noguera Pallaresa
Barranc de Moredo

Small streams on the Comamala plateau

scree slope and walk E to the **Estanys de Tartera** (2375m), which can be seen from the pass. Walk between the lakes and cross a stream, then climb SSE, following yellow makers, and arrive at the

5.30 Coll de Curios (2455m, signpost), a large pass. Don't go down to the two largest Calberante lakes but climb E on a path marked with some cairns along a tiny stream to the highest and smallest **Estany de Calberante** (2490m). Walk along its southern shore and climb E on a vague track to the

6.10 Coll de Calberante (2610m). From here descend steeply to the large **Estany Major de la Gallina** (2490m) and walk around the lake. Continue along its northern shore until you've found the place where the descent to Refugi Enric Pujol starts; the *refugi* and the three Gallina lakes can be seen from here.

Don't go down in a straight line but follow the yellow markers that bend a little to the right. The route initially stays level, until you twice cross the stream coming down from the first lake. Then go down to the second lake. Still closely following the yellow markers, scramble down carefully a few metres, continue finding your way

The Gallina lakes leading to Refugi Enric Pujol

through a maze of beautifully polished rocks and reach the third lake.

Follow the markers along this most northern Gallina lake to the place where its outflow runs in a narrow, deep gully. Cross a wooden bridge over the water and climb a few metres to

7.25 Refugi Enric Pujol (2290m). ◄ The hut, also called Refugi Mont Roig, is owned by the FEEC and sits on a bluff close to the imposing east face of the Mont Roig, overlooking the lake as well as the Estany de Llavera, down below to the east. It is a solid, unmanned hut, with bunk beds for nine hikers. It's worth spending the night here.

The ascent of Mont Roig starts from the refuge and takes 3hr 15min (return) – see 'Summit 8'.

SUMMIT 8

Mont Roig (2868m) from Refugi Enric Pujol

Start	Refugi Enric Pujol (Day 28/29)
Distance	4km
Total ascent/descent	560m
Grade	F
Time	3hr 15min; allow 1hr 45min to reach the summit

From Refugi Enric Pujol the two summits of Mont Roig (also called Mont Rouch) can be clearly seen: the French summit (2868m) and the Spanish summit (2864m). The east face of the mountain is quite impressive and has a narrow gully covered with snow practically all summer. The ascent is somewhat rough, but not difficult in the high summer season, when snow has vanished from the slopes below the frontier ridge. There is no path that leads to the frontier ridge and there are just a few cairns here and there. The direction, however, should be obvious. A little care is needed on the ridge leading to the summit. The views from the summit are spectacular, but what will strike you most of all is the remarkable contrast between the fresh green French mountains and the much more barren Spanish sierras.

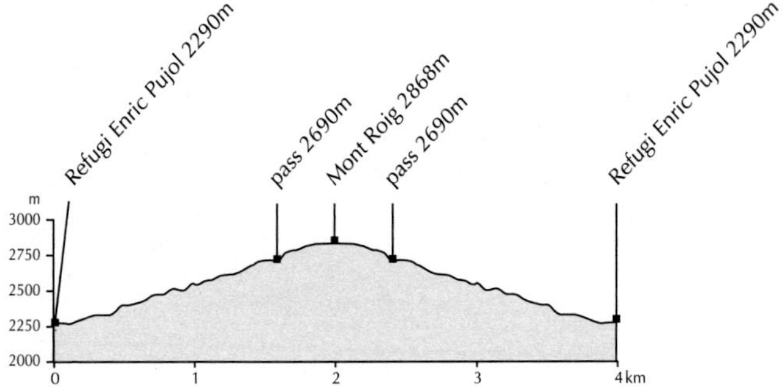

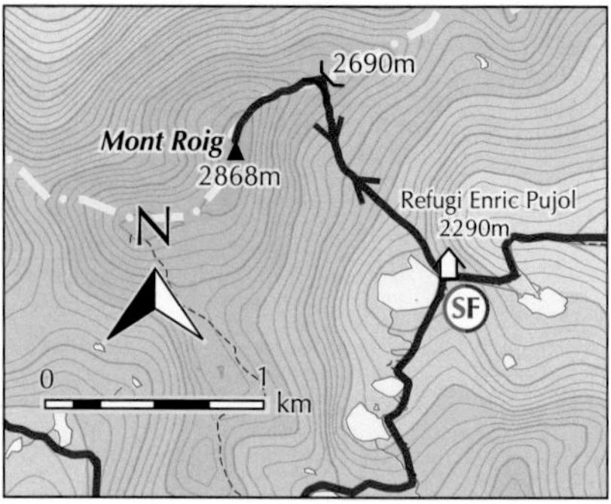

0.00 Refugi Enric Pujol (2290m). From the refuge, gain height NW and aim for the pass, clearly visible ahead, as you work your way up through grass and rocks. Early in the season there may be a few snowfields that have to be crossed. Finally climb through scree to reach a **pass** on the frontier ridge (2690m). Don't go into France but turn left and climb SW on the ridge. Here and there you'll have to avoid a tiny rocky eminence on the ridge, but it won't be too difficult to reach the summit of

1.45 Mont Roig (2868m – the French call this the Mont Rouch de France), which is marked with a large cairn. Take the same route on your way down to the refuge.

DAY 29

Refugi Enric Pujol to Refugi de Certascan

Start	Refugi Enric Pujol
Distance	13.5km
Total ascent	1045m
Total descent	1095m
Grade	2
Time	7hr 15min
Map	Rando Editions Mapa Excursionista, 1:50,000, no 22: Pica d'Estats–Aneto
Route	Via the hamlet of Noarre and the Coll de Certascan (2605m)
Note	The steep east side of Coll de Certascan may be snow-covered in early summer; proceed with care.

A beautiful walk through otherwise inaccessible alpine landscapes, where only few trekkers come. Several sections have no path and no more than a few cairns, and early in the season there may be snow on the far side of the Coll de Certascan, but despite this there should be no major difficulties. A variant route for hikers who need food supplies is described in Variant 5.

0.00 Refugi Enric Pujol. From the refuge, follow the cairns along the stream and go down in the direction of Estany de Llavera. The path turns left before reaching the lake to go down steeply, staying very close to the stream that descends in small cascades. Reach the upper section of a valley, stay left of the stream and walk SSE on polished rocks. Keeping the stream on your right-hand side, arrive at a small plateau and cross a minor stream that comes from the left (1929m).

Climb a few metres and follow the path, which becomes level, then cross a small ravine and go down again. Cross a stream and then a very short climb brings you to an open, marshy field with a traditional stone shepherds' hut: Cabana de lo Fangassal (sometimes

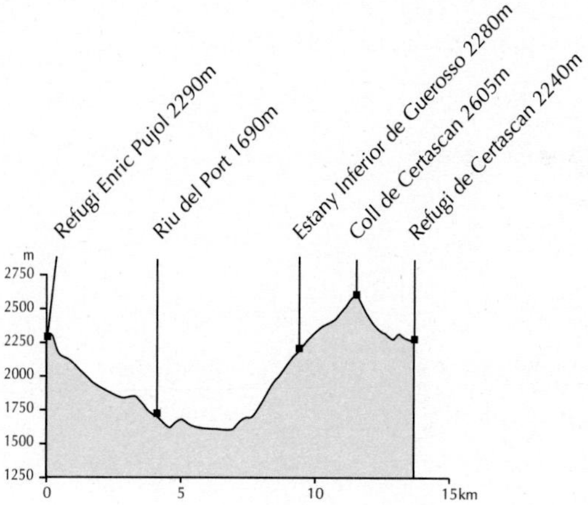

in use by a shepherd, five places). Keeping the plateau on your left, descend gently SE and enter a forest with pine trees and birches. After crossing a couple of streams you'll finally come out of the forest to arrive at the

2.15 Riu del Port (1690m). Cross the stream by a footbridge, enter a forest and walk S for about 15min on a more or less level path, crossing several minor streams in a marshy area, until you arrive, after having climbed a few metres, at a dirt road (which goes towards Tavascan) on a hairpin bend (1700m, signpost). ◀ Go S down this road for a few minutes to reach a signpost that indicates the route to Noarre. Leave the road, turn left and follow a level path in the forest; keep walking in the same direction at a junction and the easy-to-follow path will bring you to

Variant 5 describes an alternative route to Noarre via Tavascan, should you need supplies. It takes 4hr 10min to reach Noarre from this point via the variant.

3.00 Noarre (1600m), a small hamlet that consists of a few (farm)houses in an open field, close to the Riu de Noarre. Many buildings have been recently renovated and are being used as summer residences. ◀ Go down to a junction (signpost) and continue to another junction a few metres further on where a signpost indicates the

Noarre is remarkable for being cut off from what we call 'the civilised world': it has no road access.

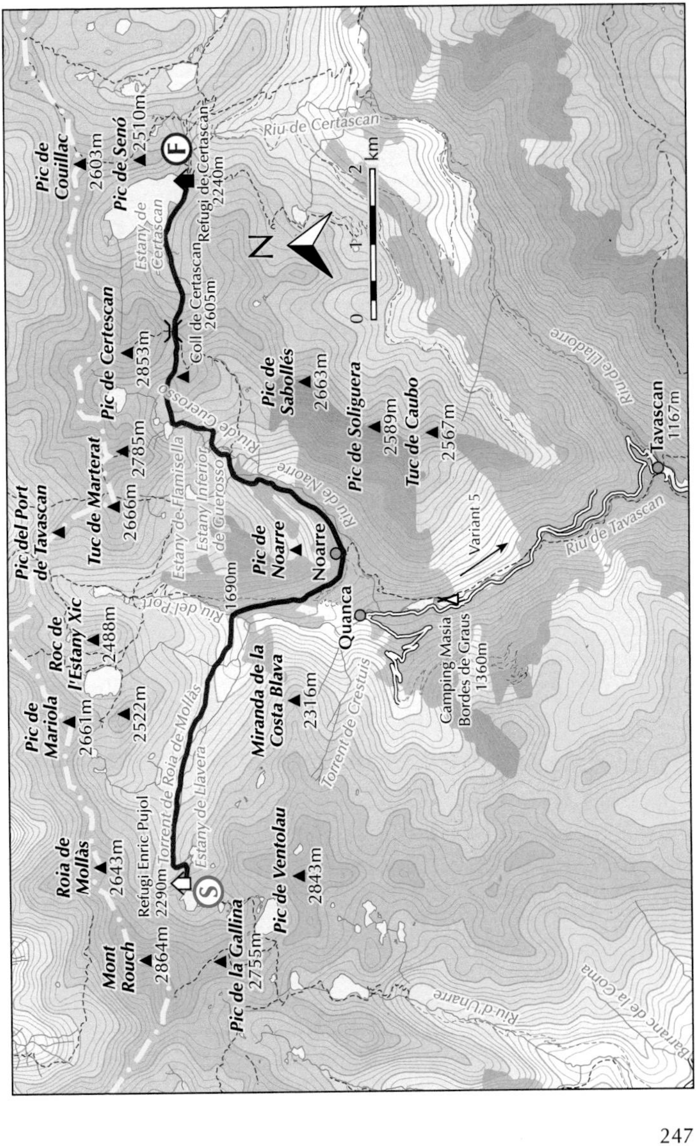
Pic de Couillac
2603m
Pic de Senó
2510m
F
Estany de Certascan
Refugi de Certascan
2240m
Riu de Certascan
N
0
1
2
km
Coll de Certascan
2605m
Pic de Certescan
2853m
Pic de Sabollés
2663m
Pic de Soliguera
2589m
Tuc de Caubo
2567m
Riu de Lladorre
Tavascan
1167m
Riu de Tavascan
Variant 5
Riu de Naorre
Riu de Guerosso
Estany Inferior de Guerosso
Estany de Flamisella
Tuc de Marterat
2785m
2666m
Pic del Port de Tavascan
Pic de Noarre
Noarre
1690m
Riu del Port
Quanca
Camping Masia Bordes de Graus
1360m
Roc de l'Estany Xic
2488m
Pic de Mariola
2661m
2522m
Miranda de la Costa Blava
2316m
Torrent de Crestuis
Torrent de Roia de Mollàs
Estany de Llavera
Refugi Enric Pujol
2290m
S
Roia de Mollàs
2643m
Pic de Ventolau
2843m
Mont Rouch
2864m
Pic de la Gallina
2755m
Riu d'Unarre
Barranc de la Coma

Estany de Llavera on the way to Noarre

route to Refugi de Certascan. Turn left and walk NE, noting an isolated house on your left above. Follow the path and climb gently NE between birch trees; eventually the path bends to the left and climbs steeply in zigzags in a mixed forest.

Cross the stream coming from Estany de Flamisella (about 2000m, just below a small waterfall) and continue the ascent. Soon you'll arrive at a beautiful marshy plain, with the Riu de Noarre winding through it. Walk along the plain, keeping the stream on your right-hand side, until you reach a signpost. Turn left and follow the marks NE on a rough rocky slope. The route gradually approaches the Riu de Guerosso, which descends in cascades. Climb steeply N on rough terrain to the small

5.00 Estany Inferior de Guerosso (2280m). Cross the outflow and climb steeply E until the path (which becomes faint at times) turns left and climbs N, with a stream on your left-hand side. Cross a small ravine and climb to the tiny Estany Mitja de Guerosso (2350m). Pass the lake and a small waterfall and a little higher you'll find Estany Blau de Guerosso (2370m). Here the final climb to the Coll de Certascan begins. The route makes

A waterfall close to the Coll de Certascan

a sharp turn to the right, then you follow a line of cairns as you climb straight ahead ESE on rough terrain to the

6.15 Coll de Certascan (2605m), a small gap in the ridge south of the Pic de Certascan (2853m). ▶ Go down on the steep east side of the pass. The descent soon eases, the route turns left and you pass a snow-meter and a small tarn (at a distance on your right). Cross the main stream (at 2342m) and walk towards the large **Estany de Certascan**. Near the lake (fine places for a bivouac) you have to cross the stream twice. The path then bends away from the stream; walk above the southern shore of the lake and follow the undulating path to

The ascent of Pic de Certascan starts from here and takes 1hr 10min (return) – see 'Summit 9'.

7.15 Refugi de Certascan (2240m). The hut is surprisingly not situated at the lake, but a little hidden at a distance from it. Manned from June until late September, 40 places, meals available, owned by the FEEC, tel 973 623 230.

VARIANT 5

To Noarre via Tavascan

Start	Dirt road to Tavascan (Day 29)
Finish	Noarre (Day 29)
Distance	16km
Total ascent	770m
Total descent	830m
Grade	1
Time	4hr 10min

This variant allows you to buy supplies in Tavascan, stay overnight at a campsite and reach Noarre the next day, by an alternative route.

Tavascan is a small mountain village that has gained popularity because of its isolation. You can find restaurants here, an outdoor shop (gas for sale) and a small grocery store.

Follow the Haute Route as described for Day 29 until you arrive at the dirt road coming from Tavascan (1700m). Go down this road until you arrive at the tarmac road, then turn left, pass the tiny hamlet of **Quanca**, and continue past a dammed lake on your left-hand side. A little further on you'll find **Camping Masia 'Bordes de Graus'** (1360m, bar/restaurant and a refugi, tel 973 623 246 or 973 623 206). It'll take you 45min to get here. Pitch the tent before heading down to Tavascan.

Continue via the hiking path that starts near the playground, or go along the road, and walk 5km to Tavascan (also called Tabescan, 1167m). It will take you 1hr to get there and 1hr 30min to get back to the campsite, but hitchhiking might well work too.

The next day, follow the old track from Graus to Noarre: leave the campsite at the back (near the playground) and go down to the Riu de Tavascan. Turn left and follow the stream for a few moments until you arrive at a bridge. Cross the bridge and follow a clear path to

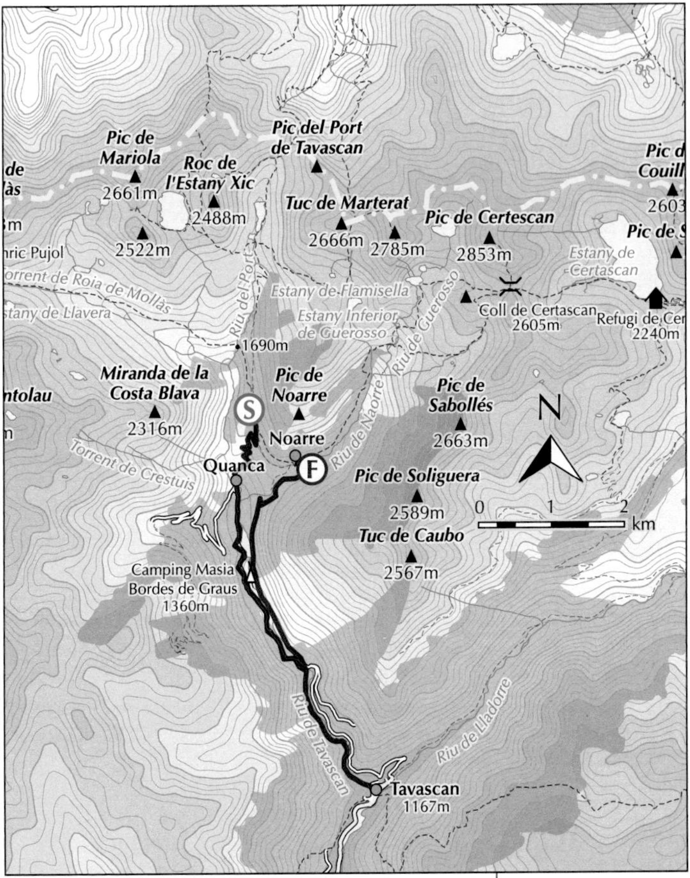

Noarre, with plenty of signposts. In less than 1hr you will be in **Noarre**. ▸

To continue on the Pyrenean Haute Route, see Day 29.

SUMMIT 9

Pic de Certascan (2853m) from Coll de Certascan

Start	Coll de Certascan (2605m) (Day 29)
Distance	2km
Total ascent/descent	235m
Grade	F
Time	1hr 10min; allow 40min for the ascent

The Pic de Certascan dominates the vast region between the Mont Roig (2868m) in the west and the Pica d'Estats (3143m) in the east. This summit is worth the extra effort because of the extensive views it offers: all the summits of the Aigüestortes region, the Besiberri massif, the snow-covered summits of the Maladeta massif, the vertical east face of the Mont Valier (2838m) in France, Mont Roig, the Pica d'Estats, the Estany de Certascan and numerous sun-baked Spanish sierras. It's an uncomplicated, rough ascent in summer over a scree slope and finally on boulders.

0.00 Coll de Certascan (2605m, see Day 29). A few metres west of the pass you'll notice some cairns that indicate the route to the Pic de Certascan. Climb steeply N on a more or less clear trail through scree and gain the

On Pic de Certascan, with the view opening up after a climb in the clouds

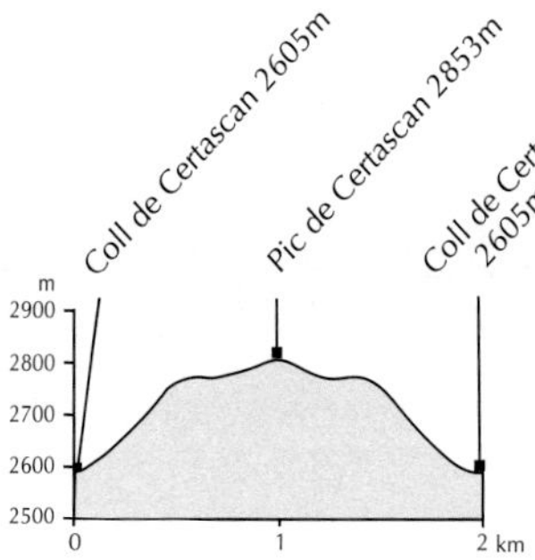

ridge that leads to the summit. Stay close to the ridge as you climb. Go around the west side of a rocky eminence as the end of the ascent approaches and finally climb on boulders to the top of the

0.40 Pic de Certascan (2853m). Follow the same track back to the Coll de Certascan.

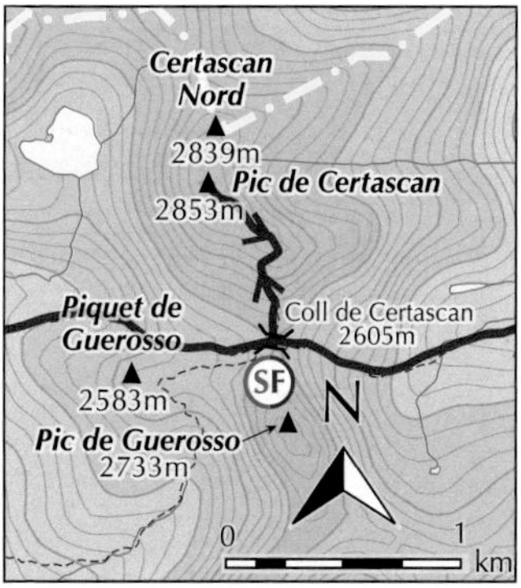

DAY 30

Refugi de Certascan to Refugi de Baborte/del Cinquantenari

Start	Refugi de Certascan
Distance	12.5km
Total ascent	1190m
Total descent	1060m
Grade	2
Time	5hr 10min
Map	Rando Editions Mapa Excursionista, 1:50,000, no 22: Pica d'Estats–Aneto
Route	Via Pla de la Borda (1440m) and the Coll de Sellente (2488m)

This stage first descends on easy paths to Pla de la Borda before taking you through great mountain scenery to the foot of the most western 3000ers in the Pyrenees. The Baborte lakes are a delightful place to spend the night. The stage ends at an unmanned refuge so you will need to bring food.

0.00 Refugi de Certascan. From the refuge, go down E to a small lake (2205m) and walk along its north shore. Continue descending, keeping left of a stream that cascades down, and arrive at a stream. Cross it and go down to a junction. With the dam (on your right below) in sight, continue S (ignoring the path going E) and go down to a dirtroad. Cross the dirtroad and continue descending S. At 1850m you find a small stream on your right side, which you soon leave again. Continue descending all the way to a junction at

1.35 Pla de la Borda (1440m), where you reach the Cami de Boavi, a dirtroad with Riu de Lladore just below. Turn left and follow the Cami de Boavi to Pla de Boavi (1470m). Continue E past this plain and soon reach

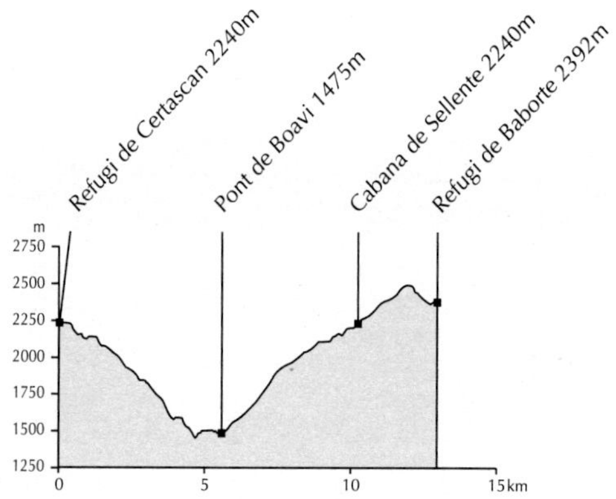

1.50 Pont de Boavi (1475m). Cross the stream on this footbridge and walk SE on an obvious path (white-and-red marks from here on) to enter a forest with large pine trees. Climb gently in zigzags until you arrive at the Riu de Sellente, cross the stream by a footbridge and follow the path as it bends away from the stream to soon arrive at a junction (signpost).

Overlooking the Pyrenees' most western 3000ers near Refugi de Barborte

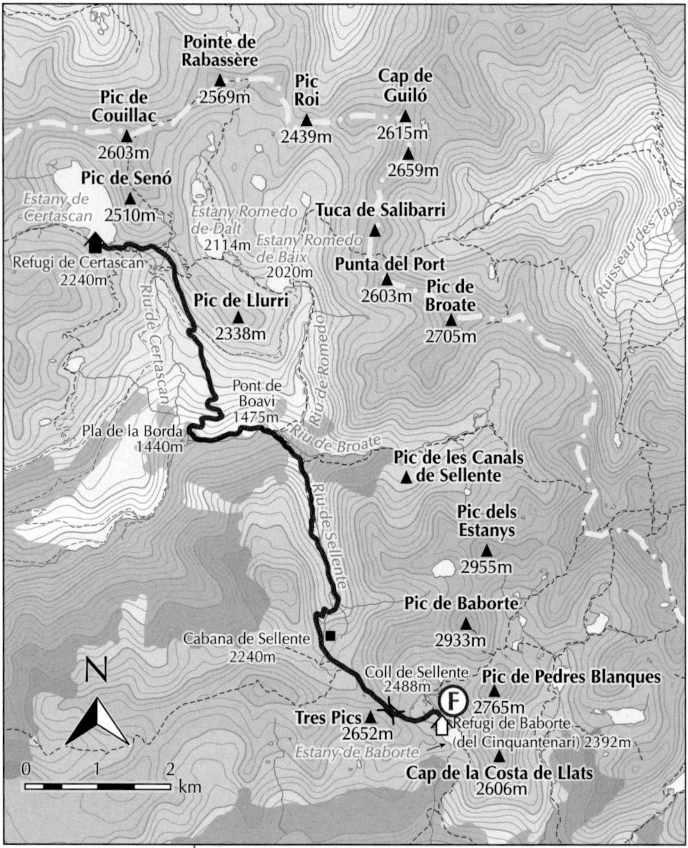

Turn right and climb SSE on a path that approaches the Riu de Sellente. Cross the stream after a rocky section (1830m) and climb above the west side of the Riu de Sellente. Re-cross the stream at 2020m and walk along the east side of a large plateau in the upper section of the valley. At the end of the plateau the path bends to the right, crosses several minor streams and goes up in a few large zigzags to arrive at what is left of

4.10 Cabana de Sellente (2240m), situated besides a small flat area. Cross a stream and walk S through the plateau. The route becomes faint, but as you climb SSE you'll find cairns that lead easily to a false col. Cross the false col, go down a little on a small path (notice two tarns on your right below) and climb straight ahead to the

4.55 Coll de Sellente (2488m), a large saddle, where the Refugi de Baborte comes in sight. Go down on a steep scree slope and continue through grass. Cross a stream near a small lake and improvise a little as you climb to the unmanned, orange-coloured

5.10 Refugi de Baborte (2392m, officially called Refugi del Cinquantenari, but nobody uses that name), situated on a bluff and overlooking the largest Baborte lake. The solid unmanned hut has places for nine. Alternatively, there are many fine places to bivouac near the lake.

DAY 31

Refugi de Baborte/del Cinquantenari to Étang de la Soucarrane

Start	Refugi de Baborte/del Cinquantenari
Distance	10km
Total ascent	820m
Total descent	970m
Grade	2
Time	5hr 20min
Map	Rando Editions Mapa Excursionista, 1:50,000, no 22: Pica d'Estats–Aneto
Route	Via the Port de Boet (2509m)

A relatively easy walk on clear paths. Only the last stage to Port de Boet requires some improvisation. Étang de Soucarrane is a beautiful place for a bivouac. There is no accommodation at the end of the stage, but you can stop at Refugi de Vallferrera or push on to El Serrat.

0.00 Refugi de Baborte. From the hut, go SE down towards the lake and walk along its eastern shore. When you are close to the outflow, turn left and climb steeply

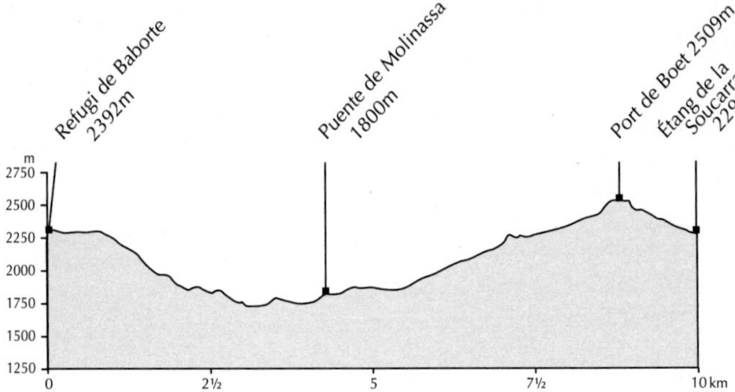

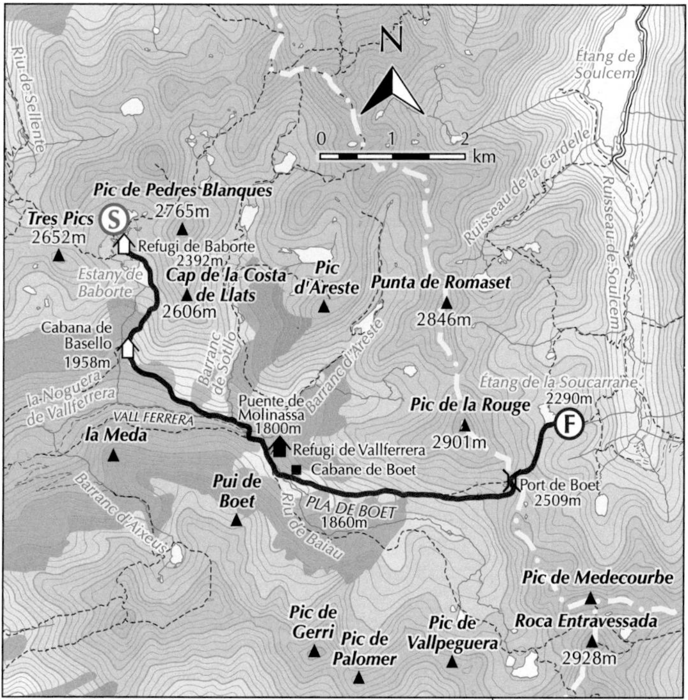

for a few moments to a minor pass, then descend S rather steeply through grass and scree on a path that bends away from the stream. Cross an area with some pine trees and the Cabana de Basello comes in sight. Go down in an open valley towards the *cabana* and arrive at

1.00 Cabana de Basello (1958m, only good as an emergency shelter, sleeps 2), situated on the edge of a small plateau. The path forks here (signpost); go left from the *cabana*, where you'll find a clear path to Vall Ferrera. Go down between bushes and enter a forest, then keep walking NE until you reach the floor of the Vall Ferrera. Cross the Barranc de Sottlo by a footbridge (1740m) and climb E along the Noguera de Vall Ferrera to the

The climb to the Port de Boet

2.00 Puente de Molinassa (1800m), a bridge on the Noguera de Vall Ferrera. Cross the bridge and climb a few metres to reach a parking area, then turn left and walk up a dirt road. After 5min you'll arrive at another parking area; find a signpost and turn left towards Pla de Boet. Climb a little and then follow the road, ignore a turn to Refugi de Vallferrera (tel 973 641 681) and walk to the

2.30 Pla de Boet (1860m), a beautiful flat area. Cross the Riu de Baiau several times using footbridges and walk towards Cabane de Boet (1900m, closed). Pass the *cabane* and two stone walls that are used to give salt to animals and follow a path that goes generally E in the direction of Port de Boet. At first the path is clear but later you'll have to depend on cairns for direction. When the cairns also disappear, continue E, pass the tiny lake of Estanyet de Port de Boet (2495m) very close to the pass and arrive at the

4.40 Port de Boet (2509m, signpost), a wide border pass. Descend E on the French side and follow the white-and-red markers. After passing a stone building with a grass roof, arrive at:

5.20 Étang de la Soucarrane (2290m). There are many good places for a bivouac at this beautiful lake.

DAY 32

Étang de la Soucarrane to Refugi de Sorteny

Start	Étang de la Soucaranne
Distance	15.5km
Total ascent	1090m
Total descent	1415m
Grade	2
Time	6hr 45min
Map	Rando Editions Mapa Excursionista, 1:50,000, no 21: Andorra–Cadí
Route	Via Port de Rat (2537m) and the Estanys de Tristaina

Today the Haute Route enters Andorra, where you will be treated to a short visit to the beautiful lakes in the Circ de Tristaina. An area worth exploring! After a hike along rivers and a less interesting section on tarmac road, you enter the Sorteny nature park. Hikers in need of food supplies can go off-route at El Serrat to a supermarket in a nearby village.

0.00 Étang de la Soucaranne. Pass the lake by its south shore until you reach the outflow. Cross the stream, turn right and follow the path left of the stream. While walking down you'll lose sight of the stream, after which you soon reach a not-so-obvious junction on a balcony (**2150m**). The path to the left is well used, whereas the path to the right is less clear; take the path to the **right** and after a few metres reach the same stream coming from Étang de la Soucarrane.

Cross the stream and follow a more or less even path S, then cross another stream (possibly dry in summer) and continue S. After crossing a further stream you'll reach an obvious path with yellow marks (**2090m**); turn left and follow this path towards the dirt road below, crossing the Ruisseau de Médecourbe as you descend. The path gradually becomes rockier, and you reach the road at a hairpin bend (**1974m**).

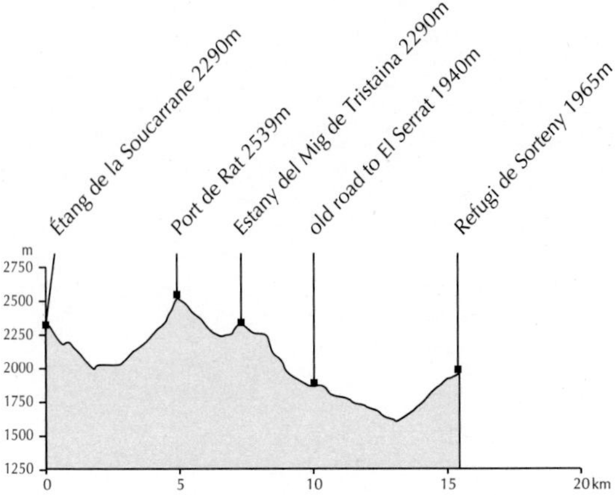

Walk up the gradually ascending road to the east side of the valley. Notice cairns on your left next to the road, a little before the next hairpin bend. In the same place you'll find white-and-red markers on the right side of the road; turn right and follow the path with the white-and-red markers, which climbs with the Ruisseau de Rat on your right. The path crosses the road several times and continues to climb SE, gradually moving away from the Ruisseau de Rat. At **2310m** the path goes N for a couple of minutes, after which you continue E in zigzags to the

2.55 Port de Rat (2539m, sign-post), a pass on the French-Andorran border. ◂ Descend E, following the white-and-red markers, and at 2440m the path turns NNE. Continue until you reach a road that goes down in hairpin bends. Follow the path that cuts NNE across the bends and arrive at bar/restaurant **'La Goma'** (2235m, drinks and snacks available). Turn left at the building and climb NE on an obvious path to the

The Arcalís ski resort is in front of you.

The Port de Rat leads you into Andorra

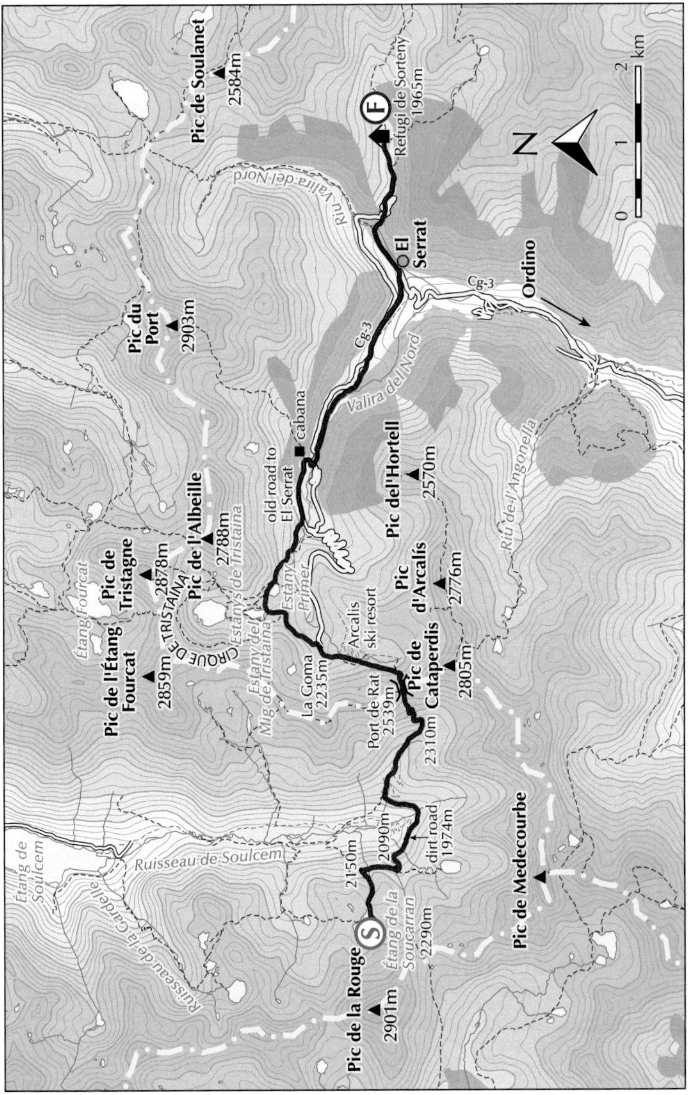
Pic de Soulanet
2584m
Refugi de Sorteny
1965m
F
Riu Valira del Nord
N
0 1 2 km
El Serrat
Ordino
Cg-3
Pic du Port
2903m
Cg-3
Valira del Nord
cabana
old road to El Serrat
Pic del'Hortell
2570m
Riu de l'Angonella
Pic de Tristagne
2878m
Pic de l'Albeille
2788m
Estanys de Tristaina
Étang Fourcat
Pic de l'Étang Fourcat
2859m
CIRQUE DE TRISTAINA
Estany Primer
Estany del Mig de Tristaina
Arcalis ski resort
Pic d'Arcalís
2776m
La Goma
2235m
Pic de Cataperdis
2805m
Port de Rat
2539m
2310m
Pic de Medecourbe
dirt road
1974m
2090m
2150m
Ruisseau de Soulcem
Étang de Soulcem
Ruisseau de la Gardelle
S
Étang de la Soucarran
2290m
Pic de la Rouge
2901m

4.00 Estany del Mig de Tristaina (2290m), the middle of the three lakes. Cross the outflow on the south side of the lake by a footbridge and continue E to **Estany Primer** (2250m). Pass this lake on its north shore, continue E close to the lake's outflow, and from there descend towards a small dam below. Carefully cross a short steep section and continue going down with the stream on your right. Close to the dam, start following an obvious path SE and go down to the **old road to El Serrat** (1940m).

Turn left and follow the road E, pass a *cabana* (good shelter, sleeps 2–3) on your left and go down a few metres to a gate in the bridge over the Riu de Tristaina. Go through the gate in the bridge and follow a path between trees, with the stream on your right. Arrive at a place with a picnic area on your right and continue SE to an open field that brings you to the CG3 road to El Serrat. ◄

Every half an hour buses run along this road, allowing access to a supermarket (see below).

Turn right and follow the road for 1.4km (ignore the road left to the Sorteny valley) as far as a sharp turn. Turn left just before this turn and follow a dirt road (signpost Sorteny, yellow-and-red marks). The dirt road very soon becomes a path which you follow along the Riu Valira del Nord. Turn right at a junction on the path and reach another dirt road, then turn right and follow this dirt road which makes several zigzags (two shortcuts are indicated) before arriving at a small botanical garden on your right. Continue on the road, cross a stone wall and finally reach

6.45 Refugi de Sorteny (1965m), a hut with 50 places (of which 10 are free of charge) and a large menu, tel 846 446.

At this point you may want to buy supplies. The closest supermarket is 10km south from El Serrat on the CG3 road. There are buses running every hour between El Serrat and Ordino (check www.montmantell.com for the schedule). The supermarket (tel 840 181) is situated on the left side of the road, between Ordino and La Massana. On the way back it is possible to take the bus all the way to the entrance of the Vall de Sorteny natural park. From there it takes about 30min to get to Refugi de Sorteny.

DAY 33

Refugi de Sorteny to Refugi de Cabana Sorda

Start	Refugi de Sorteny
Distance	12.5km
Total ascent	1385m
Total descent	1055m
Grade	2
Time	6hr 25min
Map	Rando Editions Mapa Excursionista, 1:50,000, no 21: Andorra–Cadi
Route	Via the Collada dels Meners (2713m)

A beautiful but physically demanding stage through a real mountain wilderness in the north of Andorra. Route-finding is very easy thanks to the markers along the trail. The stage ends at an unmanned hut so you will need to bring food.

0.00 Refugi de Sorteny. Pass the refuge on its north side and walk ENE on a path left of a stone wall, with red-and-yellow markers. The Riu de Sorteny is at a distance

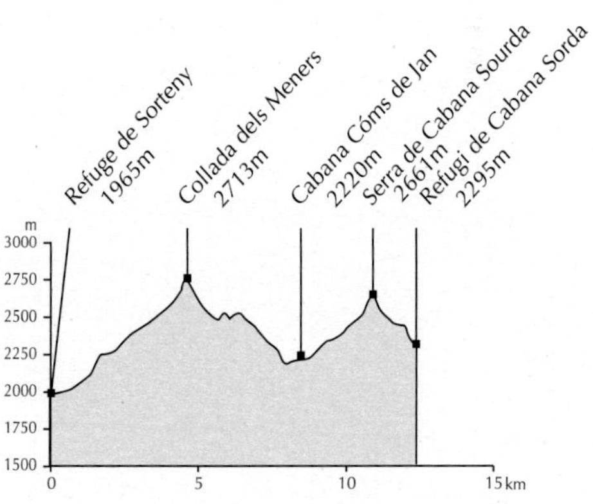

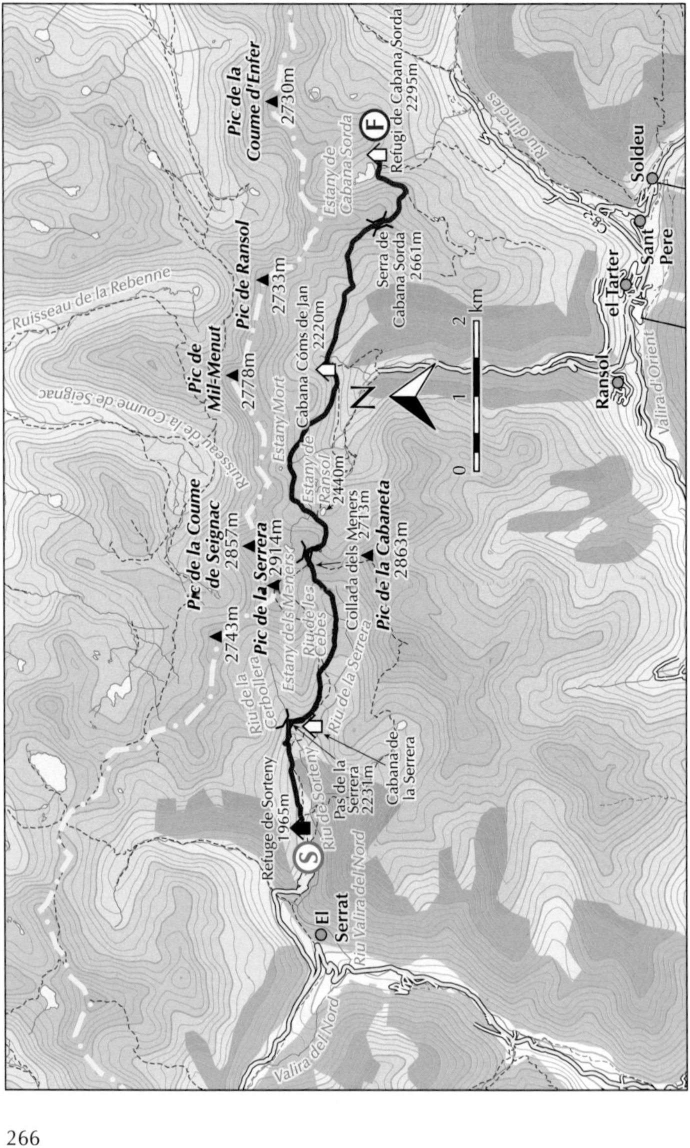
Pic de la Coume d'Enfer
2730m
Pic de Ransol
2733m
Pic de Mil-Menut
2778m
Pic de la Coume de Seignac
2857m
Pic de la Serrera
2914m
2743m
Pic de la Cabaneta
2863m
Collada dels Meners
2713m
Ruisseau de la Rebenne
Ruisseau de la Coume de Seignac
Estany de Cabana Sorda
Refugi de Cabana Sorda
2295m
Serra de Cabana Sorda
2661m
Cabana Cóms de Jan
2220m
Estany Mort
Estany de Ransol
2440m
Estany dels Meners
Riu de les Cebes
Riu de la Cerbollera
Estany dels Meners
Riu de la Serrera
Refuge de Sorteny
1965m
Riu de Sorteny
Pas de la Serrera
2231m
Cabana de la Serrera
El Serrat
Riu Valira del Nord
Valira del Nord
Riu d'Incles
Soldeu
Sant Pere
el Tarter
Ransol
Valira d'Orient
CS-
S
F
N
0
1
2
km

Cabana Cóms de Jan

on your right. Pass a marshy area, cross several minor streams and follow the obvious path which gradually approaches the Riu de la Cebollera coming from the left. Cross this stream at 2159m by a footbridge.

The path bends to the right and climbs in short zigzags to a pass, the **Pas de la Serrera** (2231m). From here go down a few metres, notice **Cabana de la Serrera** on your right below, and continue climbing with the Riu de Serrera on your right-hand side. Cross the **Riu de les Cebes** (2353m), pass a multicoloured pole, continue E and climb rather steeply to the

2.00 Collada dels Meners (2713m; also called Coll de la Mina), a gap in the ridge between the Pic de la Serrera (2914m) and the Pic de la Cabaneta (2863m). Notice an emergency shelter just beneath the pass.

Descend on a steep scree slope on the east side of the pass. Notice Estany dels Meners (2619m) at a great distance on your left and go down on a clear track E, then S and finally E towards **Estany de Ransol** (2440m). Walk around the north side of the lake and arrive at a junction, where Cabana Cóms de Jan is indicated on a stone. Turn left and follow the yellow-and-red marks that branch off to the left.

Climb gently to 2510m and follow an almost level path E, then cross the outflow (possibly dry in summer) of the small **Estany Mort** and start descending SE. Turn right at a junction and keep descending in the same direction. At 2200m the route turns NE; climb the last few metres to the

3.40 Cabana Cóms de Jan (2220m) – a small, solid hut with metal beds that has been divided into two parts. There are 10 places, and a water point at the side of the building. It is possible to bivouac.

To continue, follow the path E from the *cabana* and cross the Riu de Rialb near a tiny lake. Climb E towards the ridge ahead of you and after a short descent arrive at a small flat area, then cross a stream. The track, which climbs again, bends to the right, then left and after a very short descent (just past a false col) arrives at another stream. Climb towards the ridge on a rough track which becomes very steep, then cross a small ravine. The route bends a little to the right, and you arrive on the

5.10 Serra de Cabana Sorda (2661m), separating the Vall de Ransol from the Vall d'Inclès, with fine views. ◄ Descend E on a steep slope, and follow the yellow-and-red marks on a reasonably clear path. The route makes a surprising swing to the left and is flat for a short while. Descend again to arrive on a ridge south of the Estany de Cabana Sorda. (The lake and the hut stay hidden until the final descent.) Follow the ridge briefly, then turn left and go down on a small path (steep slope, care required) towards the **Estany de Cabana Sorda**, seen ahead of you. Descend steeply to the lake, which has a small dam, cross a stream and climb a few metres to

If you turn left and follow the ridge for a few moments you'll get a superb view over the Estany de Cabana Sorda.

6.25 Refugi de Cabana Sorda (2295m), an unmanned, solid hut with 10 places.

DAY 34

Refugi de Cabana Sorda to l'Hospitalet-près-l'Andorre

Start	Refugi de Cabana Sorda
Distance	17km
Total ascent	920m
Total descent	1775m
Grade	2
Time	8hr 20min
Map	Rando Editions Mapa Excursionista, 1:50,000, no 21: Andorra–Cadí
Route	Via Col de l'Albe (2539m), Couillade des Pédourès (2265m)

Today the haute route leaves Andorra again, but not before visiting some of its finest corners.

0.00 Refugi de Cabana Sorda. Ignore a path with yellow marks that goes E (to Estany Anrodat) from the hut and instead follow the yellow-and-red marks that go down S

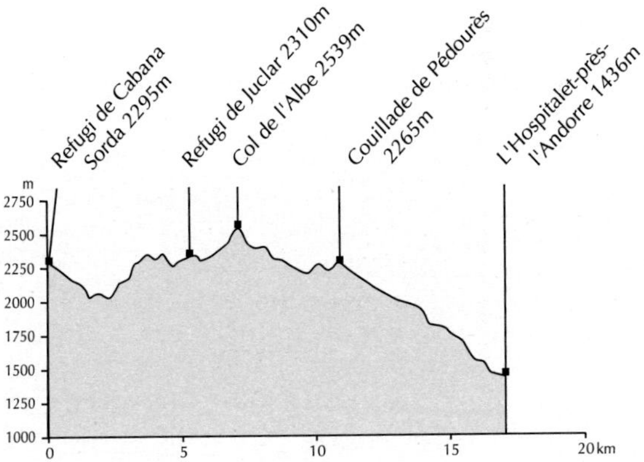

for a short while, close to the stream, and then bend to the left. The easy-to-follow path stays high above the Vall d'Inclès and finally descends NE to a junction (signpost). Ignore the path that goes straight on to Port d'Inclès and turn right to the floor of the valley.

Cross two small streams without bridges and then a third one by a footbridge, turn right and after a few metres notice the white-and-red marks of the **GRT** (Grande Route Transfrontalier) painted on a rock. Turn left and follow the GRT, which climbs steeply S.

Soon the route turns SE; at 2200m the climb eases briefly and then continues steeply E. Climb to a pass (2365m) and then descend to a small tarn that you pass on its south shore. Climb E to the next pass (2348m) and descend E towards a wide path next to the stream coming from Estany de Juclar. On reaching the wide path, turn left, cross a bridge and climb to

2.30 Refugi de Juclar (2310m, hut manned from June to September, good meals, 43 places, tel 678 145). From the hut, follow a path marked with yellow paintflashes close to the south shore of the **Estany Primer de Juclar**. Cross a footbridge between this lake and the **Estany Segon de Juclar** and start the climb to Collado de Juclar (2442m). Don't cross the frontier yet, but turn right on the pass and follow white-and-red marks to

3.55 Col de l'Albe (2539m, indicated on a rock), on the Andorran-French border. Descend E of the col on a steep scree slope towards Étang Haut de l'Albe (2355m).

Hikers between Col de l'Albe and the Juclar lakes

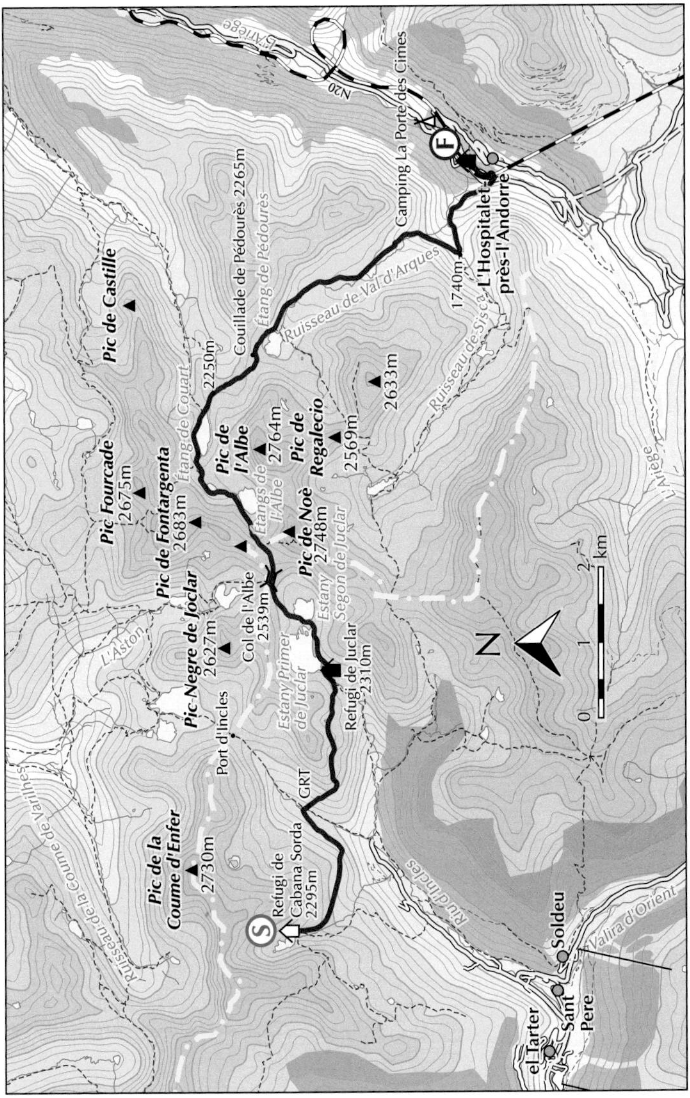
Pic de Castille
Couillade de Pédourès 2265m
Étang de Pédourès
Camping La Porte des Cimes
N20
L'Ariège
F
L'Hospitalet-près-l'Andorre
1740m
Ruisseau de Val d'Arques
2250m
Étang de Couart
Pic Fourcade 2675m
Pic de Fontargenta 2683m
Pic de l'Albe 2764m
Pic de Regalecio 2569m
2633m
Ruisseau de Sisca
Étangs de l'Albe
Pic de Noè 2748m
Estany Segon de Juclar
Col de l'Albe 2539m
Pic Negre de Joclar 2627m
L'Aston
Estany Primer de Juclar
Refugi de Juclar 2310m
Port d'Incles
GRT
Pic de la Coume d'Enfer 2730m
S
Refugi de Cabana Sorda 2295m
Ruisseau de la Coume de Varilhes
Riu d'Incles
Valira d'Orient
Soldeu
Sant Pere
el Tarter
L'Ariège
N
0 1 2 km

The descent soon eases; pass the lake on its west shore, staying well above the water level. Follow cairns that lead you N along the lake's outflow and pass Étang Bas de l'Albe and a few smaller tarns. The route now turns E and you descend again steeply to

5.15 Étang de Couart. Pass the lake on its north shore. Don't turn left past the lake, but go SE, still following the white-and-red markers, which lead you to a place above the chaos of rocks. Climb over polished stones to a minor pass (**2250m**) and soon after this the path goes down. Pass a pluviometer (a device for measuring rainfall), cross a stream and climb again to arrive at a large pass: the **Couillade de Pédourès** (2265m). Descend ESE on a clear path that bends a little to the left, to reach

6.30 Étang de Pédourès (2165m), which has a small dam on its east side. Walk above the north shore a little distance from the lake and descend SE through a small valley along the **Ruisseau de Val d'Arques**. Beyond a small plateau the path bends a little away from the stream and goes down gently. Continue to a small dammed lake and walk above its north shore, then continue descending SE until you arrive at an old stone bridge on the stream.

Cross the stream, go S down an obvious path, walk underneath an EDF (Electricité de France) pipeline, and arrive at a footbridge on the Ruisseau de Sisca (**1740m**). Cross the bridge and go ESE down to the village of l'Hospitalet, walking twice below the same pipeline. Arrive at a road near the village (signpost); cross the road, walk a few metres to the right, then turn left and follow a small road that brings you to the centre of

8.20 l'Hospitalet-près-l'Andorre (1436m). Walk along past the church and turn left and then right to reach the gîte d'étape l'Hospitalité, tel 06 74 87 05 05, . It's a very fine, comfortable gîte with great food.

The campsite is located outside of the village: continue walking past the gîte, cross the railway, turn right and follow the N20 for 600 metres until you find **Camping La Porte des Cimes** on your right. For more information about l'Hospitalet see the introduction to this section.

SECTION 5: L'HOSPITALET-PRÈS-L'ANDORRE TO BANYULS-SUR-MER

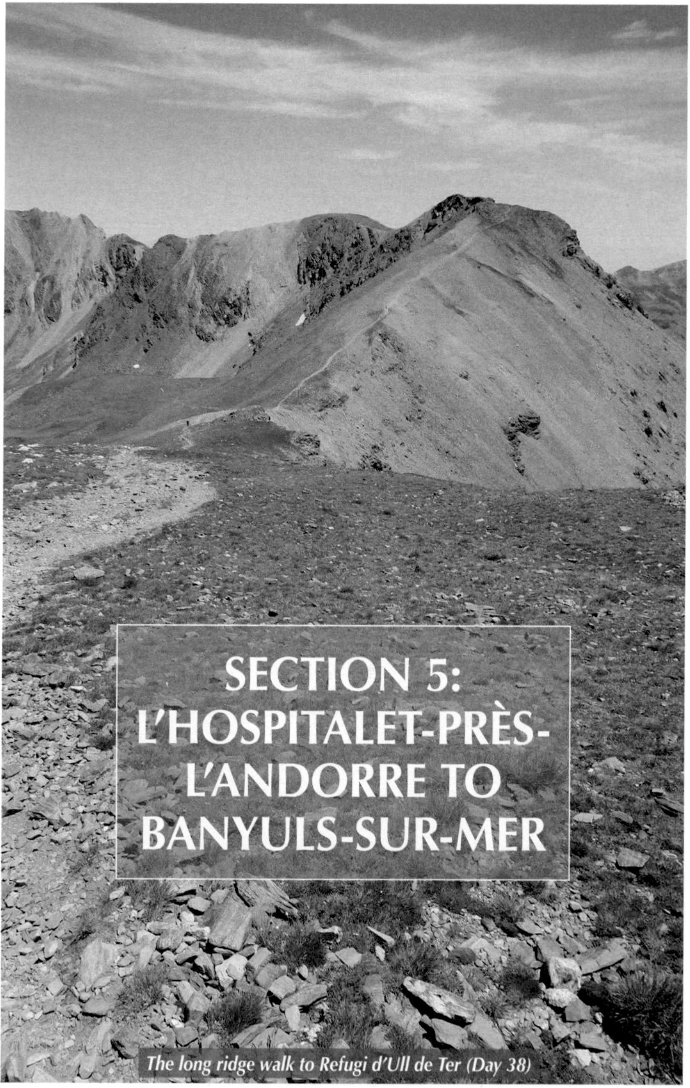

The long ridge walk to Refugi d'Ull de Ter (Day 38)

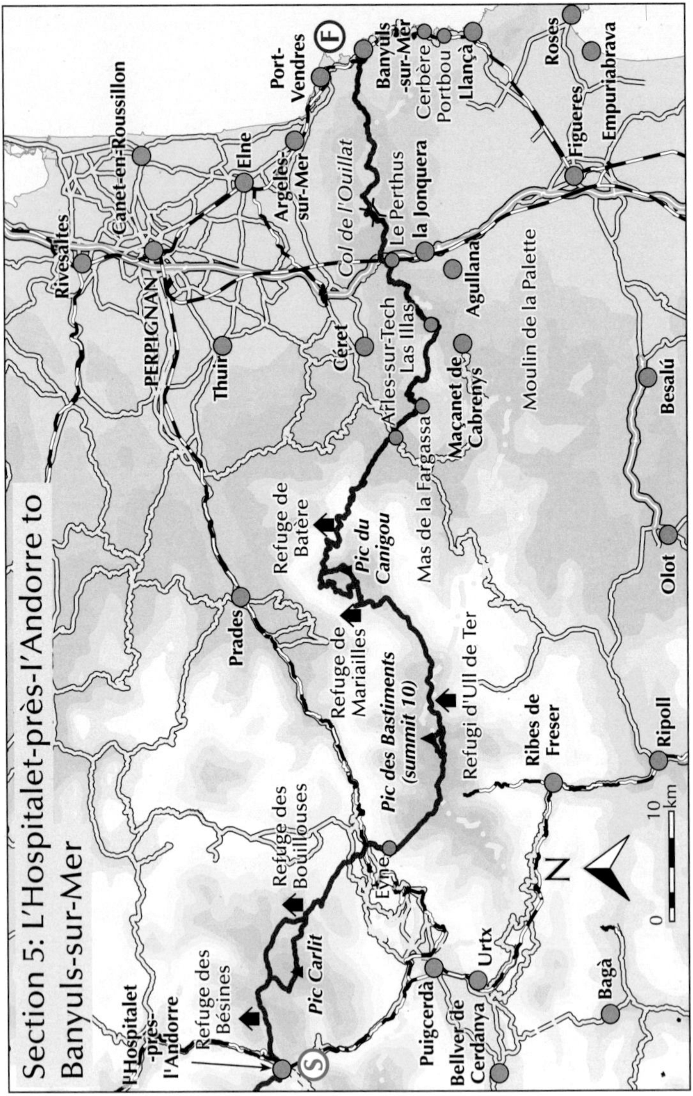
Section 5: L'Hospitalet-près-l'Andorre to Banyuls-sur-Mer
L'Hospitalet-près-l'Andorre
Refuge des Bésines
Pic Carlit
Refuge des Bouillouses
Eyne
Puigcerdà
Bellver de Cerdanya
Urtx
Bagà
Pic des Bastiments (summit 10)
Refugi d'Ull de Ter
Ribes de Freser
Ripoll
Refuge de Mariailles
Prades
Pic du Canigou
Refuge de Batère
Mas de la Fargassa
Olot
Arles-sur-Tech
Las Illas
Maçanet de Cabrenys
Moulin de la Palette
Besalú
Thuir
PERPIGNAN
Rivesaltes
Canet-en-Roussillon
Céret
Elne
Argelès-sur-Mer
Col de l'Ouillat
Le Perthus
la Jonquera
Agullana
Port-Vendres
Banyuls-sur-Mer
Cerbère
Portbou
Llançà
Figueres
Roses
Empuriabrava
0
10
km
N

THROUGH THE EASTERN PYRENEES TO THE MEDITERRANEAN SEA

Every stage of the Haute Route has its challenges and this fifth and last one is no different. First, the walk from l'Hospitalet-près-l'Andorre to Banyuls-sur-Mer is long. The 10 days (some quite long) described in this section make it the longest of the five. Secondly, there are a few serious obstacles to be tackled.

The most challenging mountain appears on the second day: Pic Carlit, at 2921m the highest mountain of the eastern Pyrenees. The impressive west face of Pic Carlit might well appear intimidating. In case of bad weather, there is an easy variant by which you can avoid Pic Carlit (Variant 6). Other high, but less difficult obstacles are found on Day 38, when you do a classic walk in the Catalonian mountains that involves a long stretch on the frontier ridge. On Day 40 you finally have to face one of the most famous mountains of the Pyrenees: Pic du Canigou (2784m). The Haute Route leads to the summit of this mountain.

Furthermore, the weather conditions in the eastern Pyrenees could turn the final section into a real battle. Beyond the Carlit massif, the climate gradually becomes Mediterranean. In short, this means heat and drought. Particularly on the last three days, the high temperatures and fewer water points can add extra challenges. All you can do is make a very early start in order to take advantage of the relative coolness of the early morning and refill water bottles at every opportunity.

The steep Esquerdes de Rotja on the way to Pla Guilhem (Day 39)

Overall, this last section of the Haute Route is a long walk that is not suitable for beginners and demands thorough preparation. For Haute Route walkers walking the entire route, it is a final test.

One of the most thrilling moments is the first time you catch sight of the Mediterranean Sea. If you have clear weather, it can be as soon as Day 39, from Refugi d'Ull de Ter. On the last day you will very often catch glimpses of the blue ocean as you leave the last mountains and hills behind, and later, walking through vineyards, you will see the final destination getting closer and closer. As you reach the streets of Banyuls-sur-Mer, you may well already start to miss the mountain magic. But when you finally dive into the Mediterranean Sea you'll be celebrating the journey you've completed.

If your feet are still itchy after reaching Banyuls, you can follow the Sentier Littoral (coastal trail, yellow marks) which explores the magnificent Côte Vermeille. You can either hike north towards the sandy beaches of Les Elmes and the villages of Port-Vendres, Coullioure and Argelès-sur-Mer, or South to Cerbère, the last village before the Spanish border.

PRACTICAL INFORMATION

Public transport to l'Hospitalet-près-l'Andorre

There is a railway service from Paris (Gare Austerlitz) to Latour-de-Carol. This train has a stop in l'Hospitalet-près-l'Andorre.

Facilities in l'Hospitalet-près-l'Andorre

There is a basic campsite north of the village, a tiny food shop, a post office, cash dispenser, hotel and a gîte d'étape.

Facilities in Banyuls-sur-Mer

For information on Banyuls, see www.banyuls-sur-mer.com.

It's a 1.5km walk from the beach to the campsite. Go back on the GR10 trail to the tunnel underneath the railway. Don't go through the tunnel but turn left and follow the road along the railway until you reach another tunnel underneath the railway. Turn right, go through the tunnel and go straight ahead. Turn right at the roundabout and continue to Camping Municipal 'La Pinède', tel 04 68 88 32 13. There is a supermarket on the other side of the road.

Public transport from Banyuls-sur-Mer

There is a train service from Banyuls-sur-Mer to Paris (Gare de Lyon).

Variants

Variant 6 is a bad-weather alternative to the Day 36 main route, following the GR10 trail from Refuge des Bésines to the Refuge des Bouillouses. The GR10 is also followed on Variant 7, a bad-weather alternative on Day 40, from Refuge de Mariailles to Refuge des Cortalets.

Classic summits

Pic des Bastiments (2881m) can be climbed on Day 38, leaving the main route at Pic de la Vaca and rejoining at Coll de la Marrana.

Food

Replenishment of food supplies is possible in Bolquère (Day 37, good shop), Arles-sur-Tech (Day 41, several shops) and Le Perthus (Day 43, several shops).

Maps

Rando Editions Carte de Randonnées, 1:50,000, no 8: Cerdagne–Capcir; Rando Editions Carte de Randonnées, 1:50,000, no 10: Canigou; Rando Editions Carte de Randonnées, 1:50,000, no 11: Roussillon.

Accomodation: contact details

All numbers and other information on accommodation on the Haute Route are also given in the route description.

- L'Hospitalet-près-l'Andorre: Gîte l'Hospitalité – tel 06 74 87 05 05
- Day 35: Refuges des Bésines – tel 09 88 77 35 28
- Day 36: Refuge des Bouillouses – tel 04 68 04 93 88; Auberge du Carlit – tel 04 68 04 22 23
- Day 37: Cal Paï – tel 06 08 82 00 99 and Gîte du Presbytère – tel 06 98 57 39 60
- Day 38: Refugi d'Ull de Ter – tel 619 51 49 59
- Day 39: Refuge de Mariailles – tel 04 68 05 57 99
- Day 40: Refuge des Cortalets – tel 04 68 96 36 19; Refuge de Batère tel 04 68 39 12 01
- Day 41: Camping Mas de la Fargassa – tel 04 68 31 01 15
- Day 42: Hostal dels Trabucayres –tel 04 68 66 55 38 and gîte d'étape – tel 07 76 09 65 81
- Day 43: Le Chalet de l'Albère – tel 04 68 83 62 20
- Banyuls-sur-Mer: Camping Municipal 'La Pinède' – tel 04 68 88 32 13

DAY 35

L'Hospitalet-près-l'Andorre to Refuge des Bésines

Start	L'Hospitalet-près-l'Andorre
Distance	7.5km
Total ascent	855m
Total descent	185m
Grade	1
Time	3hr
Map	Rando Editions Carte de Randonnées, 1:50,000, no 8: Cerdagne–Capcir
Route	Via Étang des Bésines (1973m)

The final section of the Haute Route begins with a very simple, short walk to a modern manned hut.

0.00 L'Hospitalet-près-l'Andorre (1436m). Turn right from the gîte d'étape, then turn right again after a few metres and go up the stairs following a signpost that

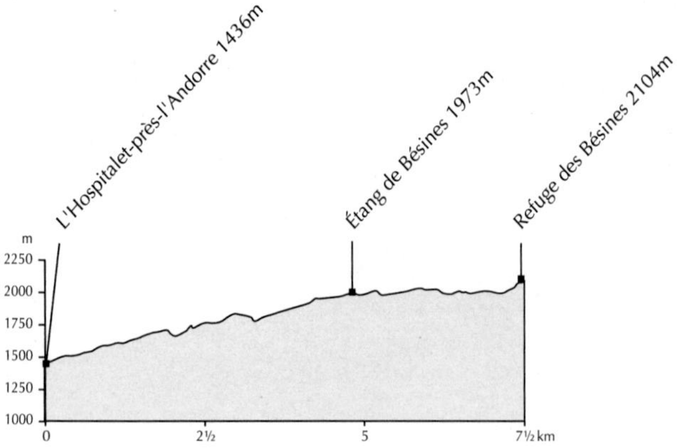

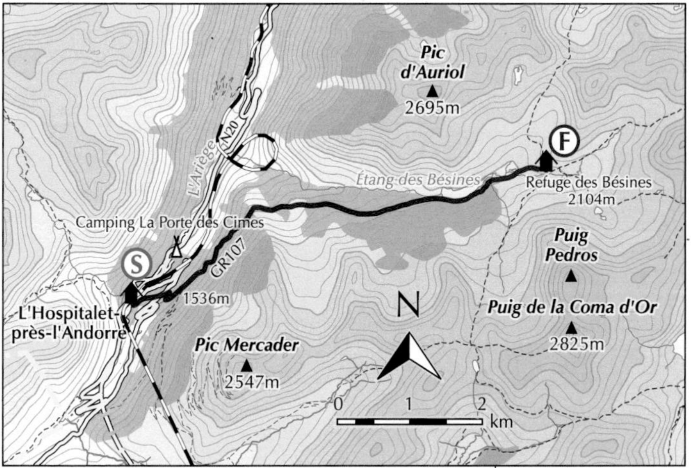

indicates the route to Refuge de Bésines. (If you spent the night at the campsite, walk back to the village along the N20, cross the railway and turn right just before Hotel du Puymorens. Turn left before you reach the gîte d'étape and find the signpost and stairs in front of you.) Leave the village and climb on a narrow path that reaches the N22, then cross the road and climb a few minutes until you arrive at a

0.30 junction at 1536m. Turn left and follow a large track (GR107, white-and-red marks) that climbs gently NE. Turn left at a junction (signpost) and climb on an easy-to-follow path in a forest. Eventually the path bends to the right, and in an open spot you cross a stream. Climb through grass and enter the forest again, then climb a little and walk E for about 30min on an almost level path to

2.25 Étang des Bésines (1973m). The path arrives at the small dam on the west side of the lake; walk along the south shore and then walk E through the beautiful flat area east of the lake. Cross a stream by a footbridge on the east side of the plateau and climb between pine trees to

Étang des Bésines

3.00 Refuge des Bésines (2104m), a modern hut, manned from June to the end of September, owned by the FFCAM, 55 places, tel 09 88 77 35 28.

Today you can either have a short hike and a long rest, or you might prefer to hike part of tomorrow's route. There are many beautiful places to pitch a tent before you reach Pic Carlit. Étang des Fourats, just before the final climb to Pic Carlit, is a particularly good choice.

DAY 36

Refuge des Bésines to Refuge des Bouillouses

Start	Refuge des Bésines
Distance	19km
Total ascent	1280m
Total descent	1380m
Grade	3
Time	8hr 45min
Map	Rando Editions Carte de Randonnées, 1:50,000, no 8: Cerdagne–Capcir
Route	Via the Col de Coume d'Agnel (2470m) and Pic Carlit (2921m)
Note	There are very steep slopes on both sides of Pic Carlit. If the weather is poor, follow Variant 6 from Refuge des Bésines to the Lac des Bouillouses.

A long, physically demanding stage that includes the exciting climb to Pic Carlit. You will see numerous lakes, all of which have their own character: from the enourmous Étang de Lanoux and the charming Étang des Fourats to the 13 lakes of the Désert du Carlit.

0.00 Refuge des Bésines. ▸ Go down a few metres in front of the hut and turn left at the signpost. Follow the GR10, which descends E to the floor of a narrow valley. Follow a stream as you climb and soon arrive at a junction with a signpost; ignore the path that branches off to the right and keep following the GR10 as it climbs NE.

Variant 6 describes a bad-weather alternative route from the Refuge des Bésines to the Refuge des Bouillouses following the GR10.

Arrive on a small plateau with the Ruisseau de Coume d'Agnel running slowly through it. Don't cross the plateau but stay on the north side of it and continue to climb NE, finally crossing the stream. Climb steeply until you reach a tiny lake (2400m) in a rocky area, then walk along the south shore of the lake and follow the white-and-red marks of the GR10 on rocks and stones as you climb to the large

View from the Col de Coume d'Agnel

Snow tends to last well into summer just below the pass.

1.30 Col de Coume d'Agnel (2470m, signpost). ◂ Descend on an obvious path, ignore a path branching off to the left (yellow-and-red marks) and walk towards the north side of a giant lake: the Étang de Lanoux. On your way down you'll pass **Estany de**

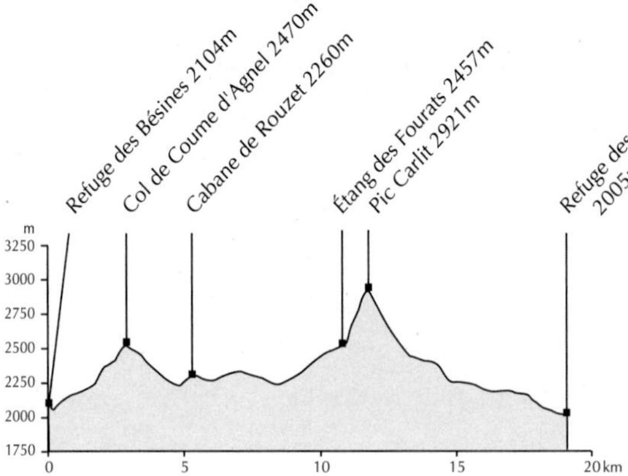

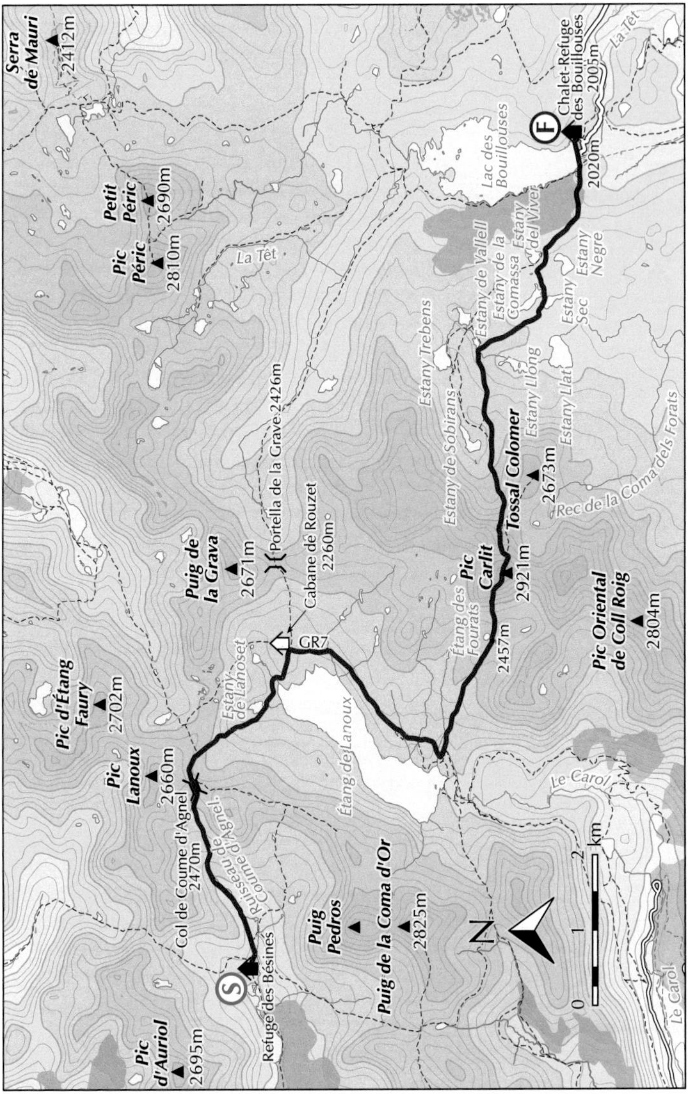
Serra de Mauri
2412m
Petit Péric
2690m
Pic Péric
2810m
La Têt
Chalet-Refuge des Bouillouses
2005m
La Têt
Lac des Bouillouses
2020m
Estany del Viver
Estany de la Comassa
Estany de Vallell
Estany Negre
Estany Sec
Estany Trebens
Estany Llong
Estany Llat
Estany de Sobirans
Tossal Colomer
2673m
Rec de la Coma dels Forats
Portella de la Grave 2426m
Cabane de Rouzet
2260m
Puig de la Grava
2671m
Pic Carlit
2921m
Étang des Fourats
2457m
Pic Oriental de Coll Roig
2804m
GR7
Estany de Lanoset
Étang de Lanoux
Pic d'Étang Faury
2702m
Pic Lanoux
2660m
Col de Coume d'Agnel
2470m
Ruisseau de Coume d'Agnel
Le Carol
Puig Pedros
Puig de la Coma d'Or
2825m
N
0
1
2 km
Refuge des Bésines
Pic d'Auriol
2695m
Le Carol

Lanoset. Keep the lake (with excellent places to bivouac) on your left-hand side, cross the outflow and continue towards the Étang de Lanoux.

Follow the path on the north side of the lake as it goes down, crosses a stream and arrives at a junction (signpost). Turn right and after a short climb go down to **Cabane de Rouzet** (2260m, sometimes in use by a shepherd). There's a junction in front of the hut: leave the GR10 (unless you'd prefer to take Variant 6), which climbs E to the Portella de la Grave, and instead follow a well-worn track above the east shore of **Étang de Lanoux** (2213m). You are now following the GR7 (white-and-red marks).

The path goes up and down for a while and crosses several streams. Finally, just before reaching the dam on the south side of the lake, go down to a small plateau with a stream meandering through it. Turn left, cross the stream and reach a small dam. Turn left again, leave the GR7 (which makes a turn to the right) and follow the Ruisseau des Fourats as you climb E on a path marked with cairns. Cross the stream on a small plateau and climb E on a path that bends away from the stream, to arrive at

4.30 Étang des Fourats (2457m), which marks the final climb to Pic Carlit. Walk along the south shore of the lake, heading E and straight ahead to Pic Carlit. It's a wonderful climb of extremes: steep and challenging, but also fun and very rewarding. Beware of stonefall as there is a lot of scree. Follow plenty of zigzags with some cairns to guide you, and finally the ascent eases a little. Climb to a pass (2910m) just below the summit of Pic Carlit (notice a small stone windbreak on your left, where it's possible to pitch a small tent). From the pass, turn right and climb to the highest summit of the eastern Pyrenees:

In the right conditions you can see the Mediterranean Sea from the summit. There are also fantastic views of the Désert du Carlit, Pico d'Estats and Andorra.

6.00 Pic Carlit (2921m, metal cross). ◀ Return to the pass, go down on a very steep scree slope on the east side of Pic Carlit and soon arrive on a ridge. Continue to descend on this very steep ridge, using your hands here and there. On finally leaving the ridge, the route bends a little to the left, crosses a tiny stream at a lake where

The impressive route to Pic Carlit as seen from Étang des Fourats

snow tends to linger, and goes down E in zigzags on a stony slope.

The stones eventually turn into grass, and the path forks (2370m). There are yellow marks from here to Bouillouses. Don't turn left on a path that descends to Estany de Soubirans (2340m) but walk E until you arrive at the tiny **Estany de Vallell** (2220m) and keep the lake on your left-hand side. Cross a stream (signpost) and after a short climb go down on an obvious track to the **Estany Sec** and **Estany de la Comassa**. Walk between the lakes and, a little later, between **Estany Negre** and **Estany del Viver**, and continue to descend in a pine forest ESE to the dam of another giant lake:

The Désert du Carlit with its 13 lakes

8.35 Lac des Bouillouses (2020m). Pass a hotel/bar/restaurant on the right which has a dormitory for walkers (Les Bones Hores, tel 04 68 04 24 22) and walk along the dam to

8.45 Refuge des Bouillouses (2005m), 200 metres SE of the Lac des Bouillouses, beside a small road (D60). The refuge is owned by the FFCAM and has 59 places, meals available, tel 04 68 04 93 88. Auberge du Carlit, only 50 metres SE of the lake, also offers accommodation and meals (40 places, tel 04 68 04 22 23).

VARIANT 6

GR10 to Refuge des Bouillouses

Start	Refuge des Bésines (Day 35/36)
Finish	Refuge des Bouillouses (Day 36/37)
Distance	16km
Total ascent	760m
Total descent	835m
Grade	2
Time	6hr 10min
Map	Rando Editions Carte de Randonnées, 1:50,000, no 8: Cerdagne–Capcir
Route	Via the Col de Coume d'Agnel (2470m) and the Portella de la Grave (2426m)

The GR10 trail from Refuge des Bésines to the Refuge des Bouillouses is a bad-weather alternative to the main route. It is a walk on obvious tracks.

0.00 Refuge des Bésines. Go down a few metres in front of the hut and turn left at the signpost. Follow the GR10,

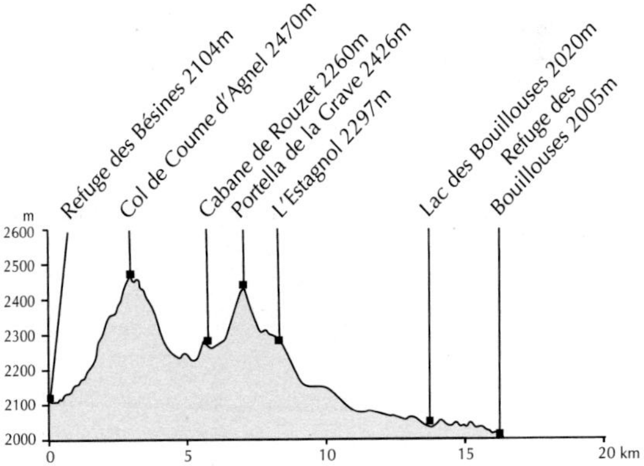

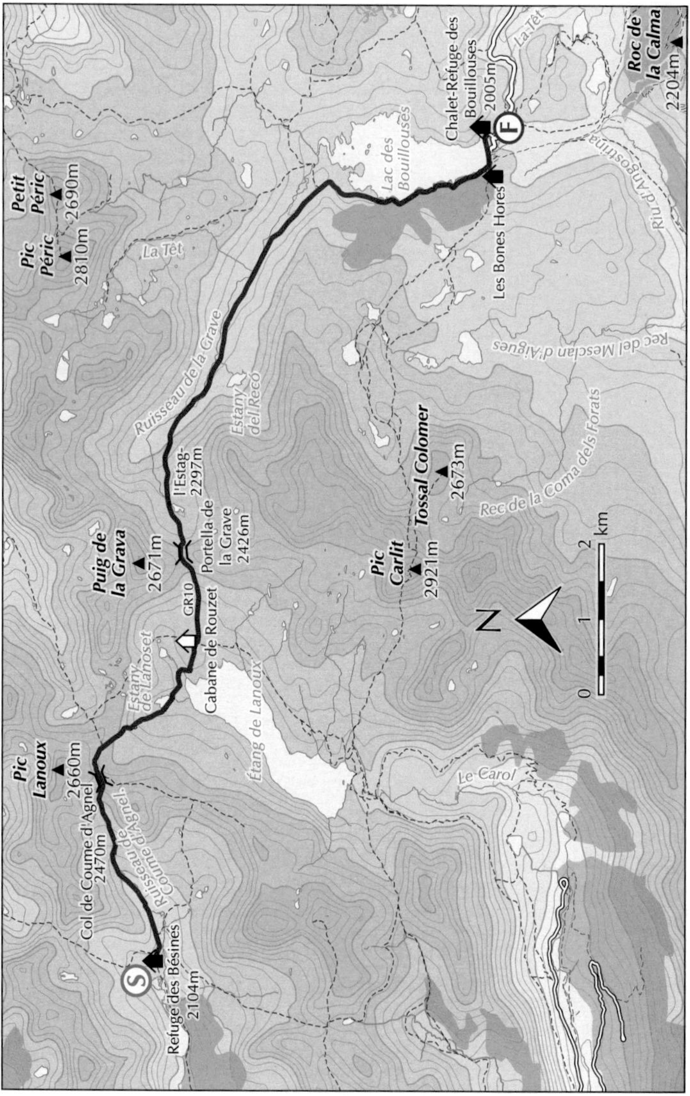

Refuge des Bésines
2104m
Col de Coume d'Agnel
2470m
Ruisseau de Coume d'Agnel
Pic Lanoux
2660m
Estany de Lanoset
Étang de Lanoux
Cabane de Rouzet
GR10
Puig de la Grava
2671m
Portella de la Grave
2426m
l'Estag-
2297m
Ruisseau de la Grave
Estany del Recò
La Têt
Pic Péric
2810m
Petit Péric
2690m
Pic Carlit
2921m
Tossal Colomer
2673m
Rec de la Coma dels Forats
Rec del Mesclan d'Aigues
Le Carol
Lac des Bouillouses
Les Bones Hores
Chalet-Refuge des Bouillouses
2005m
Riu d'Angostrina
Roc de la Calma
2204m
N
0
1
2
km

which descends E to the floor of a narrow valley. Follow a stream as you climb and soon soon at a junction with a signpost; ignore the path that branches off to the right and keep following the GR10 as it climbs NE.

Arrive on a small plateau with the Ruisseau de Coume d'Agnel running slowly through it. Don't cross the plateau but stay on the north side of it and continue to climb NE, finally crossing the stream. Climb steeply until you reach a tiny lake (2400m) in a rocky area, then walk along the south shore of the lake and follow the white-and-red marks of the GR10 on rocks and stones as you climb to the large

1.30 Col de Coume d'Agnel (2470m, signpost). ▸ Descend on an obvious path, ignore a path branching off to the left (yellow-and-red marks) and walk towards the north side of a giant lake: the Étang de Lanoux. On your way down you'll pass **Estany de Lanoset**. Keep the lake (with excellent places to bivouac) on your left-hand side, cross the outflow and continue towards the Étang de Lanoux.

Snow tends to last well into summer just below the pass.

Follow the path on the north side of the lake as it goes down, crosses a stream and arrives at a junction (signpost). Turn right and after a short climb go down to a shepherds' hut, **Cabane de Rouzet** (2260m, sometimes in use by a shepherd). Stay on the GR10, turn left and follow an obvious path that climbs E towards the Portella de la Grave, which can be seen from a distance. The easy climb ends at the:

3.00 Portella de la Grave (2426m). Descend steeply on the east side of the pass; the track soon bends a little to the left, eases somewhat and goes down ENE to a small lake:

3.20 L'Estagnol (2297m). North of the lake the GR10 bends to the right. Cross a stream and descend gently SE on a path in an open landscape with the **Ruisseau de la Grave** below on your left all the time. As you come closer to the Lac des Bouillouses, more and more pine trees appear in the valley. Cross several minor streams on your way down, then climb a few metres and you'll see the giant

5.20 Lac des Bouillouses (2020m). Go down towards the lake and soon arrive at a junction. Turn right and walk along the lake, which is 3km long. The path goes up and down between pine trees and finally arrives at the SW side of the lake. Pass a hotel/bar/restaurant on the left (**Les Bones Hores**) and walk along the dam to the

6.10 Refuge des Bouillouses (2005m), 200 metres SE of the Lac des Bouillouses, beside a small road (D60). The refuge is owned by the FFCAM and has 59 places, meals available, tel 04 68 04 93 88. Auberge du Carlit, only 50 metres SE of the lake, also offers accommodation and meals (40 places, tel 04 68 04 22 23).

DAY 37

Refuge des Bouillouses to Eyne

Start	Refuge des Bouillouses
Distance	17km
Total ascent	370m
Total descent	815m
Grade	1
Time	4hr 45min
Map	Rando Editions Carte de Randonnées, 1:50,000, no 8: Cerdagne–Capcir
Route	Via the village of Bolquère and the Col de la Perche (1579m)

A short, easy walk on tracks, road and dirt road. On the first part of the walk you are treated to a series of beautiful lakes. As the GR10 descends towards the Plateau de Cerdagne – a large plateau and the first real rupture in the mountain chain – the route slowly enters civilisation. It might take some getting used to after the mountain wilderness you've experienced. The authentic village of Eyne is a great place to rest and stay overnight, and bivouacking is allowed above 2000m in the nature reserve closeby.

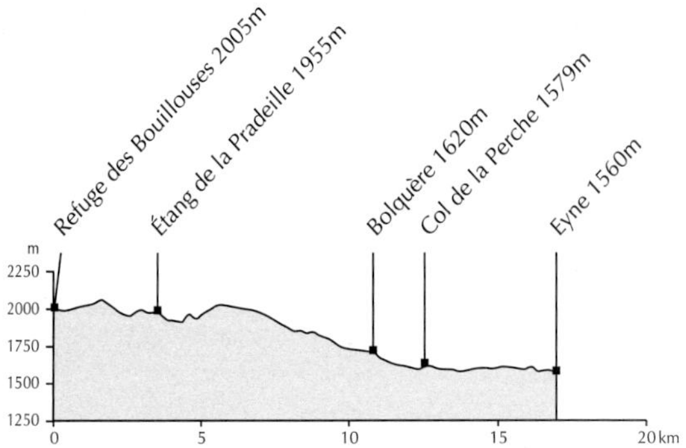

0.00 Refuge des Bouillouses. From the refuge, go down for a few minutes on the D60 until you notice a footbridge on the right side of the road. Leave the road, cross the bridge and follow a broad track. After about 40 metres the route forks; leave the GR10, turn left and climb through a pine forest on a path with yellow marks. Notice Étang Racou at a distance on your right, and a little later go down steeply to the lovely **Étang Long** (Estany Llong). Walk along the south shore of the lake and go down between pine trees to the much larger **Étang Noir** (Estany Nègre). Turn right, walk along the west shore of the lake, and when you are at the south side, the path suddenly bends away from the lake. Climb a few metres and follow the marks SW to the next large lake:

1.00 Étang de Pradeille (1955m, also called Estany de la Pradella). The Haute Route and GR10 meet again S of Étang de Pradeille on a broad track (signpost); turn left and follow this track (in fact more of a dirt road) E. It climbs initially a little and then goes down. Ignore the path that branches off to the Col del Pam (signpost) and keep walking in the same direction. Don't turn left at the next junction but go straight ahead.

Cross a ski piste, walk under a ski lift and follow the dirt road until you arrive at a junction, where several dirt

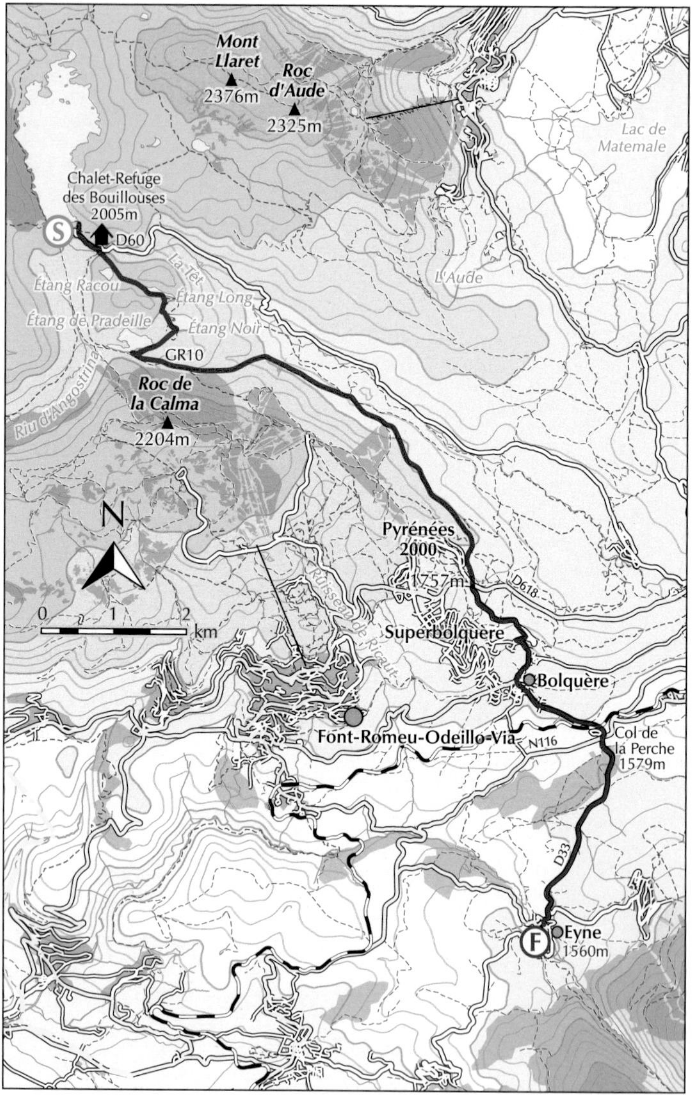
Mont
Llaret
2376m
Roc
d'Aude
2325m
Lac de
Matemale
Chalet-Refuge
des Bouillouses
2005m
S
D60
La Têt
Étang Racou
Étang Long
Étang de Pradeille
Étang Noir
L'Aude
GR10
Roc de
la Calma
2204m
Riu d'Angostrina
N
0
1
2
km
Pyrénées
2000
1757m
D618
Ruisseau de Ricaut
Superbolquère
Bolquère
Font-Romeu-Odeillo-Via
N116
Col de
la Perche
1579m
D33
F
Eyne
1560m

The Sainte-Eulalie church in Bolquère

roads meet. Turn right and climb SE on a dirt road. Notice a ski lift on your right and climb very gently for about 2km through the pine forest.

Beyond the highest point, turn right, still following the GR10, and follow a path alongside a few chalets of the Pyrénées 2000 resort. Arrive at a junction, go straight ahead and soon arrive at a junction of tarmac roads (1757m). Walk S and follow the D10c (towards Bolquère) for 10min, then leave the road, turn right and take a shortcut to miss out a hairpin. Cross the same road, take the next shortcut and enter the village of Bolquère. Continue S and walk towards the centre of

3.55 Bolquère (1620m). The GR10 goes through the village (in the centre there's a good shop, opposite the post office, and it's possible to bivouac close to the church – ask the shopkeeper). Pass the village hall (Mairie) and walk SE on the D10. ▶ Cross the railway and soon arrive at the

Notice the Bolquère-Eyne railway station on your right – France's highest regular railway station (1592m).

4.10 Col de la Perche (1579m, hotels, bars and restaurants). Cross the N116, leave the GR10 (which branches off to the left), and follow the D33 for about 3km until you arrive at the hamlet of

4.45 Eyne (1560m). There is usually an exhibition worth visiting in Maison de la Vallée d'Eyne, and there's a good restaurant in the same building. There are two hostels in the upper section of Eyne: Cal Paï (30 places, tel 06 08 82 00 99) and Gîte du Presbytère (excellent meals, tel 06 98 57 39 60; make your reservation well in advance).

Although it's appealing to stay overnight in Eyne, another good option is to continue on tomorrow's route and pitch the tent somewhere in Vallée d'Eyne – near l'Orri de Baix (2040m, a primitive stone shelter), for example. In the Eyne natural reserve walkers are allowed to pitch a small tent for the night only above 2000m.

DAY 38

Eyne to Refugi d'Ull de Ter

Start	Eyne
Distance	20km
Total ascent	1785m
Total descent	1125m
Grade	3
Time	8hr 15min
Map	Rando Editions Carte de Randonnées, 1:50,000, no 8: Cerdagne–Capcir
Route	Via the Col d'Eyne (2683m), the Col de Noufonts (2652m), the Col de Nou Creus (2796m), the Col de Tirapitz (2783m) and the Col de la Marrana (2535m)

A delightful stage that includes a long walk on a high ridge that forms the French-Spanish border. A true classic in the Catalonian mountains, this high ridge walk offers magnificent views, wonderful colours and surprisingly smooth paths. The route follows the GR11 from the Col de Noufonts to Refugi d'Ull de Ter. The last in the series of classic summits is described at the end of this route and is at the same time an alternative route between Pic de la Vaca and Col de la Marrana. On a fine day, the climb to Les Bastiments (2881m) is a great bonus.

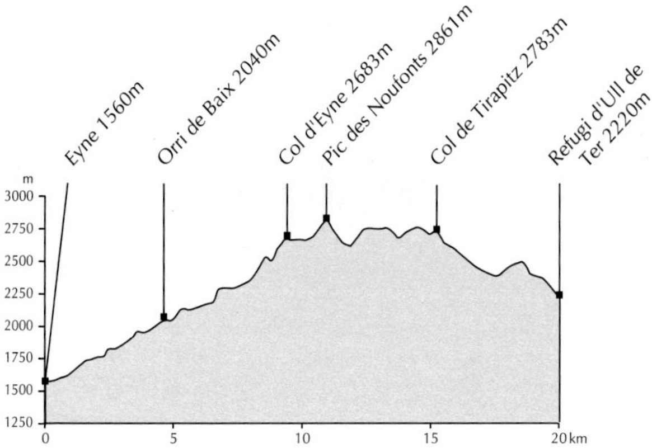

0.00 Eyne. Go down SE through the village on the D33 road that links Eyne with the village of Llo. Turn left, walk S on this road, cross a stream by a bridge and turn left again. Walk S between pastures on a large track that leads to the Réserve Naturelle de Vallée d'Eyne (just follow the signposts). Soon you'll enter a forest, and the path climbs a little steeper.

The path becomes smaller and you arrive at a junction where a large track joins from the right. Keep walking S, go through a gate in a fence and climb gently until you reach a stream that runs through a narrow valley. Cross it and climb S on the obvious path through the forest and later on through an open valley. Notice at an altitude of 2040m, on the other side of the stream, at a distance:

2.00 Orri de Baix, a primitive stone shelter. Continue to ascend, still with the stream on your left-hand side. Climb along a small rock face and walk S on a gently rising path. Fine places for a bivouac are to be found here.

The valley narrows and the path climbs above the stream until the valley reopens. Arrive at a place (about 2300m) where another stream meets the stream you have been following. Cross the right-hand stream in an area that can be marshy, and climb E through grass. Cross a

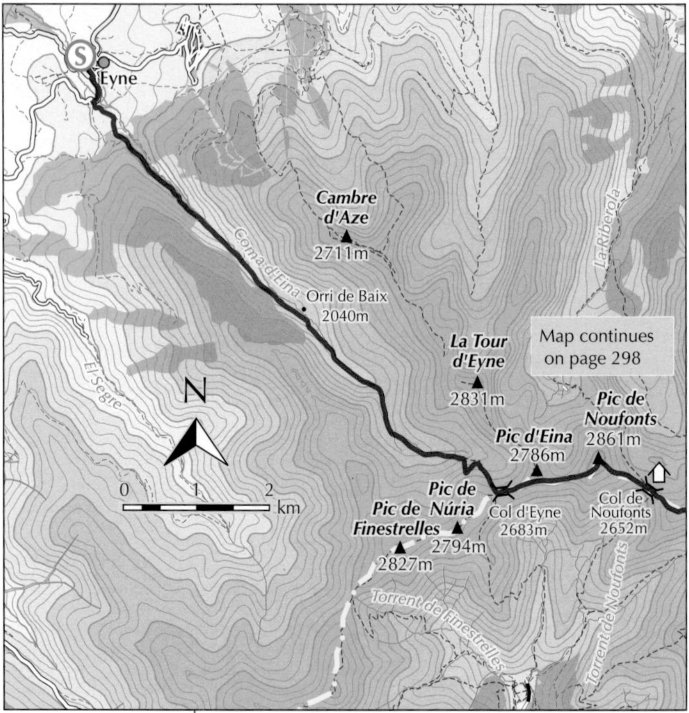

minor stream coming from the right (your last chance to take water for a long time!). The grass turns into scree as you work your way up to the Col d'Eyne. The last part of the climb is rather steep but not difficult; near the end the path bends to the right and climbs S to the

4.10 Col d'Eyne (2683m, also called Col de Nuria and Coll d'Eina), a broad saddle on the French-Spanish border between the Pic de Núria (2794m) and the Pic d'Eina (2786m). There is a signpost south of the pass: turn left and follow the ridge, initially without a path but soon you will find an easy-to-follow track. Notice a stone windbreak on your left; bivouacking on this ridgeline is an option if the weather permits.

The ridge walk to Refugi d'Ull de Ter keeps you high for a very long time

Arrive at a pass where the path forks. Don't turn left but keep the Pic d'Eina at a distance to your left. Follow the track that leaves the ridge, go around a minor summit and arrive again on the ridge at 2734m. Follow the ridge now E and climb through scree on a track which in the end bends a little to the left to reach the

4.50 Pic de Noufonts (2861m). Descend SE on the rather steep frontier ridge and arrive at the **Col de Noufonts** (2652m). Notice a stone cabane above the pass and find the white-and-red marks of the GR11, which you will follow to Refugi d'Ull de Ter. Don't turn right (that path goes down to Núria) but stay on the ridge, pass the *cabane* and climb steeply towards the Pic de Nou Creus (2799m). Beyond a minor pass the path, still on the ridge, goes up and down and arrives at the

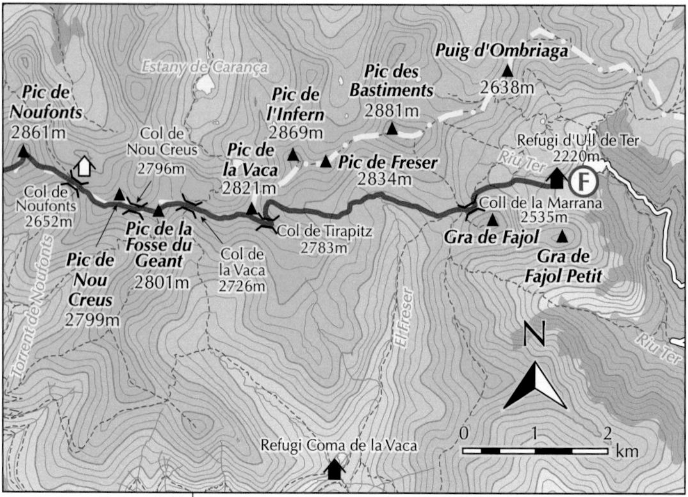

5.40 Col de Nou Creus (2796m, also called Col des Neuf Croix). Unsurprisingly, there are nine small crucifixes to be found there. Don't turn right to go down but follow the path that bends slightly to the left and goes 30 metres north of the **Pic de la Fosse du Geant** (2801m). Descend E to the **Col de la Vaca** (2726m), ignore the path that goes left to the Carança valley and another one that turns right to Refugi Coma de la Vaca, and climb rather steeply on the ridge on a brown slope towards the

6.15 Pic de la Vaca (2821m). ◂ It's not necessary to go all the way to the top; instead, go around the summit. East of the summit you have a wonderful view north of the Carança lakes. A few metres further E, for the first time since the Col d'Eyne, the path bends significantly away from the frontier ridge to go to a pass situated SE of the Pic de la Vaca:

The ascent of Pic des Bastiments starts here: it takes 2hr 55min to rejoin the Pyrenean Haute Route at Coll de la Marrana – see 'Summit 10'.

6.25 Col de Tirapitz (2783m). To the east you can see the route leading to the Coll de la Marrana. Descend steeply in Spain on a path that makes a sharp curve to the north, notice a round *cabane* at a distance to your left and go down E. After crossing several minor streams

Long views from the high ridge walk to Refugi d'Ull de Ter

you'll reach the floor of the Circo de Freser (2450m). Notice a variant of the GR11 coming from the right (from Refugi de Coma de Vaca) and climb from here E on rough terrain to arrive without any problems at the

7.40 Coll de la Marrana (2535m), situated between the Pic des Bastiments and the Pic Gra de Fajol. Descend NE, initially rather steeply, in the Circo d'Ull de Ter. The descent eases somewhat and finally you go down ESE to the

8.15 Refugi d'Ull de Ter (2220m), a hut owned by the CEC, manned from mid June until late September, meals available, 57 places, tel 619 51 49 59.

SUMMIT 10

Pic des Bastiments (2881m)

Start	Pic de la Vaca (Day 38)
Finish	Coll de la Marrana (Day 38)
Distance	5km
Total ascent	345m
Total descent	605m
Grade	F
Time	2hr 55min to the Coll de la Marrana
Warning	Parts of this route are exposed and there are sections of scrambling. Only experienced mountain walkers should undertake it.

The climb to Les Bastiments is a true high route. It has gained popularity in recent years, and for good reason: the route allows you to stay on the frontier ridge even longer, altogether you can summit three additional peaks and the scenery is magnificent. The hike is a bit more technical than today's route has been until now. A few scrambles and an exposed passage make it unsuitable for hikers who are not used to this type of terrain. For experienced hikers, the route will be pure fun. Unlike with most of the previous climbs, there's no need to go the same way down, as this route allows you to reach Coll de la Maranna a different way. From there, you continue the same route to Refugi d'Ull de Ter as described in Day 39.

Ahead, on your left, Pic de l'Infern is clearly visible, and to the right you can distinguish the wide Bastiments summit in the distance.

0.00 Pic de la Vaca (2821m). Turn left to leave the GR11, go around the summit of Pic de la Vaca and continue N and soon NE on the border ridge. ◂ Go down to 2720m and then start to climb again. At **2780m**, as you reach a passage with white rocks, turn to the left side of the ridge, go down a little and then climb steeply to an obvious path that again goes NE. Arrive at a pass (2840m) and then climb NE to the

0.45 Pic de l'Infern (2869m. Go back on the same route to the pass and descend E. Scramble a short way on a rocky section, reach the lowest point and climb E. Use

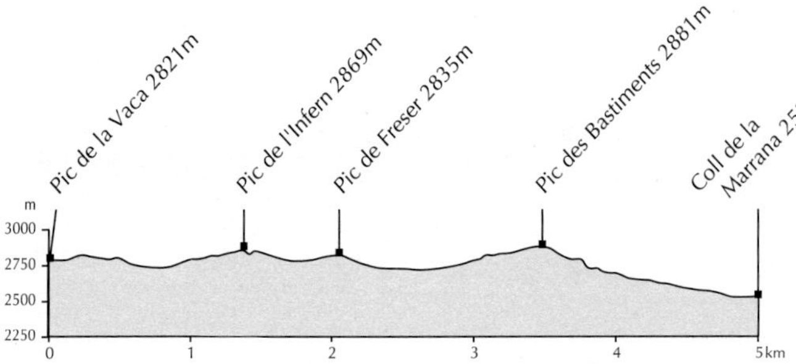

your hands again on a rocky, exposed section and then continue climbing E to

1.15 Pic de Freser (2835m). Descend NE, staying a few metres S of the ridge, until the path bends to the left and continues leading you down to the **Col de Coma Mitjana** (2704m). From the col, climb E on an obvious path to reach

2.15 Pic des Bastiments (2881m, also called Pic du Géant), a wide summit offering splendid views of the Carlit and Canigou massifs. ▶ Continue E past the actual

On a clear day you'll be able to spot the Mediterranean Sea.

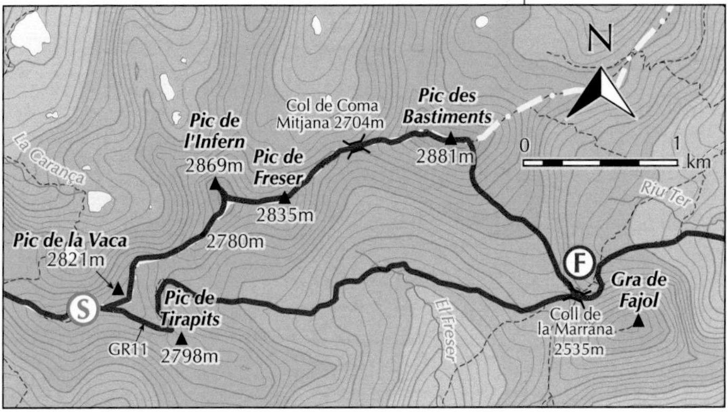

The high ridge hike to Bastiments from Pic de la Vaca: (from left to right) Pic de l'Infern, Pic de Freser and the wide summit of Bastiments

summit, turn right at a junction and go down SE on an obvious track to the

2.55 Coll de la Marrana (2535m). Here you rejoin the Day 38 route.

DAY 39

Refugi d'Ull de Ter to Refuge de Mariailles

Start	Refugi d'Ull de Ter
Distance	22km
Total ascent	820m
Total descent	1330m
Grade	2
Time	7hr 15min
Map	Rando Editions Carte de Randonnées, 1:50,000, no 10: Canigou
Route	Via the Porteille de Mourens (2383m) and the Pla Guilhem (2300m)

On today's route the possibilities for taking water are very limited, so take enough with you from the start. The Haute Route again stays high for a long time: above 2200m this time. Several large plateaux have to be crossed. Near the Roc Colom the route bends away from the French-Spanish border and goes NE towards a very popular French mountain: the Pic du Canigou (2784m).

0.00 Refugi d'Ull de Ter. Descend NE on the obvious GR11 track, cross the Riu Ter by a bridge and after about 20min reach a road (2080m) that links the village of Setcases with the ski resort of Vall Ter. Leave the GR11, turn left and climb on this road for 15min to the large parking area of Station de Vall Ter (2170m). On the right side of the building you'll find the start of the path (white-and-red marks).

Climb NE on an obvious, large track. Cross a stream (your last source of water for today) at an altitude of 2285m. Don't turn left to go to the Porteille de Mantet but climb E on a small path until you arrive at a large plateau, the Pla de Coma Armada. An obvious path in the grass brings you to the

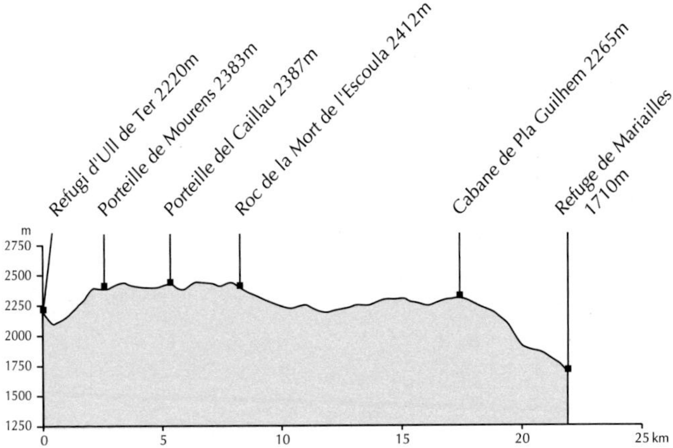

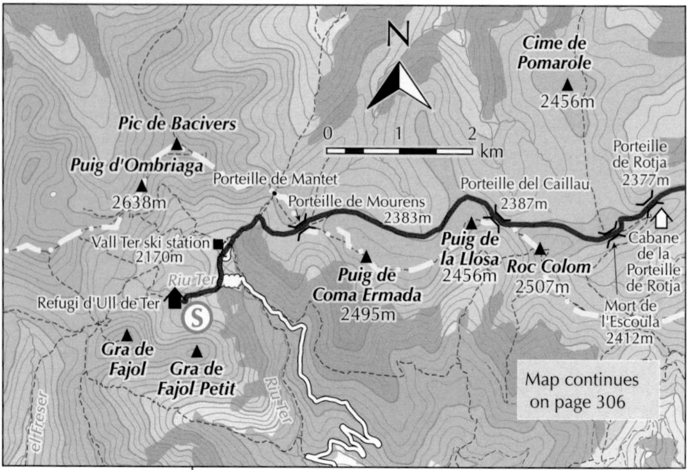

1.15 Porteille de Mourens (2383m, on the French-Spanish border). The path forks here; turn right at a sign that shows you're entering the Mantet natural reserve and climb a little E. The route has been marked with a line of large flat stones that have been set into the ground, and some cairns. Soon the path becomes level. Follow the marks that bend around the Puig de la Llosa (2456m) and reach the

2.15 Porteille del Caillau (2387m), situated south of the next plateau, the Pla de Campmagre. Walk E on a more or less level track and go around the Roc Colom (2507m, the last frontier summit higher than 2500m), ignore two tracks that stay level and follow the gently climbing track around Roc Colom. East of this mountain the rather vague path bends to the right and arrives at the Roc de la **Mort de l'Escoula** (2412m, signpost). Climb NE (no track), go through a gate in a fence and find a clear track that stays close to the ridge.

The path soon arrives a few metres below the **Porteille de Rotja** (2377m, small cabane on the other side of the pass). Keep the *porteille* on your right-hand side, go down a few metres and walk NE along the sharp, white ridge of the **Esquerdes de Rotja**. Keep close to this pointy ridge as you walk on an easy-to-follow and more or less level track.

Arrive on the ridge at the **Porteille des Avets** (signpost), keep left of the ridge and enter an area with pine trees. The path goes up and down and eventually you arrive on a dirt road. Turn right and walk a few metres to the

4.25 Collade des Roques Blanches (2252m, signpost). Turn left and follow the dirt road that climbs gently NNE. The road goes around the Puig de la Collada Verda (2403m) and leads to the **Collada del Vent** (2247m, signpost). After the dirt road has turned into a single track you again have flat stones to guide you. Follow these along a path to Pla Guilhem (2285m, signpost). The Haute Route turns N here and continues through grass. Cross a fence and walk to a small *cabane*:

5.45 Cabane de Pla Guilhem (2265m, a shepherd's hut which is closed). About 60 metres north of the cabane there's the solid, unmanned Refuge de Pla Guilhem (basic, 16 places). Continue in the same direction, now following white-and-red markers, to the **Col de**

Cabane de Pla Guilhem with its huge cairn

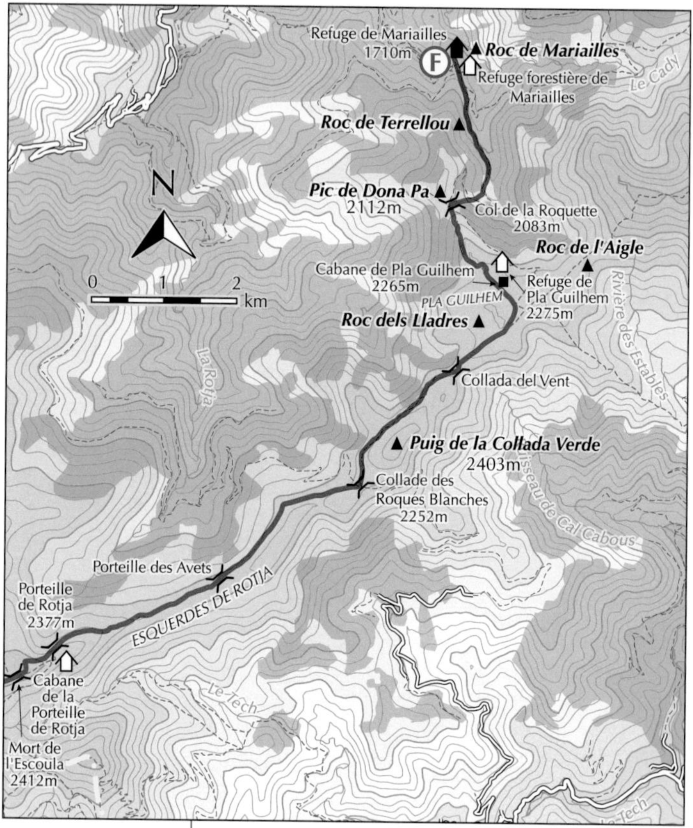

la Roquette (2083m), where you pass an iron cross (Croix de la Llipodère). Follow the path until you meet the dirt road again, and then carefully follow the white-and-red markers that immediately leave the dirt road to take a shortcut to the right.

Meet the dirt road again and immediately take another shortcut. Finally, you come back to the dirt road and turn left. Near the end of the walk you arrive at a junction of dirt roads (signpost); in front of you there's the refuge and on your right the Refuge Forestière de Mariailles (a solid building, part of which can be used by walkers). Go down in a straight line to

7.15 Refuge de Mariailles (1710m), manned from June until September, 53 places, tel 04 68 05 57 99.

DAY 40

Refuge de Mariailles to Refuge de Batère

Start	Refuge de Mariailles
Distance	27.5km
Total ascent	2025m
Total descent	2235m
Grade	3
Time	9hr 50min
Map	Rando Editions Carte de Randonnées, 1:50,000, no 10: Canigou
Route	Via the Pic du Canigou (2784m), Refuge des Cortalets (2150m) and the Col de la Cirère (1731m)
Note	The route involves sections of scrambling

A very long and strenuous hike that leads you over the Pic du Canigou (2784m). The final section of the climb is very steep and requires scrambling, but the descent from the top to Refuge des Cortalets (the classic route to the summit) is easy. This long walk can be cut in two by spending the night at Refuge des Cortalets. A bad-weather variant from Refuge de Mariailles to Refuge des Cortalets is described in Variant 7.

0.00 Refuge de Mariailles. ▸ From the refuge, walk back to the *refuge forestière*, where a signpost indicates the route to the Pic du Canigou. Take the left path, and after crossing the Ruisseau de Llipodère (1686m) by a footbridge the path bends to the left and climbs gently NE. Cross a minor stream after a short section SE and continue to climb NE to the **Col Vert** (1861m, signpost), where you arrive at a gate.

Variant 7 describes a bad-weather alternative route from the Refuge de Mariailles to the Refuge des Cortalets following the GR10.

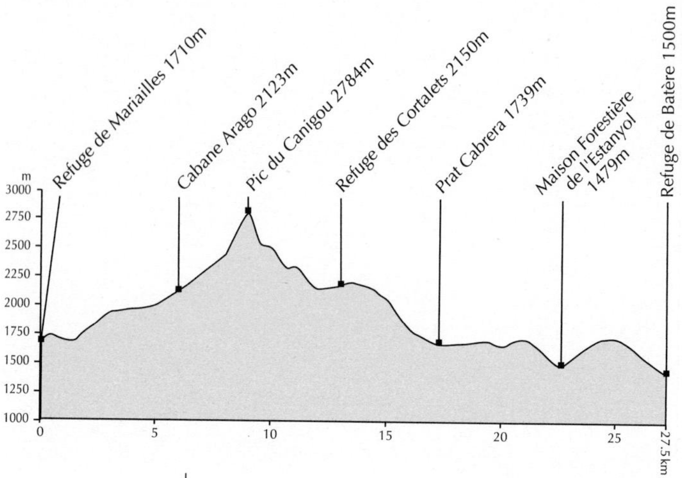

En route to the Canigou under the morning sun

Go through the gate and climb E on the clear path, passing several more gates, and go finally down a few metres to the Ruisseau de Cady (1964m, confluence of

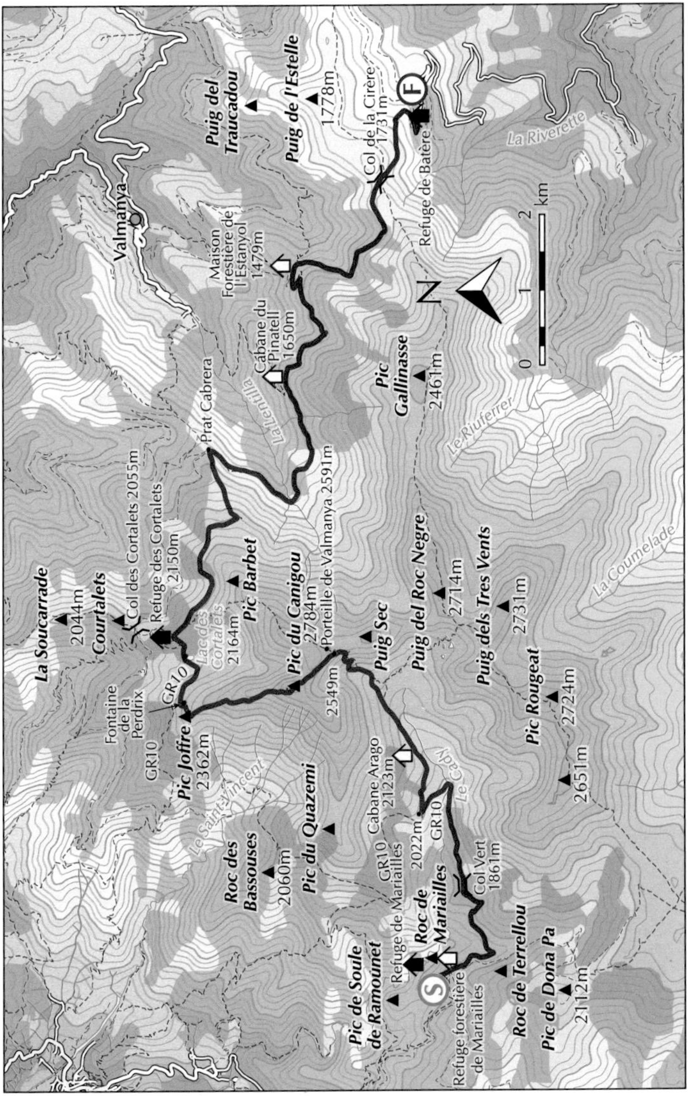
La Soucarrade
2044m
Courtalets
Col des Cortalets 2055m
Refuge des Cortalets
2150m
Fontaine
de la
Perdrix
GR10
GR10
Pic Joffre
2362m
Lac des
Cortalets
2164m
Pic Barbet
Pic du Canigou
2784m
Porteille de Valmanya 2591m
2549m
Prat Cabrera
La Lentilla
Cabane du
Pinatell
1650m
Maison
Forestière de
l'Estanyol
1479m
Valmanya
Puig del
Traucadou
Puig de l'Estelle
1778m
Col de la Cirère
1731m
Refuge de Batère
F
La Riverette
Pic
Gallinasse
2461m
Le Riuferrer
N
0
1
2
km
Puig Sec
Puig del Roc Negre
2714m
Puig dels Tres Vents
2731m
La Coumelade
Pic Rougeat
2724m
2651m
Le Cady
Cabane Arago
2123m
2022m
GR10
GR10
Le Saint-Vincent
Roc des
Bassouses
2060m
Pic du Quazemi
Col Vert
1861m
Roc de
Mariailles
Refuge de Mariailles
Pic de Soule
de Ramounet
S
Refuge forestière
de Mariailles
Roc de Terrellou
Pic de Dona Pa
2112m

two streams). Cross the streams and walk for about 15min NW on the GR10 trail. Leave the GR10 at a junction (**2022m**, signpost), turn right (the bad-weather variant starts here – see below) and climb on a path with yellow marks. Finally arrive at

There are many possibilities to pitch the tent here, and the next morning you can be the first to reach Pic du Canigou.

2.00 Cabane Arago (2123m, six places, small but cosy unmanned hut, water point). ◂ Continue following the yellow marks in the Vallon de Cady on a path that climbs gently NE. Cross a tiny stream and arrive at a minor plateau, where the path climbs gently in long zigzags.

Pass a fountain at 2400m (Font Nostra), and arrive at a junction (**2549m**, no signpost). Ignore the path that

Scrambling up the Canigou cheminée

branches off to the right to the Porteille de Valmanya (a pass, also yellow marks) and follow the path that stays below the pass. Climb NW on rocky terrain towards the Pic du Canigou until you reach a *cheminée* (a stone staircase, 2696m).

> Unlike most other *cheminées*, this **passage** was made in 1896 using dynamite, to make the climb from the east accessible to a wider group – although the easier climb from the north remains far more popular.

Climb carefully (watch out for stonefall) through this staircase to the

4.00 Pic du Canigou (2784m, large crucifix and a table d'orientation). ▶ The descent to Refuge des Cortalets presents no difficulties. Descend N in zigzags on an obvious path to the **Pic Joffre** (2362m); go around the summit and make a sharp turn to the right, then cross the ridge and go down E towards Cortalets, seen ahead of you. After the **Fontaine de la Perdrix** (water point) the GR10 joins in from the left. Go down generally E on an obvious path to the small **Lac des Cortalets** (2164m), keep left of the lake and follow the path to

You probably won't be the only person on this peak, which offers massive views of the eastern Pyrenees and the Mediterranean Sea.

5.20 Refuge des Cortalets (2150m), hut owned by the FFCAM, 105 places, manned from June until late September, meals and snacks available, tel 04 68 96 36 19. ▶ From the hut, the Haute Route follows the white-and-red marks of a GR10 variant to Prat Cabrera. Go to the back of the refuge and arrive at a junction with a signpost. Ignore the main track of the GR10, which goes down N to the Col des Cortalets (2055m). Instead turn right and climb SE in a pine forest on an obvious path. The path soon forks (signpost); ignore the route to the Crête du Barbet and turn left.

Take plenty of water before you continue.

Keep climbing, and soon you leave the forest and the path becomes level. Enter another pine forest, pass the remains of an aeroplane, climb a few metres and pass a minor col. Go down a few metres and the path, which turns right, levels out in an open landscape. Go through a gate in a fence and continue in the same direction until the route makes a sharp turn left (2060m).

Descend NE, enter a pine forest and arrive at a fence. Follow the fence, go through a gate and keep following the fence on its left side. Finally go down between pine trees until you arrive at **Prat Cabrera** (1739m), where you meet the dirt road that leads to Cortalets (signpost).

Turn right and leave the road at once. On your right side you'll find a clear and generally level path on the steep slopes of the Canigou massif. Follow this magnificent trail, the Balcon du Canigou, initially SW and then E, crossing a few streams to arrive near **Cabane du Pinatell** (1650m, unmanned hut, eight places, woodstove, water point), on your left below the path. The path stays more or less level for a while and then goes down in a few zigzags through a forest to the

8.15 Maison Forestière de l'Estanyol (1479m, unmanned basic hut with eight places, fireplace, water point), where the climb to the Col de la Cirère begins.

Ignore the path that goes N from here to Valmanya and instead follow the path that bends to the right (white-and-red marks). ◄ Ignore a path that leads to some old mines and climb S, initially rather gently but later more steeply in a forest. After a pass and a short descent, cross a stream. The path bends to the left and climbs ESE to the

In August there are plenty of raspberries here.

9.15 Col de la Cirère (1731m, signpost). Descend ESE on an eroded path that soon bends to the left. Notice the Tour de Batère (an ancient signal tower) on your left, far away. Arrive at a small concrete construction and go down to the start of a dirt road. Pass a ruin and follow the dirt road, which becomes a tarmac road. Follow this winding road for a few minutes until you arrive at

9.50 Refuge de Batère (1500m), left of the road and offering fine views. The hut has 38 places, tel 04 68 39 12 01. Great meals, hot tub outside. Open from May until mid October. There are excellent places to bivouac 200 metres W of the refuge, past an old building.

VARIANT 7

GR10 to Refuge des Cortalets

Start	Refuge de Mariailles (Day 39/40)
Finish	Refuge des Cortalets (Day 40)
Distance	16.5km
Total ascent	1395m
Total descent	925m
Grade	2
Time	6hr

This is a useful variant in case of bad weather. The GR10 trail curves around the Canigou. It will almost certainly takes two days to reach Refuge de Batère if this variant is taken.

0.00 Refuge de Mariailles. From the refuge, walk back to the *refuge forestier*, where a signpost indicates the route to the Pic du Canigou. Take the left path, and after

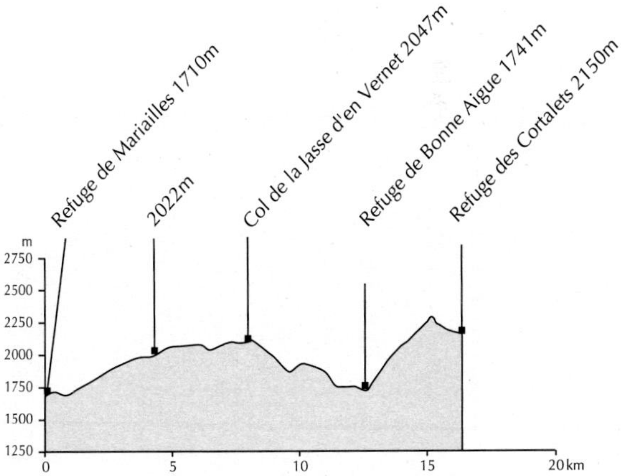

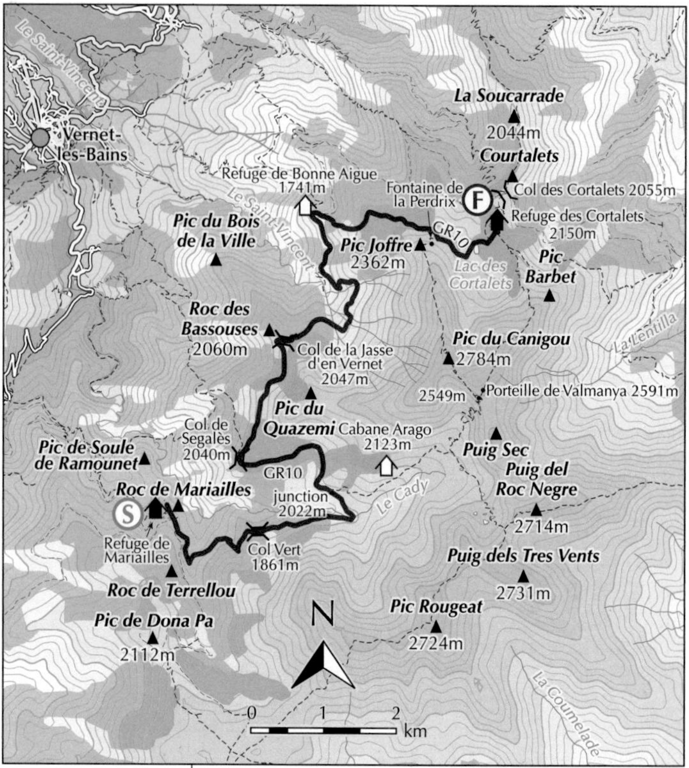

crossing the Ruisseau de Llipodère (1686m) by a footbridge the path bends to the left and climbs gently NE. Cross a minor stream after a short section SE and continue to climb NE to the **Col Vert** (1861m, signpost), where you arrive at a gate.

Go through the gate and climb E on the clear path, passing several more gates, and go finally down a few metres to the Ruisseau de Cady (1964m, confluence of two streams). Cross the streams and walk for about 15min NW on the GR10 trail until you reach a **junction at 2022m**. Don't turn right but follow the GR10, which climbs gently N. The path crosses a few giant rock slopes (very easy) and bends W to go to the

2.10 Col de Segalès (2040m, signpost). Don't turn left (yellow marks), but walk NNE on a path that climbs a little until it reaches 2100m, then it becomes almost level and finally goes down a little to the

2.45 Col de la Jasse d'en Vernet (2047m). Descend NE on an obvious track until you arrive at an open area full of rocks and boulders. Cross this area (called Les Conques; 1880m) with care, as the boulders are not always stable. Go down to cross another rock slope (Roc dels Isards, 1820m) and then descend WNW to a dirt road (1740m). Climb N on this road to

4.15 Refuge de Bonne Aigue (1741m), an unmanned hut with a water point (not always working). Leave the hut on your left, below, ignore a path branching off to the left (to Vernet-les-Bains) and continue on the dirt road for about 50 metres. Leave the road (waymarked), turn right and climb steeply ESE in a number of zigzags between pine trees.

Arrive at an open field, where you pass the beautiful Orri de la Casteille (an ancient *cabane*, 1966m) on the left. Continue to climb, and the path makes a swing to the left and arrives at a rocky bluff (excellent views). Continue on the path, which turns to the right and climbs gently SE, until you arrive finally near **Fontaine de la Perdrix** (2253m, water point) at a junction. You are now on the main track of the Haute Route again. Turn left and follow the Haute Route, which in 15min reaches

6.00 Refuge des Cortalets (2150m), hut owned by the FFCAM, 105 places, manned from June until late September, meals and snacks available, tel 04 68 96 36 19. To continue on the Pyrenean Haute Route, see Day 40.

DAY 41

Refuge de Batère to Mas de la Fargassa

Start	Refuge de Batère
Distance	20km
Total ascent	890m
Total descent	1695m
Grade	2
Time	7hr 20min
Map	Rando Editions Carte de Randonnées, 1:50,000, no 10: Canigou
Route	Via the Col de la Descarga (1393m), the village of Arles-sur-Tech and the Col de Paracolls (902m)

The Haute Route goes all the way down to Arles-sur-Tech (282m), where you're greeted by palm trees. It's a pleasant and easy descent, but the following climb to the Col de Paracolls is steep and the summer heat may add an extra challenge. The Haute Route follows the GR10.

0.00 Refuge de Batère. Leave the hut and go down on the road for about 700 metres to arrive at the **Col de la Descarga** (1393m), where the road makes a sharp curve

Wild boar at dawn close to Refuge de Batère

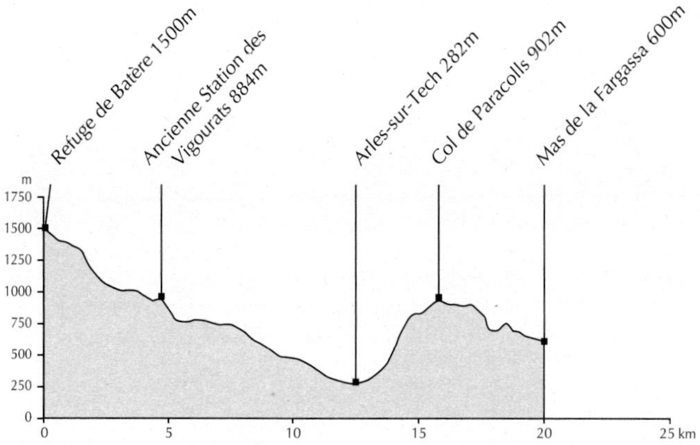

to the right. The GR10 leaves the road here; don't turn left but go down E on a (sometimes steep) path. Arrive at a dirt road (1037m), cross it and take a shortcut, which leads you through the Can Cor ecological community. Turn left at another dirt road and follow it as it gently descends. After a left turn the road enters a forest; leave the road on a hairpin bend and follow a level path to the

1.20 Ancienne Station des Vigourats (884m, signpost), Els Vigorats in Catalan. Pass the ruins of the building and turn left, then go down through the forest and arrive back at the road. Cross the road and go down to the floor of the valley where you'll reach a stream. Cross the stream and arrive at a dirt road after a short climb, then turn right and follow the road to climb S and arrive at a junction. Turn right again and follow the road until the GR10 leaves the road and turns right, then follow a path that descends and arrive finally at a junction (654m). Turn right here and walk to the

2.20 Site de Jacouty (620m), where there is the skeleton of a building on the left. Keep descending SE, follow a ridge in an open area and enter a forest. Ignore a path to a dolmen and reach the dirt road at a hairpin bend (signpost), turn right and follow the road for a minute,

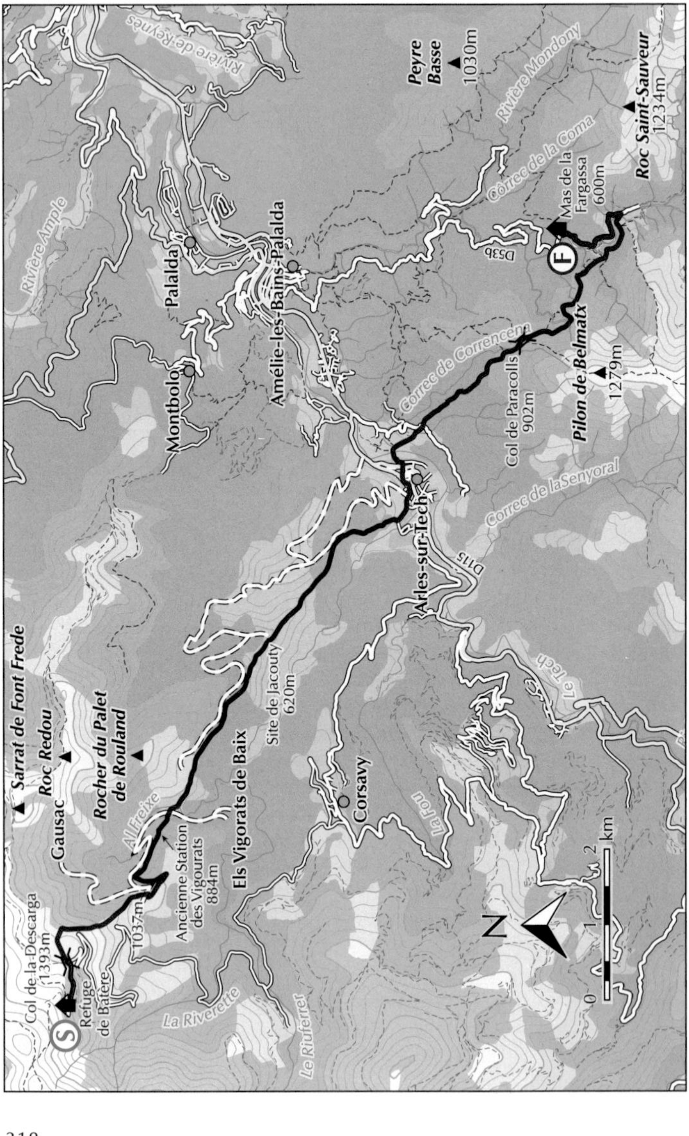
Rivière de Reynes
Peyre Basse
1030m
Rivière Mondony
Roc Saint-Sauveur
1234m
Côrrec de la Coma
Mas de la Fargassa
600m
F
D53b
Rivière Ample
Palalda
Amélie-les-Bains-Palalda
Montbolo
Correc de Correncena
Col de Paracolls
902m
Pilon de Belmatx
1279m
Correc de laSenyoral
Arles-sur-Tech
D115
Le Tech
Sarrat de Font Frede
Roc Redou
Rocher du Palet de Rouland
Gausac
Al Freixe
Site de Jacouty
620m
Els Vigorats de Baix
Corsavy
La Fou
Ancienne Station des Vigourats
884m
1037m
Col de la Descarga
1393m
S
Refuge de Batère
La Riverette
Le Riuferrer
N
0 1 2 km

then turn right and go down through a forest to the village of

3.30 Arles-sur-Tech (282m). Turn left and go down to a junction, then turn left again and walk towards the centre. Follow the markers of the GR10, which will lead you around the old centre, and go down to the **D115** near the former station of Arles-sur-Tech. Cross the road and follow a road that will lead you to the Tech river, and cross the river by a long footbridge.

On the other side, follow a concrete road for a few metres, turn left and then follow a path that climbs. Soon you will cross a dry stream. Enter an open field and climb SE; the path bends a little to the left and climbs in a forest to a small tarmac road. Turn right, follow the road for just a few metres and then leave the road to take a shortcut. Return to the road and follow it before turning left to climb on a path SE. Eventually the path becomes very steep on an eroded slope. After a long climb you'll enter a forest of sweet chestnut trees. The path becomes less steep, turns right at a junction and reaches the

5.35 Col de Paracolls (902m), an open spot in the forest with a view of the Roc de Frausa. Descend S through forest, then climb a little and the path becomes level. After crossing a tiny stream the path turns left and climbs a little more to a ruined house (870m). Here the route bends sharply to the right, stays flat for a while and then goes down in a number of zigzags to the floor of a valley. Cross another tiny stream and follow the path that climbs N.

At a ruined house, the route bends to the right. Take the left path at a junction and go down to a stream, cross it and turn left. Follow the stream and climb finally to the road, the D53b. Turn left and follow the road for 1.2km (ignoning a GR10 sign to a path on your right after 1.1km) to:

7.20 Mas de la Fargassa (600m), on the left of the road. This ecological tourist farm is mainly a holiday resort for families, but they also accommodate hikers in a dormitory (14 places) and a campground. Hikers are requested to arrive after 16h and depart by 8.30. Vegetarian meals available, tel 04 68 39 01 15.

DAY 42

Mas de la Fargassa to Las Illas

Start	Mas de la Fargassa
Distance	16km
Total ascent	1255m
Total descent	1345m
Grade	2
Time	6hr 15min
Map	Rando Editions Carte de Randonnées, 1:50,000, no 11: Roussillon
Route	Via the Roc de Frausa (1450m), the Col du Puits de la Neige (1289m) and the Col de Lly (713m)

This walk involves the last long climb of the Haute Route. The climb to Roc de Frausa (also called Roc de France), on the French-Spanish border, goes through beautiful forests. In poor visibility it is possible to bypass the Roc by sticking to the GR10. After a brief visit to Spain the Haute Route returns to France, where you can spend the night in the hamlet of Las Illas, having enjoyed the local cuisine.

0.00 Mas de la Fargassa. Return to the D53b road, turn right and after 100m leave the road at a signpost signed for GR10. Turn left onto the GR10 and climb NNE through the forest to an open spot where the route bends to the right. Walk up and down on a winding path, notice the tiny community of Montalba d'Amélie on your left below, cross the Ravin de la Coume and go down to

0.45 Montalba d'Amélie (543m), which has a chapel and a water point (Fontaine Dubois). Good places for a bivouac are easily found here. Turn right at a small iron cross before reaching the hamlet, climb SE through a forest and arrive at a dirt road (724m, signpost). Turn right and follow the road, which climbs gently. At a junction turn right, cross a fence and climb on a road that bends to the right and arrives at

The tiny hamlet of Montalba d'Amélie has a beautiful chapel and graveyard

2.00 Mouli Serradou (833m), an old mill that has become a ruin. The path bends sharply to the left and climbs steeply S to arrive at the

2.45 Col Cerda (1058m, signpost), an open spot on a ridge. Turn left here and climb SE between shrubs and bracken. Eventually you'll enter a beautiful beech forest,

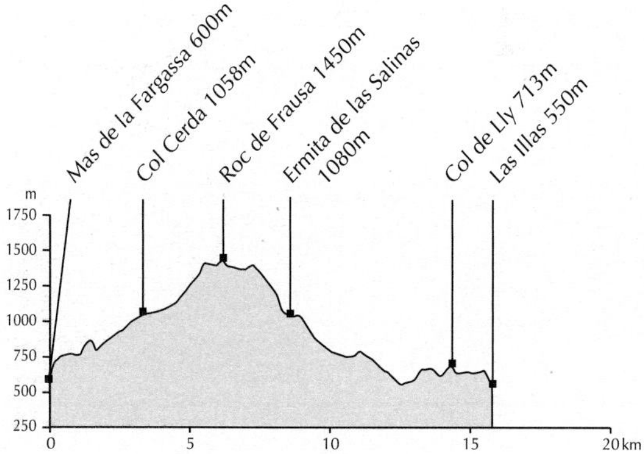

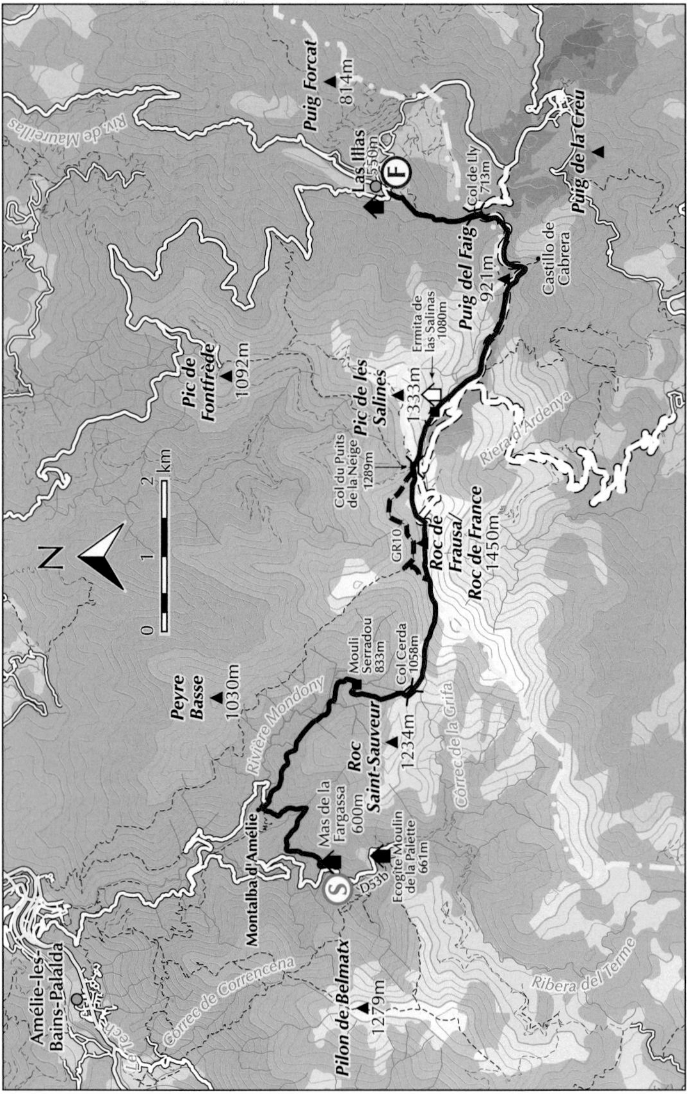
Puig Forcat
814m
Riv. de Maureillas
Las Illas
550m
F
Col de Lly
713m
Puig de la Creu
Puig del Faig
921m
Castillo de Cabrera
Ermita de las Salinas
1080m
Pic de Fontfrède
1092m
Pic de les Salines
1333m
Riera d'Ardenya
N
0
1
2
km
Col du Puits de la Neige
1289m
GR10
Roc de Frausa/ Roc de France
1450m
Peyre Basse
1030m
Mouli Serradou
833m
Col Cerda
1058m
Rivière Mondony
Roc Saint-Sauveur
1234m
Còrrec de la Grifa
Mas de la Fargassa
600m
Montalba d'Amélie
S
D53b
Ecogîte Moulin de la Palette
661m
Amélie-les-Bains-Palalda
Le Tech
Còrrec de Correncena
Pilon de Belmatx
1279m
Ribera del Terme

in which the path climbs steeply. The route approaches the frontier ridge and stays a few tens of metres below it, and then finally you leave the forest and arrive on the ridge. Walk to a junction, leave the GR10, and keep following the ridge on a path with yellow marks.

Bad-weather route bypassing the Roc de Frausa
In poor visibility it makes no sense to go to the Roc de Frausa. Just follow the GR10, which leads without any problems to the **Col du Puits de la Neige**, and from there follow the Haute Route as described below.

Keeping a small rock face on your right-hand side (the Roc de Frausa Occidental; 1417m), make a short descent and then climb to the highest summit:

3.45 Roc de Frausa (1450m, today's highest point). Walk E on the frontier ridge towards an antenna and a concrete border stone (1415m). Pass the antenna and follow a small concrete road. Leave the road where it makes a sharp curve to the right. Left of the road you'll find a path marked with yellow paintflashes; go down on the ridge, initially through open landscape and then through a beech forest. Keep on the French side of the ridge as you go down to

4.15 Col du Puits de la Neige (1289m, signpost). Turn right, cross the frontier by a cattle grid and follow the path to Las Salinas, which is signposted at the left of the road you entered. Descend SE on an obvious path (yellow marks) between trees until you arrive at a dirt road. Notice a shrine on your right and a water point in a small building below the road.

Turn left and follow the road to the **Ermita de las Salinas** (1080m). Meals and drinks may be available in summer, when the *ermita* is open for tourists Thur–Sun. For the rest of the year the building is closed, but there is a non-guarded, basic refuge for hikers (12 places).

Walk along the building and follow a path to a useful water point E of the *ermita*. Turn right just before the water point, then turn left a few metres further on and make a short descent. Cross the Ribera de les Salines

The Haute Route takes you back to civilisation in the final days

and follow a level path with red-and-yellow marks in a pine forest until you reach a dirt road. Turn left and after a few metres a signpost indicates the Coll de les Cordes. Continue SE on the dirt road, which goes down. Notice the ruins of Castillo de Cabrera on a hilltop at a distance on your right; beyond the ruins, cross a cattle grid and the road makes a large curve to the left and goes NE to the

5.40 Col de Lly (713m, signpost), which is found between border stone no 557 and a house at a point where the road touches the border. Turn left and go through a gate in a fence to reach another road, then turn right and leave the road at a fence with a closed gate.

Follow the sign to Las Illas and go down left of the fence to the hamlet of

6.15 Las Illas (550m). The first building you reach is Hostal dels Trabucayres, a hotel with an excellent restaurant, tel 04 68 66 55 38. A little further, next to the *mairie* (town hall), there is a gîte d'étape (14 places) where you can cook your own meal in the well-equipped kitchen, tel 07 76 09 65 81. Finally, there's a very convenient place to bivouac 100 metres N past the *mairie*, on a flat grass field with picnic tables.

DAY 43

Las Illas to Col de l'Ouillat

Start	Las Illas
Distance	23km
Total ascent	1280m
Total descent	895m
Grade	2
Time	6hr 30min
Map	Rando Editions Carte de Randonnées, 1:50,000, no 11: Roussillon
Route	Via the Col du Perthus (280m)

A varied walk on road, track and dirt roads. Except for at the start, the Haute Route follows the GR10 trail today, so route-finding is easy. There are lots of supermarkets in Le Perthus, the last point at which you need to replenish your food supplies. Col de l'Ouillat is a fine place to spend the last night before you arrive at Banyuls-sur-Mer; the views from the pass onto the Canigou massif are magnificent and there is a nice atmosphere in the gîte.

0.00 Las Illas. Walk N through the village and follow the D13 (in the direction of Maureillas) for a short while. The GR10 branches off to the left at a junction with the grass field for camping in front of you: leave the GR10,

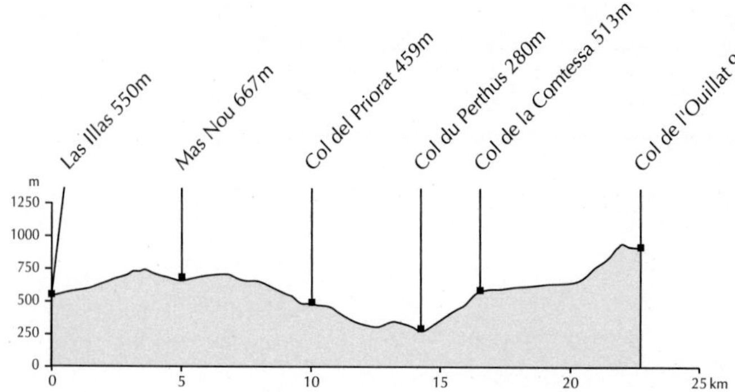

turn right and climb on a tarmac road (Route de Manrell) towards the houses of Super Las Illas. Soon the Route du Cortal comes in from the left but you continue climbing. Turn sharply right at the next junction and sharply left at the one after that.

Continue climbing in zigzags, still on the same Route de Manrell, alongside the houses of Super Las Illas. Ignore two roads on your right, continue straight on and soon arrive at the **Col de Figuer** (685m, no signpost), where the tarmac road ends. Turn left and walk NE on a dirt road that climbs a little. Ignore several other dirt roads coming in from left and right, and stay on the main dirt road.

Eventually the dirt road starts to descend and enters a beautiful beech forest. As you come out of the forest the GR10 comes in from the left and you arrive at a farm: **Mas Nou** (667m), with an information sign. From here you follow the GR10 again, keeping the farmhouse on your left-hand side. The road bends to the right and arrives a little later at a junction near a small wooden construction; don't turn left but follow the road that climbs NE for a short while and then descends. Ignore the dirt road that branches off to Maureillas, and continue on the dirt road to the

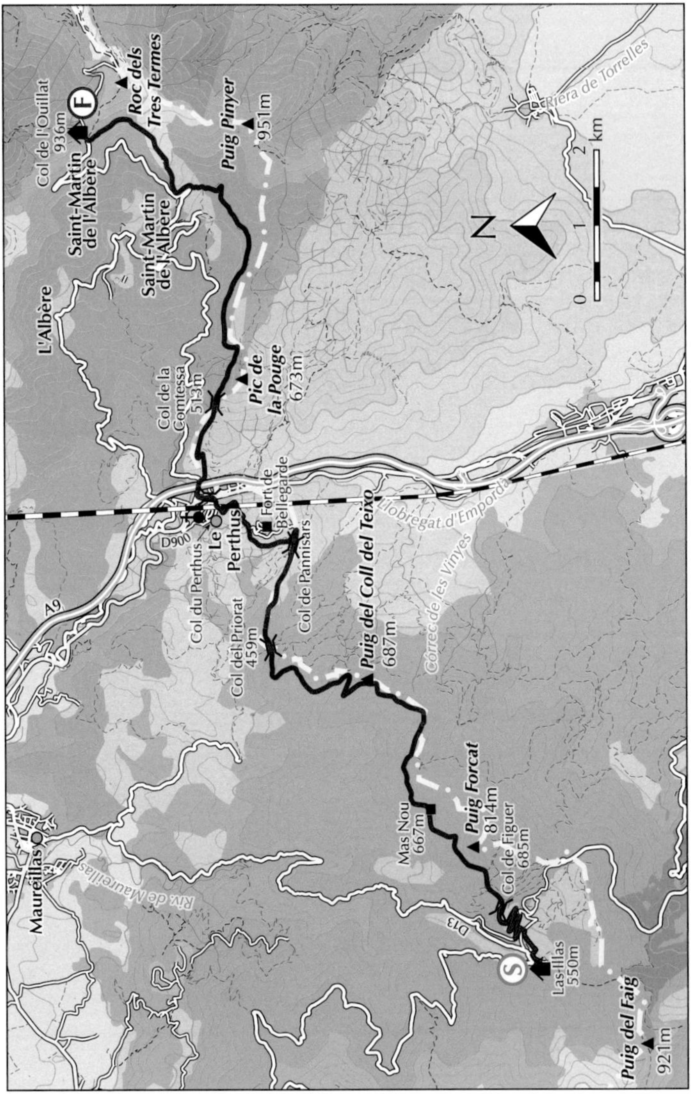
Col de l'Ouillat
936m
F
Roc dels Tres Termes
Puig Pinyer
951m
Saint-Martin de l'Albère
Saint-Martin de l'Albère
L'Albère
Col de la Comtessa
513m
Pic de la Pouge
673m
Riera de Torrelles
N
0
1
2
km
A9
D900
Le Perthus
Col du Perthus
Fort de Bellegarde
Col de Pannisars
Llobregat d'Empordà
Puig del Coll del Teixo
687m
Còrrec de les Vinyes
Col del Priorat
459m
Maureillas
Riv. de Maureillas
D13
Mas Nou
667m
Puig Forcat
814m
Col de Figuer
685m
S
Las Illas
550m
Puig del Faig
921m

2.25 Col del Priorat (459m, border stone no 565 on your right). Don't turn left or right but continue in the same direction on a path that starts next to a large green water container. Follow this narrow path, which goes up and down in a cork oak forest, to the **Col de Pannisars** (signpost) where you'll see the Ruines de Pannisars on your left. Continue to a junction where you have the large **Fort de Bellegarde** (built in 1679) in front of you. Follow the GR10 markers to the left and then continue on the road that takes you around the fort. Finally, follow the Rue du Fort to reach the

3.40 Col du Perthus (280m), on the D900.

The frontier village of **Le Perthus** is essentially one long street with numerous shops, supermarkets and restaurants. It is often overcrowded, noisy and probably not a place where a hiker would want to stay for long! The green benches on the steps in front of the church are a rare quiet spot in this chaos.

Turn left on the D900 and walk to the north section of Le Perthus, then take the D71 that branches off to the

Cork oak forest near Col du Perthus

right. Walk under a giant viaduct (autoroute **A9**) and notice a signpost (Le Perthus, 283m). Leave the D71 here, turn right and follow the dirt road on which the GR10 climbs into Spain.

Turn left before a cattle grid and follow the dirt road until the GR10 markers lead you onto a small path to the left. Go through an opening in a fence at border stone 580 and walk back into France at the **Col de la Comtessa** (513m, signpost). From here continue climbing SE until you reach a junction with a metal gate on your left. Turn left, pass the gate and follow a dirt road for over 1hr.

Just before reaching Saint-Martin de l'Albère, leave the dirt road, turn right and follow a path. Very soon you leave this path to follow another path on your left. Turn right just before reaching an asphalt road and continue NW on a path where GR10 markers keep you on the right track. Eventually the path turns left, passes a few buildings and arrives at

6.30 Col de l'Ouillat (936m), where you'll find the gîte d'étape Chalet de l'Albère (40 places, open all year, bar/restaurant with great views, tel 04 68 83 62 20) situated next to the road along the Forêt Domainiale des Albères. About 100 metres beyond the gîte there is a picnic area where you can bivouac. ▶

Don't leave anything unguarded as cows roam free here!

DAY 44

Col de l'Ouillat to Banyuls-sur-Mer

Start	Col de l'Ouillat
Distance	22.5km
Total ascent	920m
Total descent	1855m
Grade	2
Time	8hr 25min
Map	Rando Editions Carte de Randonnées, 1:50,000, no 11: Roussillon
Route	Via the Pic Neulos (1256m), the Pic des Quatre-Termes (1156m) and the Pic de Sailfort (981m)

A tough stage due to its length. Hot weather could make hiking a challenge; be sure to take enough water. The final part of the Haute Route involves a long walk on the frontier ridge – on a fine day the views of the Mediterranean Sea and the Côte Vermeille are amazing.

This is a great spot for watching the sunrise.

0.00 Col de l'Ouillat. The GR10 to Banyuls-sur-Mer is indicated on a signpost near the gîte d'étape. Follow a path that climbs SE through a pine forest and arrives at a ridge, then turn left and follow an almost level path to the **Col des Trois Termes** (1095m), next to a road.

Follow a path just above the road along a fence on the border and walk to **Pic Neulos** (1256m, large antenna). ◂ Cross the road, go clockwise around the fence on the top and ignore a large track that branches off to the left. East of Pic Neulos, go down on the French side of the border on a path that approaches a dirt road. Keep the road below on your left-hand side and walk E, pass the Tagnarède water source (your last source of water for a long time) and continue to the

1.30 Refuge de la Tagnarède (1045m, unmanned, solid shelter owned by the FFCAM, 12 places), next to

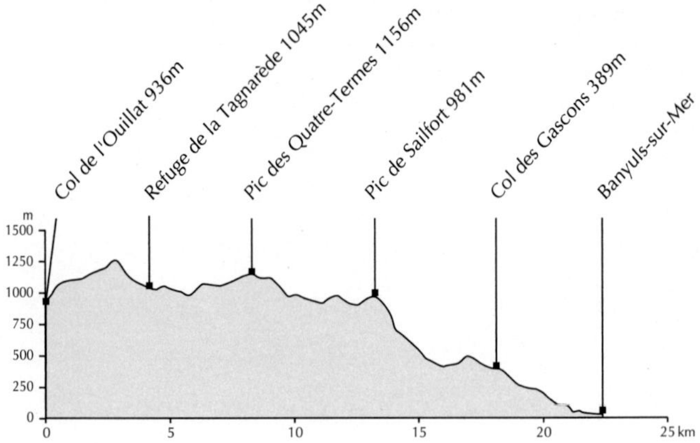

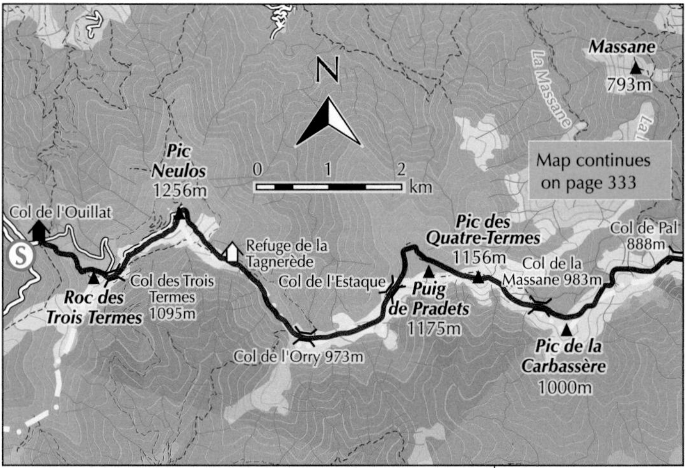

a forest and very close to the border. Walk SE on a path to the **Col de l'Orry** (973m), then climb ENE. Pass border stone 585, walk through a beautiful beech forest and go down to the **Col de l'Estaque** (border crucifix no 586). Keeping the dirt road on your left, climb ENE in a straight line on the frontier ridge to the

3.30 Pic des Quatre-Termes (1156m). Walk clockwise around the summit and go down steeply on the ridge to the **Col de la Massane** (983m, possible water source), then continue in the same direction towards the Pic de la Carbassère (1000m), where the route bends to the left. Arrive at the **Col del Pal** (888m) and climb, generally E, to the

4.50 Pic de Sailfort (981m). ▶ Leave the border ridge and descend E on a steep ridge, avoiding rocky sections by skirting below them. During the descent, at a minor pass (561m), the route bends a little to the left. Keep right at a junction and follow a ridge. Stay a little to the left and below this ridge, and go down gently NE to arrive at a pass that can be seen from afar:

This is a good place to enjoy the magnificent views of the Côte Vermeille.

6.10 Col de Vallauria (416m, signpost). A dirt road crosses the col. Take the path that climbs NE and soon

The route approaches the point at which the Pyrenees plunge into the Mediterranean Sea

crosses a ridge (456m, **Col de Formigou**), and walk on an almost level path along a steep slope above the dirt road. Arrive at a junction on a ridge, turn right and go down steeply to the

6.55 Col des Gascons (389m). A small road (the D86) touches this pass; turn right and go down on the road for about 50 metres. Turn left and take two waymarked shortcuts (beware: the path is very steep and eroded) to return to the road. Leave the road again and follow a path that passes a water point (Fontaine de les Falgeras, 282m). The path reaches the road, which you follow this time. Notice a house and a *table d'orientation* on your right and continue for a few metres until the road turns right. Here you are on the

7.20 Col de Llagastera (256m). Leave the road, take dirt road no AL73 (indicated – the one on the right) and climb E. Ignore a dirt road that branches off to the left and cross the ridge. Go down towards Banyuls, soon taking a shortcut on your right, and continue to go down on dirt roads, taking several shortcuts and following the markers of the GR10 carefully.

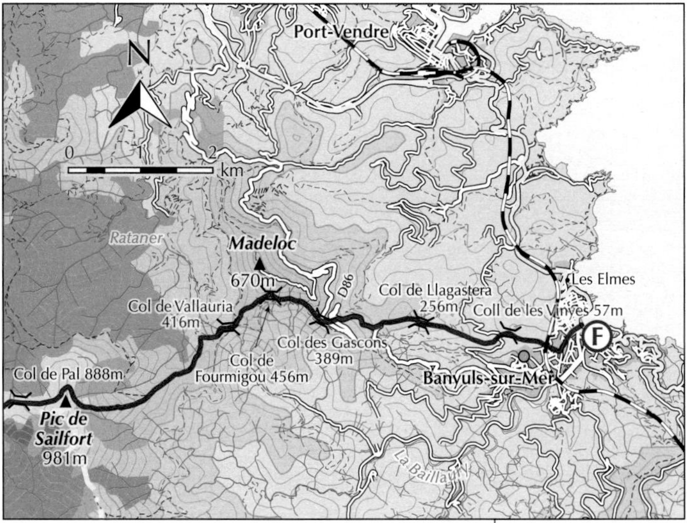

Arrive finally on a small road (**Coll de les Vinyes**, 57m). Cross this road, follow another road straight ahead and turn right at the next junction. Follow a dirt road, notice a sports field on your right below, pass a house and take a path that goes down steeply between vineyards to reach a small road. Here turn left, go through a tunnel underneath the railway line and continue in the same direction. Follow a small channel and continue to a road, then turn left and walk to a junction. Turn left and follow this road E until you finally arrive at the beach of

8.25 Banyuls-sur-Mer where there are hotels, shops, cash dispensers, campsites, bars, restaurants, banks, a railway service to Paris, and a tourist office (at the beach). The railway station is situated in the NW section of the village. Just before arriving at the beach the GR10 markers bend to the right and will lead you to the Hotel de Ville, where the track in fact ends. ▸ Hikers who want a camping spot with a view to the Mediterranean Sea can find beautiful places along the Sentier Littoral (coastal path, yellow marks) towards Port-Vendres. Along the

There is a piece of art on the building that marks the end/start of the long walk.

Sunrise from the Sentier Littoral close to Banyuls-sur-Mer

same path you can find the nearest sandy beach, the Plage des Elmes.

For more practical information see the introduction to this section.

APPENDIX A

Useful contacts

This book's facebook group
PyreneanHauteRoute

General tourist information

France
www.franceguide.com

Spain
www.spain.info

Catalonia
www.catalunyaturisme.cat
www.publintur.cat

Aragon
www.turismodearagon.com

Andorra
www.visitandorra.com

Pays Basque
www.tourisme64.comwww.guide-du-paysbasque.com

National parks

Parc National des Pyrénées Occidentales
www.pyrenees-parcnational.fr/fr

Parque Nacional de Ordesa y Monte Perdido
www.ordesa.net

Aigüestortes national park
http://parcsnaturals.gencat.cat/ca

Mountain forecasts

Meteo France
www.meteofrance.com

Mountain forecast
www.mountain-forecast.com

Meteoblue
www.meteoblue.com

Snow Forecast
www.snow-forecast.com

Meteoalarm
(extreme weather warnings)
www.meteoalarm.eu

Railway information

Eurostar services
www.eurostar.com

Other European railway services
www.raileurope.com

French railway (including TGV)
www.sncf.com

Mountain huts and gîtes d'étape

All gîtes and refuges in France
www.gites-refuges.com

All manned and unmanned mountain huts in the Pyrenees
www.pyrenees-refuges.com

Maps

French Institut Geographique National
www.ign.fr

Stanfords
www.stanfords.co.uk

The Map Shop
www.themapshop.co.uk

Other useful sources of information

A good introduction to the Spanish Pyrenees (in Spanish)
www.pirineodigital.com

APPENDIX B

Glossary

The Pyrenees region is linguistically very diverse. In addition to the official state languages Spanish and French, also Basque, Aragonese, Occitan and Catalan are spoken. This is clearly reflected in the names of streams, lakes, valleys, passes, peaks, etc. Listed here below are the common terms in the local languages to refer to these landmarks.

French	English	Spanish	Catalan
Abri	Shelter	Abrigo	Abrigo
Aiguille	Pinnacle	Aguja	Agulla/agulle
Arète	Ridge	Arista	Aresta
Auberge	Hotel	Pensión/hostal	Pensió/hostal
Barrage	Dam	Presa	Presa
Bas	Low	Baja/bajo	Baix
Bois	Wood	Bosque	Bosc
Cabane	Hut	Cabaña	Cabanya/Borda
Chemin	Path/way	Camino	Cam/camí
Cime	Summit	Cima/cumbre	Cim
Cirque	Amphitheatre	Circo	Circ
Col	Col/pass	Puerto	Port
Crête	Ridge	Cresta	Cresta/coma/serra
Dalle	Slab	Placa	Placa
Danger	Danger	Peligro	Perill
Droite	Right	Derecha	Dreta
Eaux	Waters	Aguas	Aigües
Éboulis	Scree	Pedrero	Pedrera/tartera
Église	Church	Iglesia	Església
Ermitage	Hermitage	Ermita	Ermita
Escalade	Climbing	Escalada	Escalada
Étang	Lake	Lago/estany	Estany/llac
Ferme	Farmhouse	Finca	Finca

French	English	Spanish	Catalan
Fontaine	Fountain/spring	Fuente	Font
Gauche	Left	Izquierda	Esquerra
Gave	River/stream	Arroyo	Rierol
Gorge	Gorge	Barranco	Barraca
Gourg	Tarn/lake	Lago/Ibón	Estany/llac
Grand(e)	Great	Gran/grande	Gran
Grange	Barn	Borda	Borda
Grotte	Cave	Cueva	Cova
Haut	High	Alto/Altura	Alt/allau
Herbe	Grass	Hierba	Herba
Hébergement	Accommodation	Alojamiento	Alojamiento
Horaire	Timetable	Horario	Horari
Hourquette	Col/gap	Puerto	Port
Maison	House	Casa	Casa
Mine	Mine	Mina	Mina
Montagne	Mountain	Montaña	Muntanya
Moulin	Mill	Molino	Molí
Nègre	Black	Negro/negra	Negre
Neige	Snow	Nieve	Neu
Paroi	Wall	Pared	Paret
Pas	Pass/step	Paso	Pas
Pente	Slope/meadow	Falda/cuesta	Clots
Pic	Summit	Pico	Cap
Pierre	Stone	Piedra	Pedra
Piste	Dirt road	Piste	Pista
Pont	Bridge	Puente	Pont
Port	Pass/col	Puerto	Port
Pré	Meadow	Prado/pradera	Pla/Prat
Refuge	Hut	Refugio	Refugi
Rivière	River	Rio	Riu
Rocher	Rock	Roca	Roca/roc

French	English	Spanish	Catalan
Rouge	Red	Rojo/roja	Roig
Ruisseau	Stream	Torrente/arroyo	Rierol/torrent
Sentier	Path/track	Sendero	Sender
Sommet	Summit	Cima	Pala
Tortueux	Winding	Tortes	Tortuoso
Vallée	Valley	Valle	Vall

APPENDIX C

Facilities table

Day	Location (italic) or overnight stop	Altitude	Total time	Intermediate time	Hotel	Bar/ restaurant	Shop	Bank/ ATM	Post office	Manned hut/gîte	Unmanned hut/cabane	Campsite
	Hendaye	*0m*			x	x	x	x	x			x
	Col d'Ibardin	*317m*		*4hr 30min*		x	x					
1	Col de Lizuniaga	230m	8hr 15min		x	x						
2	Arizkun	280m	7hr 15min		x	x	x					
3	Aldudes	370m	5hr		x	x	x		x	x		
4	Roncesvalles	930m	5hr 45min		x	x						
5	Egurgui	850m	6hr 45min									
	Chalet Pedro	*990m*		*3hr 20min*		x						
6	Col Bagargui	1327m	5hr 15min			x	x			x		
7	Cabane d'Ardané	1330m	7hr 15min								x	
8	Source de Marmitou	1851m	8hr 30min									
9	Lescun	900m	3hr		x	x	x		x	x		x
10	Refuge d'Arlet	1986m	6hr 45min							x		
11	Candanchu	1550m	6hr 30min		x	x	x					

Day	Location (italic) or overnight stop	Altitude	Total time	Intermediate time	Hotel	Bar/ restaurant	Shop	Bank/ ATM	Post office	Manned hut/gîte	Unmanned hut/cabane	Campsite
	Astun	*1710m*		*1hr*	x	x						
12	Refuge de Pombie	2032m	6hr 20min							x		
	Refuge d'Arremoulit	*2265m*		*5hr 5min*						x		
13	Refuge de Larribet	2072m	8hr 10min							x		
	Cabane de Doublas	*1563m*		*1hr 15min*							x	
14	Refuge Wallon	1866m	8hr 20min							x		
	Refuge des Oulettes de Gaube	*2150m*		*5hr*						x		
15	Refuge de Baysellance	2651m	7hr 20min							x		
	Barrage d'Oussoue	*1834m*		*2hr*							x	
	Cabane de Lourdes	*1947m*		*2hr 35min*							x	
	Cabane de Sausse-dessus	*1900m*		*3hr 20min*							x	
16	Gavarnie	1365m	5hr 20min		x	x	x	x	x	x		x
	Refuge des Espuguettes	*2027m*		*2hr*						x		
17	Héas	1500m	6hr 45min		x	x				x		x
	Cabane de l'Aguila	*1900m*		*1hr 15min*							x	
	Cabane des Aires	*2131m*		*Variant 1hr 45min*							x	
18	Parzán	1100m	10hr		x	x	x	x				
	Cabana de los Caballos	*2320m*		*3hr 30min*							x	

Day	Location (italic) or overnight stop	Altitude	Total time	Intermediate time	Hotel	Bar/ restaurant	Shop	Bank/ ATM	Post office	Manned hut/gîte	Unmanned hut/cabane	Campsite
	Camping Forcallo	*1650m*		*6hr 45min*								*x*
19	Refugio de Viados	1760m	7hr 15min							x		
	Cabana d'Añescruzes	*2075m*		*1hr 25min*							*x*	
	Cabane de Prat-Cazeneuve	*2020m*		*4hr 50min*							*x*	
20	Refuge de la Soula	1690m	6hr 30min							x		
21	Refuge du Portillon	2571m	6hr 15min							x		
	Hospital de Benasque	*1800m*		*5hr 5min*	*x*	*x*						
22	Refugio de la Renclusa	2140m	6hr 45min							x		
	Refugio de Mulleres	*2390m*		*5hr 50min*							*x*	
23	Refugio de Conangles	1555m	8hr							x		
24	Refugi de la Restanca	2010m	7hr 15min							x		
	Refugi de Colomers	*2120m*		*3hr 45min*						*x*		
25	Salardú	1270m	7hr 15min		x	x	x	x		x		
26	Refugi Gràcia Airoto	2200m	7hr 35min								x	
27	Alós d'Isil	1270m	3hr 30min								x	
	Refugi del Fornet	*1375m*	*4hr 45min*							*x*		
28	Refugi Enric Pujol	2290m	7hr 25min								x	

Day	Location (italic) or overnight stop	Altitude	Total time	Intermediate time	Hotel	Bar/ restaurant	Shop	Bank/ ATM	Post office	Manned hut/gîte	Unmanned hut/cabane	Campsite
	Camping Masia 'Bordes de Graus	*1360m*		*Variant 45min*		x						x
	Tavascan	*1167m*		*Variant 1hr 45min*	x	x	x					
29	Refugi de Certascan	2240m	7hr 15min							x		
30	Refugi del Cinquantenari	2392m	5hr 10min								x	
31	Étang de la Soucarrane	2292m	5hr 20min									
32	Refuge de Sorteny	1965m	6hr 45min							x		
	Cabana dels Meners	*2210m*		*1hr 20min*							x	
	Cabana Coms de Jan	*2220m*		*5hr 40min*							x	
33	Refugi de Cabana Sorda	2295m	6hr 25min								x	
	Refugi de Juclar	*2310m*		*2hr 30min*						x		
34	L'Hospitalet-près-l'Andorre	1436m	8hr 20min		x	x	x		x	x		x
35	Refuge de Bésines	2104m	3hr							x		
	Cabane de Rouzet	*2260m*		*2hr 10min*							x	
36	Refuge des Bouillouses	2005m	8hr 45min							x		
	Bolquère	*1620*		*3hr 55min*	x	x	x		x			
	Col de la Perche	*1579m*		*4hr 10min*	x	x						

Day	Location (italic) or overnight stop	Altitude	Total time	Intermediate time	Hotel	Bar/ restaurant	Shop	Bank/ ATM	Post office	Manned hut/gîte	Unmanned hut/cabane	Campsite
37	Eyne	1560m	4hr 45min			x				x		
38	Refugi d'Ull de Ter	2220m	8hr 10min							x		
	Cabane Arago	*2123m*		*2hr*							x	
	Refuge des Cortalets	*2150m*		*5hr 20min*						x		
39	Refuge de Mariailles	1710m	7hr 15min							x		
40	Refuge de Batère	1500m	9hr 50min			x				x		
	Arles-sur-Tech	*282m*		*3hr 30min*	x	x	x	x	x			x
41	Mas de la Fargassa	661m	7hr 20min							x		x
	Ermita de las Salinas	*1080m*		*4hr 45min*		x					x	
42	Las Illas	550m			x	x				x		
	Col de Perthus	*280m*		*3hr 40min*	x	x	x	x	x			
43	Col de l'Ouillat	936m	6hr 15min			x				x		
	Refuge de la Tagnerède	*1045m*		*1hr 30min*							x	
44	Banyuls-sur-mer	0m	8hr 25min		x	x	x	x	x			x